RENAISSANCE SOCIETY OF AMERICA
REPRINT TEXTS 15

Tudor Historical Thought

by F. J. LEVY

Published by University of Toronto Press
Toronto Buffalo London
in association with the Renaissance Society of America

Printed on acid-free paper

National Library of Canada Cataloguing in Publication

Levy, F.J. (Fred Jacob)
Tudor historical thought / F.J. Levy.

(Renaissance Society of America reprint texts 15)
Reprint. First published: San Marino, Calif.: Huntington Library, 1967.
Includes bibliographical references and index.
ISBN 0-8020-3775-5

1. Historiography – Great Britain – History – 16th century.
2. Great Britain – History – Tudors, 1485–1603 – Historiography.
I. Title.   II. Series.

DA315.L48 2004   942.05'.07'22   C2003-907287-8

University of Toronto Press acknowledges the financial assistance to its publishing
program of the Canada Council for the Arts and the Ontario Arts Council.

University of Toronto Press acknowledges the financial support for its publishing
activities of the Government of Canada through the Book Publishing Industry
Development Program (BPIDP).

For
SARAH, MARIAN, *and* DEBBY

Contents

Preface

Ideally, a book intending to explore the changes in historical think-ing from the time of Caxton to that of Bacon should progress in strict chronological order. But more than one facet of histo-riography altered, and the alterations did not all occur simul-taneously. Perhaps, then, a division by subject matter would be more appropriate; that approach takes one into the danger of writing several books bound up in one cover. The inevitable result is a compromise.

The late medieval chronicle may be seen as a compilation, loosely organized, whose author had no firm grasp of the essential differences between past and present, who thought of the events of a hundred years before his own time as occurring in a context identical to the world in which he himself lived. Because history writing had to be didactic, and because the lessons were those of personal morality and of the workings of Providence, it was diffi-cult to decide what was relevant and what was not, and the result was that most medieval chronicles worked on the principle of in-cluding as much as possible. Nor did these didactic motives en-courage either accuracy or the criticism of sources. What mattered was whether the lesson was clear.

This was the structure that was to be altered. The importation of Italian humanism introduced first, and most important, the con-cept of anachronism. The past was different from the present. But the Italians found a new purpose for the historian as well. Personal morality was still to be taught, but civic humanism emphasized the active role of the individual in his society, and that might be encouraged as well. The ideal inhabitant of Tudor England was not the monk but the citizen. Because society was important, and because society was identified with the state, history writing was centered on the personality of the monarch, and this meant that the rather formless narrative of the medieval chroniclers was hammered into a new, more organized, form.

The same ideas entered England by another route as well. The concept of anachronism was one of the most important ideas underlying the Reformation. No longer did men think of the church as a continuous organism: instead, they contrasted the church now with the church then, and were displeased with the comparison. At the same time, the humanists had forged weapons of source criticism that enabled the ecclesiastical historians to sort out the pure from the spurious and permitted them to build up a much clearer picture of what the ancient church was like. And because Reformation controversies were bitter, the church historians found it necessary to publish the original documents from which their revised portrait of the development of the church was drawn.

There was still more to be gained from the humanists. Vitally interested as they were in the history of the classic past, they soon found that narrative was not the only way to investigate their chosen subject. Instead, they became antiquaries and posed questions about institutions: about ancient coinage, the Roman Senate, or the various Roman provinces. England, too, had been part of the Roman Empire and thus had a place in the classical world. To discover what that place had been required the use of new sources of information, some of them narrative, but many material. Where were the Roman roads? What inscriptions had survived the ages, and what did they mean? What could be done with coins? And once these questions had been asked (and, perhaps, answered) about the Romans, there was no reason why a similar series of questions could not be asked about the history of post-Roman England.

The chroniclers had not been idle while these changes were taking place, and although the changes were absorbed slowly, they were absorbed. The organization of chronicles altered; the chroniclers became more conscious of the problems involved in selecting their materials. At the same time, they had much more material to contend with than had their predecessors. The humanists, the church historians, and the antiquaries had left an enormous legacy of new information that had to be fitted in.

And the new idea of the active citizen required that history be popularized and supplied to classes of men previously untouched by scholarly developments. Supplying such information to the citizenry was one of the self-imposed duties of a humanist historian; and the growing realization that education was important, together with the patriotism engendered by the Reformation and the struggle with Spain, meant it would be taken in by those for whom it was intended. But popularization, in some of its forms, raised new problems. The inclusiveness that persisted in the chronicles could not survive stage presentation, and the playwrights (together with the poets, who had similar difficulties) learned how to sort out the essential from the irrelevant.

The radical condensation carried out by the playwrights and poets was based, however, on a method of selection which was literary rather than historical. The importation of the histories of Machiavelli and Guicciardini supplied a more historical method. An increase of interest in the subject of the state had been evident throughout the century; now men took the inevitable next step and focused their attention on politics. Politic historians no longer asked how men should act so as to pass the tests of moral behavior; instead, they asked what would work in a secular, political society. The new question meant a narrowing of focus; that is, it provided a means for selecting some of the materials of history as more important than others. It could be carried too far, to the point of mere political aphorism. But taken together with the new sources and the new means of analyzing them, the politic method could be made to yield histories very different from those written a century before.

These are the problems I have posed in this study, together with some suggestion of the answers I propose. In the course of writing this book, I have amassed an astonishing quantity of debts. Some are to the authors whose works I have read so often that by this time my footnotes can acknowledge only part of what I owe: Lily B. Campbell, Leonard F. Dean, Denys Hay, Sir Thomas Kendrick, E. M. W. Tillyard. Some again are to my teachers at Harvard University, Professors Myron P. Gilmore and Wilbur K. Jordan. Moreover, completion of this book would have been impossible without a variety of financial support. I thank Harvard's History Department for sending me to England in 1958, allowing me to incorporate much unpublished material in my dissertation on

William Camden; the American Philosophical Society, through its Boies Penrose Fund, paid for another trip in 1961; a fellowship from the Folger Shakespeare Library made possible a year of uninterrupted research in the most pleasant of surroundings; and the Huntington Library awarded me a grant-in-aid during the summer of 1965 to complete my work. The University of Washington has been generous in its aid: grants from the Agnes Anderson Fund of the Graduate School permitted me to take two summers for research and writing and also paid for a great deal of microfilming and typing. Dr. Louis B. Wright of the Folger allowed me to impose on his kindness and was persuaded to read the manuscript, and Professor French Fogle of the Claremont Graduate School very kindly read the chapter on politic historians. The manuscript also gained a great deal from the careful ministrations of the Publications Department of the Huntington Library, and I am especially grateful for the time spent on it by my editor, Mrs. Anne Kimber. Like every scholar, I have abused the patience of librarians: I thank them for their forbearance as well as for their help.

Such a list, however long, is still inadequate. For omissions I apologize, and I am conscious that my thanks are hardly sufficient recompense for many kindnesses. As for my family, it is enough to say that they were willing to follow wherever the road led. Thus, whatever there is of value in this book may be attributed to others. The errors, however, are mine.

Quotations in the body of the text are given as they appear in the originals, except that u and v, i and j have been altered to agree with modern usage and contractions have been expanded; the same is true of book titles, but the capitalization of these has been modernized.

F. J. L.

Seattle, Washington
September 1966

Tudor Historical Thought

Introduction

Any study of a subject over the span of more than a century will be about change, and whether the change is called development, progress, degeneration, process, revolution, or collapse does not alter the fundamental point. Yet the inevitable desire of a historian to record flux may mean the omission (or at least the neglect) of a substratum of ideas shared by those of whom he writes, and this omission, by exaggerating differences, may distort the picture. The difficulty is that the similarities are often hidden very deep indeed and are commonly held far below the level of discourse. It is possible that the very men who shared in the great fund of sixteenth-century historical ideas may not themselves have realized it. One can only wonder what the eager purchaser of a Caxton chronicle might have said if he had been handed a copy of Sir Robert Cotton's *Henry III*. By all the obvious indices—style, content, purpose—the two books differed. Yet their authors saw the universe and the earth within it in much the same way. The differences and what accounted for them will be the tale told by the ensuing seven chapters; the similarities had best be looked at here and now.

The men of the sixteenth century saw the universe as orderly.[1] Even the greatest of the cataclysms that disrupted the comparative quiet of the late Middle Ages—the Reformation—did nothing to alter that view. The world was the creation of God, and His work had purpose and order. More than that, everything in creation was intimately linked to everything else, not only because of a tie to God but because God established a network of interrelationships among all his creatures. This universe was like a vast web, a net, which quivered everywhere whenever any part was touched. Man

[1] E. M. W. Tillyard, *The Elizabethan World Picture,* Vintage Books (New York, n.d.), gives the best general description, and I have leaned heavily on it; but Tillyard is not concerned with history writing.

3

was but one of God's creatures, more important perhaps than most because of his part in the drama of salvation but not to be ranked with the angels. And man, like all other creatures, was susceptible to the stirrings of the cosmos as well as being one cause of them. So much was sure: men knew that the structure existed and understood some of its details, but only God was omnipotent and omniscient. Man could increase his understanding, and the effort involved was not prohibited. The universe was not only orderly but also comprehensible, and the purpose of most writing—theological, historical, even scientific—was to make men more aware of their place in God's great scheme.

The historian thus was one of the explicators of the universal harmony; like the others, he suffered from the limitations of possessing an understanding that was only partial and—perhaps worse—from not knowing even the extent of his own ignorance. But if history were to be useful for more than explication, and all agreed that it was, then the historian had somehow to find a place for man's free will. How much of a place? The answer came to depend on the precise delimitations of the realms of Reason, Fortune, and Providence.[2] The proportions were mixed according to the taste of the historian, according to his purpose and what it was that he wished to teach. The man who wrote about the past because he believed that this would help rulers in the present would minimize Fortune and Providence in order to glorify Reason; the predestinarian theologian might come close to equating the power of Fortune with the Providence of God and might emphasize both at the expense of man's puny Reason. Almost always the shifts were alterations of emphasis, not of substance: Providence, Fortune, Reason were not to be altogether denied. The assumed area of the unknown was thus alterable by definition; indeed, it was not to be limited any other way. A man might decide how far he could understand and beyond what point his understanding would fail him. But he might decide, too, to deepen his understanding within the realm allotted him. A theologian, such as John Bale or John Foxe, might decide that God had given man a wide area of knowledge, because (at the same time) God

---

[2] Howard R. Patch, *The Goddess Fortuna in Medieval Literature* (Cambridge, Mass., 1927), esp. pp. 8–34.

had filled that area with Scripture. If only Scripture were interpreted rightly, then man could see a very large part of God's plan. So all efforts were bent on decoding the mysteries of the book of Revelation, where surely the answer was to be found. Or the connection between microcosm and macrocosm, between man's little world and the great world around him, would seem to offer a clue. Changes in the patterns of the stars must somehow be reflected in changes in the patterns of men, and thus historians of sober mien could be found studying astrology. A major alteration in the heavens—a comet, a nova—meant a cataclysm on earth; the birth of a disfigured child indicated a dislocation in men's affairs. The analysis of portents and omens was a commonplace. Numerology, whether scriptural or secular, was a promising field for study. Since there was a pattern in the universe, this was an obvious way of seeking to elucidate it. Whether a man used omens or numbers is not a good test for judging his value as a historian: the excellent Italian, Francesco Guicciardini, was enamored of portents, and the pioneering political scientist, Jean Bodin, was a numerologist, while the young William Camden spent much time working out astrological problems.[3] An interest in these matters was a mark of maturity, and the historians involved probably thought of themselves as extending the range of man's knowledge. The test, if there is a test here, is in whether these ideas were pushed beyond the available evidence; or, to look at this another way, a man was a bad historian if he used portents or astrology to replace analysis rather than to assist it.

Implied in all of this was the notion that history somehow repeated itself. If the purpose of the historian were to demonstrate the workings of God, then the repetitiveness of history would be relatively unimportant, as Christian history was essentially a straight line running from the Creation through the Incarnation to the Second Coming. But even within this frame it might be desirable to show that morality was important, and then it had to be

[3] E. Fueter, *Histoire de l'historiographie moderne*, trans. É. Jeanmaire (Paris, 1914), tends to use omens, etc., as a yardstick; but see F. Guicciardini, *The Historie of Guicciardin*, trans. Geoffrey Fenton (London, 1618), pp. 31–32; Jean Bodin, *Method for the Easy Comprehension of History*, trans. and ed. Beatrice Reynolds (New York, 1945), pp. 223–236; William Camden, British Museum, Cotton MSS, Julius F.xi, foll. 70^v–71^r, 151^v–152^v, etc.

assumed that similar situations would offer similar moral choices. If not, then men could not learn from the past how to improve themselves. The same situation existed if the lesson were political. The humanist Sir John Cheke, discoursing on the restoration of religion, compared Henry VIII to the kings of the Old Testament:

> And since the divine providence is not tied to any one age of mankind, or single nation, but is universally diffused throughout all the periods of all nations and times; when we see the same sequel of real events in those, whose studies, and pains, and favour, have been all of them laid out in the reformation of religion; shall we doubt in believing it to be the same cause which the Scripture assigns to have been in the best of kings? And ought we not, among others, to think ourselves moved by their example? [4]

It was the same line of argument that caused men to investigate omens and portents. Once the conception of the universe as a vast interconnected web was accepted and it was assumed as well that similar causes produced similar events, then a knowledge of portents and what followed them was essential:

> Whereas . . . all thinges under Heaven, are filled with the presence of GOD by his divine power and gratious government, and that nothing can be hid from his heavenly or supercelestiall view: . . . most manifest is it therefore . . . that whatsoever hath bene, is, or shal be to proceede, either Celestiall or Terrestriall, can not be without the fore-ordinance and providence of God, who sending these fore-warnings, as instrumentes to former ages, doth by the like wonderful shewe of manifest appearance foretel no lesse dangers to happen among the generation of this last posteritie. [5]

Others have labored to collect portents and have thus warned their countries of dangers to come: a patriot now could do no less than notify his fellow citizens of the brink on which they stood and over which they would inevitably plummet "unlesse some speedie amendment be found in time acceptable unto God."

Plainly the didacticism of all the sixteenth-century historians

---

[4] "A Treatise of Superstition," in John Strype, *The Life of the Learned Sir John Cheke* (London, 1821), p. 193.

[5] Stephen Batman, *The Doome Warning All Men to the Judgemente* (London, 1581), Dedication, fol. ¶.ii ʳ⁻ᵛ.

was not a conscious choice but was inherent in their very idea of how the universe worked. History that did not teach was utterly inconceivable, and if any changes occurred during the course of the sixteenth century, these had to do not with whether history should teach but with what it taught. In broad terms, the possibilities may be divided into three, ranging from the highly theological to the highly secular. A historian such as the German Bishop Otto of Freising adopted a teleology from St. Augustine and used his history to exemplify the world order: the two cities, the four empires (and the *translatio imperii*) all were preludes to the return of Christ. More common was the use of history to teach moral values. Almost all of the great medieval historians had that idea in their minds, though the degree of emphasis naturally varied. But the idea of what made a man good was itself undergoing change. Not only was a division opening between a man's public and private characters—witness the attacks on the saintly Henry VI for not keeping the peace—but new virtues were added to the canon. Some were the virtues of a good knight, which did not prevent their being secular. The enthusiasm for fame had nothing religious about it, and so even before the advent of humanism and of the idea of *virtù* men were already shifting their ideals. In the course of the sixteenth century that process accelerated. The division between public and private character became more pronounced until, in the end, Machiavelli separated them altogether. But the process was going on even before Machiavelli's influence became strong in England, and the politic historians of the early seventeenth century merely concluded a chain of development which had been in the forge for centuries.

The shift away from the theological to the secular meant a narrowing of focus. No longer was man to be considered in all of his capacities: the emphasis was shifting from the realm of life to that of politics. Similarly, the introduction of the concept of anachronism meant that all of history could no longer be considered as somehow contemporaneous. Once Alexander the Great was removed from the category of knighthood—and he had for centuries been thought of as a knight—then the category itself grew smaller. Once the idea of anachronism took hold, the background of a man or an event assumed more importance, and historians came to seek after those things which made for uniqueness rather than for similarity. The past became fragmented, and the pieces grew ever more discrete. So, gradually, the universal history of the Middle Ages died out. The decline was aided by an increase in patriotism. Just as the interest in history revived, as it did more or less contemporaneously with the Tudors, the divisions of the Wars of the Roses ended, and men no longer felt that their loyalty belonged to one or the other of the warring factions but to England. The Reformation, by cutting some of the ties binding England to the common body of Catholic Christendom and by raising up new enemies to force Englishmen into a common purpose, served to increase the power of the new national feeling. And the emphasis on English as a language equal in its potentialities to any other—a legacy of the very early Renaissance by way of Chaucer, and of the Reformation with its insistence on the vernacular—operated in the same way. Men wanted to read English history first.

New ways of writing history were obviously required. The idea of anachronism meant that the whole history of England needed to be rethought. The emphasis on the secular, and especially on the political, meant that the standards of accuracy had to be revised. More important still, the techniques of ordering the materials of the past required a total overhaul. The stuffed annals of the old days gradually became unworkable in the new context. Finally, the new imports from the Continent had to be absorbed. The end product of all these changes still bore a resemblance to the chronicle of the fifteenth century, but by the end of the first quarter of the seventeenth century that resemblance had vanished from the sight of all but the most observant.

I

The Late Medieval Chronicle

By the fifteenth century the art of writing chronicles had nearly vanished. Those monasteries which in their prime had encouraged some member of the scriptorium to devote a part of his time to recording events now themselves no longer flourished. Except at St. Albans, where the long and illustrious tradition of chronicling was now revivified by Thomas of Walsingham, and Canterbury, where Thomas of Elmham wrote of Henry V, the early years of the century saw the extinction of the monastic chronicles. What historical enthusiasm remained in the monasteries was devoted to the copying and enlarging of treatises on the origins of monastic life, and these, while antiquarian, began as *apologia* for the monks vis-à-vis the friars and, one suspects, an increasingly indifferent secular population.[1]

If the chronicle could no longer flourish in the cloister, was there any other soil in which it might take root? The problem is complicated by the lack of standing of history in the general context of medieval thought. Medieval curricula had no place for history except insofar as it might be subsumed under rhetoric. The prevailing scholasticism concerned itself more with the eternal verities than with the transitory flux of human events, and except as another proof of God's orderliness history was excluded from the territory of the reigning queen of the sciences, theology. Nor

[1] For later medieval historiography, C. L. Kingsford, *English Historical Literature in the Fifteenth Century* (Oxford, 1913); V. H. Galbraith, *Historical Research in Medieval England* (London, 1951); Denys Hay, "History and Historians in France and England during the Fifteenth Century," *Bulletin of the Institute of Historical Research*, XXXV (1962), 111–127. See also the relevant discussions in Dom David Knowles, *The Religious Orders in England*, 3 vols. (Cambridge, Eng., 1948–59), and C. S. Lewis, *The Discarded Image: An Introduction to Medieval and Renaissance Literature* (Cambridge, Eng., 1964), pp. 174–185.

could secular authority see much reason to encourage chronicling. On some rare occasions the country might be searched for evidence supporting the crown's claim to Scotland; occasionally one feels that the St. Albans chroniclers, particularly Matthew Paris, had a quasi-official status, but a royal historiographer after the French model simply did not exist, and St. Albans never held the same position as S. Denis. History writing in fifteenth-century England held no official position, and its haven in the monasteries was gradually closing.

The result was the decline and termination of the classic medieval Latin chronicle. Its readership had always been limited to the educated, and whatever view one takes of the extent of literacy in the Middle Ages, this group can never have been a very large one. A revival of chronicling depended on the demands of a new audience, and this turned out to be an audience of laymen with some education and with interests only in certain specific aspects of the past. For them the chronicles had to be written in English. The groups involved were the wealthier merchants, mostly but not exclusively in London, and some members of the wealthier landed class, and what they wanted to read was a kind of general history slanted in the one case toward city history and in the other toward heroic legendry. The works that they read were the *Polychronicon* of Ranulph Higden, as Englished by John of Trevisa, and the chronicle of the *Brut*.

Both the *Polychronicon* and the *Brut* were early published by Caxton, and both ran through a large number of editions. Of the two, the *Polychronicon* covered the wider ground, since it at least purported to include the history of the world; the *Brut* was more strictly a British history, though non-British material was by no means entirely excluded. Geoffrey of Monmouth's version of the early history of the Britons permeated both works, but while it lay as the foundation of the *Brut,* it was tempered in Higden's work by his use of a wide range of other English, and of foreign, historians. The *Brut* was somewhat more manageable than the *Polychronicon:* where the latter required in excess of two hundred leaves to reach the Anglo-Saxon invasions, one version of the former arrived at the same point in merely thirty-three.[2] One result of the

---

[2] *Cronycle of England* (London: R. Pynson, 1510).

greater brevity was a wider popularity, and so it was the manuscripts of the *Brut* that were usually kept up to date, with the paradoxical result that it is more full for the later reigns (Edward III's, for instance) than the *Polychronicon*. Again, one must wonder how much of the popularity of the *Brut* was due to its greater concentration on British history, to its enthusiasm for the tales of Arthur's heroism at home and abroad, at a time when patriotism was encouraged by the adventures of Henry V. Thus, not surprisingly, those city chronicles that do not stand alone are usually found grafted onto some version of the *Brut*.[3]

Even a cursory examination of the two books indicates that their compilers shared some common characteristics. The most obvious, and that most widely diffused through the two works, was a belief in the orderliness of the universe. Whatever the role of Providence, human affairs were not controlled by chance. However far away from their schema the compilers moved, their theological framework remained visible. The crucial events in man's history were those related in the Old and New Testaments, with the Incarnation at the very center. So there was, in each book, a framework based on the ages of the world, combined with another derived more specifically from British history. The *Polychronicon*, as befitted a universal history intended for an age sorely lacking in geographical knowledge, opened with the dimensions of the world, and not until sixty leaves of description were past did Adam make his appearance. Thereafter a new book marked the advent of the revolutions in the history of man: the destruction of the Temple and the transmigrations of the Jews (traditionally the fifth age) began the third book; the birth of Christ opened the fourth. Then the scene shifted to England. Book Five began with Vortigern, that is, with the coming of the Anglo-Saxons; Book Six saw the arrival of the Danes, Book Seven that of William the Conqueror. Caxton introduced an eighth book, taking the story from 1358, where Higden and Trevisa had left it; but his *liber ultimus* was a matter of convenience whose chronological dimensions are meaningless. This was obviously a compromise between two systems which were essentially in opposition. The theological view of his-

[3] City chronicles are discussed in Kingsford, *English Historical Literature,* and also in his edition of *Chronicles of London* (Oxford, 1905), as well as in Ralph Flenley, *Six Town Chronicles of England* (Oxford, 1911).

tory was predicated on the idea that after the Incarnation man moved through a world in which the thought of heaven and hell was omnipresent and in which the most important event was impending rather than already past: the Second Coming. However, the millenarian fervor of the early Christians was gone; the Second Coming was clearly in the future, but that future seemed increasingly remote. The closest that one could come to theology, in terms of historical organization, was to argue the idea of the four monarchies, but whatever might be said for that theologically, its usefulness in terms of a history oriented toward Britain was minimal. Hence, the emphasis shifted away from a theological toward a secular and national system of organization, and rather than concentrate on the Roman Empire as the last of the four monarchies, the *Brut* and the *Polychronicon* concentrated on Britain. A general idea of order, of course, survived the shift even so; and the more specific idea of the omnipotence—and omnipresence—of God was as appropriate to national as to theological history.

If man's stay on earth was brief and its sole purpose was to effect his entrance into heaven—and all of this was implied in the theological view of history as well as, of course, in the teachings of Christianity—then the reading of history should play its part in enabling man to achieve his goal. It did so by teaching man what to do and what to eschew, not in a political sense (that is, what works and what does not) but in a moral one. History could serve as the example illustrating a precept; reading in the chronicles gave a man experience of various places without the necessity of travel; more than that, history could furnish a man with vicarious experience, enabling him to grow old in wisdom without growing old in years. In short a reader of the chronicles could avoid the sort of errors which, if repeated often enough, might lead him to damnation.[4]

In most cases the moral teaching of the chronicles was general: it applied to all sorts and conditions of men, though in the nature of things the lessons were most appropriate to the ruling orders.

[4] W. J. B. Crotch, ed. *The Prologues and Epilogues of William Caxton,* Early English Text Soc., O.S., No. 176 (London, 1928), pp. 64–65 (prologue to *Polychronicon*).

Occasionally some author might be more specific. John Hardyng tried to influence royal policy by encouraging the king to seize Scotland; more to the point at issue here, he explained to Richard, Duke of York, exactly what was lacking in Lancastrian kingship—strong laws, rigorously enforced—and how a strong moral stand by the ruler would improve the lot of all Englishmen, not only politically but morally as well. Hardyng's former patron, Sir Robert Umfraville, served as an example of an honest and fearless knight, a good servant to his king, a good friend to his neighbors, a good master to his household. And Umfraville, as seen by Hardyng, well illustrated the moral bias of the English chroniclers, for he was presented as a model of righteousness rather than as a pattern of chivalry, though he would have served well for either.[5]

Indeed, this same moral bias raises some other basic problems. It has been assumed that history, to fifteenth-century writers, was a record of past events. There is some evidence, however, that even this simple definition is insufficiently elastic. A record of past events, to be sure, was included under the rubric of history, but so were other narratives. In fact, any truthful-seeming narrative might be called a history; the word could be used to mean no more than story. Caxton, although he made the point that "yf the terryble feyned Fables of Poetes have moche styred and moeved men to pyte / and conservynge of Justyce / How moche more is to be supposed / that Historye assertryce of veryte"[6] does the same, nonetheless also referred to the *Polychronicon* as containing "many wonderful historyees" and included among the last not only the deeds of men but also the description of the world.[7] Lydgate thought of his *Siege of Thebes* and his *Troy Book* as histories too, because of their truth; and Lord Berners referred to Theseus and Hercules, just after quoting Cicero's encomia on history, with no sense of incongruity.[8] It becomes evident from all of this that the

[5] *The Chronicle of Jhon Hardyng in Metre*, ed. Richard Grafton (London, 1543), foll. xxvi^{r-v}, xlvi^r; Kingsford, "The First Version of Hardyng's Chronicle," *English Historical Review*, XXVII (1912), 462–482, 740–753.

[6] Crotch, ed. *Caxton*, p. 65.

[7] Ibid., p. 67.

[8] Walter F. Schirmer, *John Lydgate: A Study in the Culture of the XVth Century* (Berkeley, 1961), pp. 47–48, 64; "The Preface of Johan Bourchier, Knyght," *The Chronicle of Froissart*, ed. W. P. Ker, Tudor Trans., 6 vols. (London, 1901–03), I, 4–5.

chief criterion for historical truth was moral utility. If a ruler, or even an ordinary citizen, could learn how to behave from a story, then it was in some sense history. The result of this view was that criticism, or even doubt, became difficult, largely because it was irrelevant. The most one might hope for was a blanket denial of responsibility: "wherfore in the writyng of this historye. I take not upon me to afferme for trouthe all that I wryte but suche as I have seen and redde in dyvers bookes"; and even this statement was preceded, a bit up the page, by a quotation from St. Augustine: "We sholde trow and worshyppe the myracles of god / and not them dyspreve by dysputacyon wonders ben not all to be un-trowed." [9]

If the moral preconceptions of the chroniclers did little to en-courage even a slight degree of skepticism, it is not surprising to discover that they did no more to cause any change in the tra-ditional methods of organization. In an illuminating introductory note, the St. Albans chronicler listed a whole series of devices which could be used to divide up, and hence understand, the past. One was a single division into the usual two periods, B.C. and A.D., here named the ages of deviation and reconciliation; another scheme, not very different, had three categories: before the law of Moses, under the law, and under the law of grace (after Christ died). There was, of course, also the well-known division into four kingdoms, as well as the less known order of Holy Scripture (under fathers, under judges, under kings, under bishops). The diversity of laws, from the laws of nature to the law of the Muslims, offered another possibility. "The fythe is. The noblynesse, or unnoblynesse in dedes And as to Thyse. It is to knowe that .vij. persones ben redde of / whom the dedes many tymes are hadde in mynde in historyes / That is to wyte / of a prynce in his reame / of a knyghte in batayll / of a Juge in his place / of a bysshop in the clergy / of a polityk man in the people / of an husband man in the hous / & of an abbot in his chyrche. And of thise are wryten many tymes. the laudes of gode men / & the punysshmentes of the cur-syd men." [10] The last would seem to be a most appropriate, if

[9] Ranulph Higden, *Polycronycon* (London, 1527), fol. iv[v].
[10] *The Cronycle of Englonde with the Fruite of Tymes* (Westminster, 1497), foll. a.i[v]–a.ii[r].

difficult, scheme of organization for one wishing to inculcate morality. In fact, as we have seen, the *Polychronicon* and the *Brut* and their immediate derivatives followed none of these methods. The divisions suggested here were basically theological, and it was only recommended that the reader keep them in mind: the actual division was a compound of theological and secular; and neither the actual divisions nor the suggested ones had anything at all to do with the stated purpose of the chronicles, promoting morality.

It is not surprising that there should have been some confusion. Not only did the authors of the *Polychronicon* and *Brut* have to make use of organizational systems originally designed for purposes different from theirs, but there was the additional problem that both works were compilations and that both then suffered from excessive accretion. To find a clear system of organization, one must turn to a work such as Lydgate's *Fall of Princes*. The *de casibus* pattern—the pattern of rise and fall—came from Boccaccio and was essentially an elaboration of the very old idea of Fortune's wheel.[11] Even here the precise purpose of the author was not always easy to fathom. In some cases the paradigm of rise and fall was used to demonstrate the mutability of Fortune, without consideration of the deserts of the victim. That was the way of life on earth: everything was changeable, and the only certainty awaited in heaven. In other cases, and these the most interesting, men struggled to climb the wheel to its top but in so doing became sufficiently sinful, because of pride or avarice, to warrant their being dashed once more to the ground from which they had so painfully raised themselves. In its most extreme form the moral became "Do not struggle; put away ambition, for success is temporary and inevitable failure leads to damnation." But a transmutation to "follow your métier as best you can, but sin not" was possible. Whatever the moral, however, an order had been imposed upon the past, and the events of a man's life could be seen as a pyramid with its top skewed toward the right: a slow rise to the heights followed by an abrupt fall. All this was to become very familiar. Cavendish organized his *Life of Wolsey* according to this

[11] Howard R. Patch, *The Goddess Fortuna in Medieval Literature* (Cambridge, Mass., 1927), and Willard Farnham, *The Medieval Heritage of Elizabethan Tragedy* (Oxford, 1956), Chs. i–iv.

principle, and the authors of the *Mirror for Magistrates* popularized it so that it became an Elizabethan commonplace.

John Hardyng worked out a different solution to the problem of
finding an operative principle in history. Unlike Lydgate, he had
to construct a consecutive narrative rather than a series of biogra-
phies, and the method used was purely chronological. But Hardyng went a step further by asking why kingdoms—and kings—
run into difficulty, and his answer, if not very sophisticated, at
least made good sense. In essence, Hardyng read the situation of
the fifteenth century back into the past and thus found a yardstick
for judging ancient rulers as well as a technique for making history
useful. "Elynguellus kyng of Brytein had greate will to here all
menne when thei came to hym, whiche is a vertue. For greate
cunnyng maketh a manne wyse and to knowe muche, and for
mischefes to fynde remedies, as my lord Umfrewill commended
never a manne, that putteth a mischief and canne fynde no reme-
die therfore." [12] The advice involved here was both political and
moral, and it is advice that was repeated throughout the book.
Cadwallader was scored for his "impotence," a defect that led to
disorder and lack of law; these then led to utter chaos and the ruin
of the land and the church. On the other hand, Henry V served as
a good example:

> Above all thynge he kept the lawe and pese
> Thurgh all Englonde, that none insurreccion
> Ne no riotes than wer withouten lese,
> Ne neyghbours werre in fawte of his correccion:
> Bot pesybly undyr his proteccion
> Compleyntes of wrongs alway in generall
> Refourmed were so undyr his yerde egall. [13]

And this lesson could be learned equally well by Henry VI or by
his opponent, Richard, Duke of York, for both of whom it was at
various times intended.

Of the fifteenth-century chroniclers, Hardyng is the only one
who was not merely embroidering work that came ready to his
hand, and one suspects that part of the reason was his close

---

[12] *The Chronicle of Jhon Hardyng*, fol. xxxv^r.
[13] C. L. Kingsford, "The First Version of Hardyng's Chronicle," p. 744.

association with poets rather than with historians. Whatever one may think of his verse—and it is difficult to find anything good in it—his choice of poetry rather than prose indicates where his allegiance lay. He had certainly read Lydgate, and that experience proved more lasting than any immersion in the chroniclers. The result was a work which could appeal to the educated lay audience for which it was created: the same audience which read Lydgate and Chaucer.[14] But a new kind of lay audience was coming into being in the fifteenth century, an audience which in most cases not only read chronicles but also wrote them. Civic patriotism was not a new phenomenon in England, and it had been exceptionally strong in London. Now with a new enthusiasm for the English language, which made the older Latin and Anglo-French chronicles obsolete, plus the gradual establishment of London as the only strong corporate body in the realm, the citizens grew more and more interested in the history of England and its reflection in the stories of their own city.

Manuscripts of London chronicles exist by the dozen, and no two are completely alike. Some are attached to the *Brut;* some begin with the traditional date of 1189, when bailiffs were first elected. What seems to have happened was that some merchant had a chronicle copied by a professional scribe, and this copy would itself include some of the continuations of the original (which continuations and how far they extended depended on the manuscript chosen); then the merchant would keep his copy more or less up to date until, later, it too might serve as the basis for a new copy for someone else. The chronicles that resulted bear evident signs of their origin. The London segments, which alone are of interest here, are nothing besides a record of events. There was no theorizing, and the bias was a local one: more so even than the monks, the city men saw the world with blinkers. The events were, for the most part, those concerning London, and even national and ecclesiastical affairs were seen narrowly. Sporadically, patriotism occasioned the inclusion of the deeds of heroic Englishmen—there was much on Agincourt; once in a while a human

---

[14] There is a reference to "Bochas" (i.e., Boccaccio) on fol. xcvii^v: I assume this refers to Lydgate's translation, *The Fall of Princes;* his intended audience—warriors and their wives and children—are apostrophized, foll. v^v–vi^r.

love of gossip led to a paragraph on the misdeeds of the mighty; and merchants whose taste ran that way might well note portents and their implications. Accuracy in detail was prized, and one result was the inclusion in the city chronicles of vast heaps of contemporary documents. Neither logic nor order was responsible for their selection; whatever came to hand—treaties, letters, speeches, lists of soldiers, accounts of panoply—was placed in its chronological slot. The authors and the readers of these chronicles were concerned with the raw materials of the past, and especially with those of their own recent past. As men more secular-minded than most, they collected the records and accounts of their city and of those national affairs that impinged on their city. Their curiosity never extended very far back into the past, nor did it run to an investigation of causes. These chronicles are preeminently records of contemporary events, and there is never any attempt to evaluate the root stock onto which each merchant grafted his own contribution.

One can see the extremes that such a system of writing made possible by glancing at the chronicles of Richard Arnold and Robert Fabyan. The haberdasher Arnold compiled a volume on the *Customs of London* of which his chronicle was only a small part; the fact that the whole frequently goes by the name of the part has only given rise to disappointment. The *Customs* was a miscellany, a kind of commonplace book, in which the ballad of the Nut-Brown Maid and a description of the Four Monarchies stood side by side with no incongruity. The encapsulated chronicle is irritatingly brief in its entries, and there is never a sign of a personal opinion. The not unimportant year 1485 serves as a typical example of Arnold's style:

> Thomas hylle mair. Richard chestir Thomas bretayn sherefs the iii. yere [of Richard III] This yere in decembre deyd Richard Chester. & for hym chosen Rauf astry and the same yere in august. The erle of Richmond wyth the erle of penprok that longe had been banysshyd came in to england and the od' [other] gentylmen that fled in to Fraunce made a felde beside leyceter and the kinge there slayn. And the erle of Richmond was crowned the xxx. day of Octibre. And aboute candylmas maried kinge Edwardes eldest doughter. And this yere in Septembre deyed Thomas

hylle, and for hym choson w stockar And he deyed the third daye after. & than was chosen Johñ ward and ocupyed tyll seint Ed. daye.[15]

Fear of commenting on fairly recent politics might explain such brevity, but in fact all the entries are about equally laconic. Arnold's chronicle seems to fit with one's idea of an early almanac, and the rest of his book serves only to reinforce the notion.

Fabyan's work was far different, although the author came from much the same background as Arnold and indeed reached the office of sheriff. The point of departure is that Fabyan was literary-minded. Naturally, he collected facts; but he was not content to do only that, and insisted on comparing accounts as well. When the accounts disagreed, Fabyan resisted the temptation to choose the most plausible—or the one that best suited his prejudices—and noted the differences, sometimes in considerable detail. Most of the time Fabyan tamely followed the lead of Geoffrey of Monmouth: the fact that Geoffrey was occasionally and demonstrably wrong did not shake Fabyan's faith in him, for the simple reason that no one else filled the unbearable gaps in early British history. Yet one does come upon passages such as that which begins: "But here I entend to leve the farther processe of myn authour Gaufride, for so myche as here he varieth from other writers of authority, as Eutropius, Titus Livius, & other, that dyd great dilygence in writynge of the dedys & acts of the Romayns, and of other peple dwellyng at those dayes in Italia, Gallia, & Germania." [16] Then followed the story of Brennus, and the telling depended as much on the *Polychronicon* as on any other source, but Fabyan did in fact refer to Livy and Eutropius, and to others as well. He did not extend his analysis to the authors he cited: there was no feeling of internal consistency, nor did Fabyan notice that some of his sources (for instance, the *Polychronicon* and Geoffrey) were not independent of each other.

Not every case was quite as clear-cut. Fabyan did doubt Geoffrey's story of the marriage of Arviragus to the daughter of the Emperor Claudius, but he doubted the form of the story rather

[15] [*Customs of London Otherwise Called Arnold's Chronicle*] ([Antwerp, 1503]), fol. [A.vii^r].
[16] *Fabyans Cronycle* (London, 1533), Pt. I, fol. xii^v.

than the fact of the marriage. The only sources used here were the *Polychronicon*, whose story Fabyan preferred, and the English chronicle (that is, the *Brut*) and its source, Geoffrey. The Romans who wrote on the subject received no mention. However, Fabyan's reasons for rejecting Geoffrey give an insight into his critical habits:

> And all be yt that myne authore Gaufryde varyeth not myche from the englyshe cronicle: I thynke in that doynge he toke example of Homerus, that wrote the dedis and actes of the Grekes / the whyche shewed and put in memory all the noble actes by them done, and specyally in the recuyll or boke made by hym of the syege of Troye. But the other dedys concernynge theyr dyshonoure / he hyde yt as mych as he myght. And in lyke maner do many other writers, which I passe over. And so Gaufride for he was a Bryton, he shewed the beste for Brytons.[17]

It was a plausible explanation. Where a similar problem occurred concerning the martyrdom of Saint Ursula, Fabyan again compared accounts, though in this case he reserved judgment and sent his readers off to the Legend of Saints as read yearly in the churches. It will be noted that Fabyan's skepticism was far from radical: he had doubts concerning details, not concerning the acts themselves, for if any deed appeared in a chronicle, then it must have taken place. As he himself said, after telling a peculiarly vivid and improbable tale of a female sorceress carried away to hell, "Thys wolde I not have shewed, but that I fynde it wryten and recorded of divers authours."[18]

Fabyan's approach was, for the fifteenth century, unusual. Higden, much earlier, had had some few doubts; and Caxton felt it necessary to defend the authenticity of Arthur by setting forth, very cogently and at length, the facts pointing to his existence.[19] By and large, however, the past, and comment on the past, was accepted without question. Nor was there anything especially new in the writers we have considered: some of their predecessors—for instance, William of Malmesbury—had thought more carefully about similar problems, and Matthew Paris and Thomas of Wals-

[17] Ibid., Pt. I, fol. xix^v.
[18] Ibid., Pt. I, fol. cxxxv^v [*recte* 136]. Fabyan was, however, skeptical of how Richard Lion-hearted received his name (ibid., Pt. II, fol. vii^r).
[19] Crotch, ed. *Caxton*, 93–94.

ingham had constructed narratives more competently. It must be admitted that the construction of a smoothly flowing narrative was not a major concern of many of the fifteenth-century chroniclers who were, instead, engaged in composing aids to the memory. In the men whose work we have examined there was no sense of anachronism; for them all history was present history, either because it expressed a theological schema that was equally valid in all times or places or, finally, because it listed facts useful to one or another group of readers. Fabyan, who approached closest to a system of criticism, nonetheless had little sense of improbability and certainly never asked whether a given event was likely to have happened in a particular place and at a particular time. Insofar as the idea of anachronism took root anywhere, it did so in the illustrations in John Rous's Warwick Roll. Rous had a strong visual sense and in depicting the earls of Warwick did manage to get the armor in correct temporal sequence. On the other hand, the same John Rous wrote a history of Britain which shows no trace of historical insight. And it was the visual rather than the analytic which characterized William of Worcester as well. There is no question that his curiosity was boundless, that he measured and examined and made use of documentation, but there was no synthesis of any sort involved, and whatever one thinks of his importance as the first of the traveling antiquaries, his importance in the history of historical writing is small.[20]

The great age of the city chronicle came in the fifteenth century. Then, with the invention of printing, every merchant who wished a chronicle could purchase one cheaply enough. Since men no longer had to copy the work of their predecessors—or have it copied—they were less inclined to master the techniques of writing chronicles. What happened, in short, was that chronicles were more widely distributed so that they were no longer limited to a

[20] T. D. Kendrick, *British Antiquity* (London, 1950), pp. 18–33; Sir James Mann, "Instances of Antiquarian Feeling in Medieval and Renaissance Art," *Archaeological Journal*, LXXXIX (1932), 254–274; Levi Fox, ed. *English Historical Scholarship in the Sixteenth and Seventeenth Centuries,* Dugdale Soc. (Oxford, 1956), pp. 129–132; K. B. McFarlane, "William Worcester: A Preliminary Survey," *Studies Presented to Sir Hilary Jenkinson,* ed. J. Conway Davies (Oxford, 1957), pp. 196–221.

few very interested persons, and the increasing rapidity with which
new editions followed one another made it unnecessary for a man
to keep his up to date himself. The result was the predictable one,
that the old London chronicle, the manuscript record of public
events, gradually degenerated into a species of half public, half
private diary. Since the new printed volumes were oriented to
London, it might be expected that some of the provincial cities
would preserve chronicles of their own. A good many do, indeed,
survive, some written by town officials out of the local records,
others by merchants of historical tastes; few are more than bare
compilations. Again the printed volumes may be blamed to an
extent, since events of national interest were fully and readily
available in them. Moreover, outside London and perhaps Bristol,
the corporate spirit was never so strong in England as it was in,
say, Italy, and in the sixteenth century London grew more and
more rapidly while the outports declined. At the same time, the
merchant aristocracy of the provincial towns was very limited in
numbers: they either knew what was happening (and what had
happened) or they had access to the records, among which, in fact,
the town chronicles might be included. Since it was these same
merchants who would have been most likely to read, and write, the
local chronicles, it is no wonder that few were produced.

The Calais chronicle, extending to 1540, exemplifies the degenerate nature of the provincial city chronicles. Its author wrote
about the history of the city, and even events of more general
importance were seen entirely in terms of their effects on Calais.
Moreover, the chronicler had no sense of discrimination at all: any
event that was at all out of the ordinary was included, regardless of
its importance: "1509, the 24. of Awgust, the 1. of Henry the
Eighth, ther came a grete swarme of bees, and light on the bole
undar the wetharcoke of S. Nicholas steple in Caleys, at xi. of the
cloke, and sat tyll iij. in the aftarnone." [21] Unlike some of the
medieval chroniclers, the author of the *Chronicle of Calais* drew
absolutely no conclusion from these mysterious occurrences, not
even a conclusion of an ominous or portentous sort. The King's
Lynn chronicle, while not so given over to trivia, nonetheless

[21] *The Chronicle of Calais in the Reigns of Henry VII. and Henry VIII.*, ed.
John Gough Nichols, Camden Soc. (London, 1846), p. 7.

resembles that of Calais in its determinedly local character: the accession of Queen Mary was seen in terms of the proclamations made in the town, the Armada in terms of the ships that King's Lynn contributed. In the latter case the three sentences on the Armada were immediately followed by another of entirely local interest: "Also in this yeare the warehouses on the northe side of Common Stayne yeard were newe buylded." There is no sense of incongruity, nor any real sense of the past, merely a feeling for the continuity of a microscopic political organism.[22]

It must not be supposed that the few London chronicles were much better. They were centered as completely on the locality, the principal difference being that London was, of course, the political cockpit of the nation. Because of the existence of the printed chronicles, the London records tend to be more idiosyncratic than their provincial cousins. The very brief chronicle for the years 1500–1545 (14 pages) was based, as all were, on the mayoral years, but the material was intended largely to illustrate the executions not only of felons but also, once the Reformation was under way, of roods and images.[23] The Grey Friars chronicle was much more full, but it too preserved its aloofness. One would have thought that a crypto-monastic record would have contained indications of feeling about the Reformation, but while there is no question that the author disapproved of the proceedings, the disapproval was very muted. Indeed, a reading of the chronicle leaves one with the impression that its author wrote with the suspicion that an agent of the king stood always behind his shoulder. The Wars of the Roses drew no comment, either on Henry IV's usurpation as beginning them, nor on Henry VII's accession as their conclusion. The brief and equally inconclusive chronicle of Arnold was probably the source of the early material, but even when the chronicle took on its own life, it remained merely a record. The annal for 1533/4 began with the Maid of Kent, continued with a hanging, and then went on to what would seem to us the major matter of the year: "And this yere was the byshoppe of

---

[22] Flenley, *Six Town Chronicles*, p. 31n; there is a discussion of provincial chronicles generally, pp. 27–38.

[23] *London Chronicle during the Reigns of Henry the Seventh and Henry the Eighth*, ed. Clarence Hopper, Camden Miscellany IV (London, 1859).

Rome('s) powre pu[t down, and] a pes concludyd with Scotlond that lastyd but a wy[le]." Perhaps the author agreed with his king that the Pope's power was excessive; there was no complaint until 1550, when the confusion of religious practice brought an exclamation of discouragement.[24]

The two fullest of the London chronicles are more respectable. Henry Machyn's account is usually called a diary, and although it is not a personal document in the sense of containing introspection, it is highly personal in its choice of what to record. Since its author had no especial interest in history writing and was in no sense writing or continuing a permanent record, Machyn's *Diary* is best ignored. The chronicle of Charles Wriothesley, Windsor Herald, is fully in the tradition of the fifteenth century. The earlier parts were copied from Arnold and the whole was intended as a continuation of him. Mayoral years provided the skeleton of organization, but the flesh with which the bones were padded consists of a wide variety of heterogeneous details. Wriothesley included a substantial bloc of raw documentation, and, the concerns of his day being what they were, sermons and scaffold speeches were numerous. It is almost needless to add that the usual quota of two-headed calves, deformed children, apparitions and spirits, and droughts and alarums were also included. From all of this no conclusions were drawn besides the obvious ones of loyalty to the crown and to the city. Wriothesley's *Chronicle* was simply an anachronism.[25]

Most of the substantial chronicles of the earlier half of the sixteenth century will concern us later. Grafton's continuations of Fabyan and Hardyng as well as his own works, Hall's *Union*, and their successors are best treated as successors of Polydore Vergil, whose Latin history they borrowed in substantial quantities. The fact that these were the major works available and that most went through several editions ought not to be forgotten here, for they

---

[24] *Chronicle of the Grey Friars of London,* ed. Nichols, Camden Soc. (London, 1852), p. 37. See also p. 67: "And the Assumpcion of our Lady was soche devision thorrow alle London that some kepte holy day and some none. Almyghty God helpe it whan hys wylle ys! for this was the second yere, and also the same devision was at the fest of the Nativitie of our Lady."

[25] *The Diary of Henry Machyn,* ed. Nichols, Camden Soc. (London, 1848); Charles Wriothesley, *A Chronicle of England during the Reigns of the Tudors,* ed. W. D. Hamilton, Camden Soc., 2 vols. (London, 1875–77).

were the great competitors of the old manuscript chronicles. But they were by no means the only ones. Some time before 1535 the printer Robert Wyer issued *A Cronycle Begynnynge at the .vii. Ages of the Worlde,* which he may well have compiled himself. In essence, the work was a highly distilled version of the *Brut,* listing only a few major events from Brutus to William the Conqueror and then giving John Lydgate's brief verses on the kings of England. The whole was so brief and so compressed as to lack almost any sort of utility: one is inclined to wonder who (if anyone) purchased it, a wonderment that the existence of only one edition exacerbates. The book entitled *A Short Cronycle* (1539/40) constitutes some improvement. Still very brief, this anonymous work at least began late, with the accession of Henry IV, and thus managed to get a few more details under each monarch. After listing the dates for the law terms, the author proceeded year by year, in each case naming the mayor of London and the sheriffs, though for many of the years no entries were supplied. Before the reign of Henry VIII the notices were kept short: the French wars of Henry V received as an entry only the laconic statement "The batayle of Agyncourte." The longest story told of the reign of Edward IV was of that king's going hunting with the mayor and aldermen of London. Not surprisingly, the later notices of Henry VIII's reign approved of his doings, and the Reformation was dealt with (comparatively speaking) in some detail. More interesting, the pro-Reformation bias was extended backward: for 1410, a bill in Parliament against the clergy's wasting of the temporalities found a place, and so, later, did the execution of Sir John Oldcastle—events which, granting the scale of the chronicle, might well have been omitted. Nonetheless, however brief, this was definitely a London chronicle and followed the pattern as clearly as could be expected.

The remaining productions of this class were cast in much the same mold as *A Short Cronycle,* that is, they were abbreviated versions of the standard fifteenth-century city chronicle. *A Cronicle of Yeres* (1552) also began with such needful information as the law terms, adding to this the eras from the creation. The latter information was required because the chronicle purported to include all English history: in fact, the period from Ascanius to Henry I was compressed onto a page, the three hundred years ensuing onto another, and not until the reign of Henry IV were the sheriffs and the mayor listed. Again, the information for Henry VIII's reign was more full, but the entries were hardly comprehensive. Where the *Short Cronycle* had ended with a brief description of England, *A Cronicle of Yeres* added lists of the roads. The entries in the two chronicles were not identical, but the spirit surely was. The work entitled *A Briefe Cronicle,* published early in Elizabeth's reign, was an expansion of its immediate predecessor. Some of the entries are verbally identical, but a calendar was added to the list of law terms, and the section on early history underwent some growth. The anti-Catholic bias was more pronounced: Thomas Becket was denounced in the approved fashion, and acts against the clergy were noticed, even if the acts of the Reformation—and the burnings under Mary—were written down without comment. The latter part of the chronicle, which is very full, is borrowed from the continuation of Fabyan; the very end is original.

The longevity of this species of miniature chronicle indicates something of its popularity. The four chronicles mentioned here constituted at once the end of the old tradition and the commencement of a new. John Stow was to continue to produce such works, and his various sextodecimo chronicles were made in the pattern of their predecessors. But where the early chronicles depended on each other, on Fabyan, and on Fabyan's continuator, Stow's ultimately became abbreviated versions of his own larger works. Nonetheless, the implication is strong that numbers of merchants— and perhaps their apprentices—felt it necessary to know something of the history of their country and their city, and if they learned only a little here, that was better than nothing, and it might even encourage them to learn more.

Some aspects of the late medieval tradition can be seen in George Cavendish's life of his master, Cardinal Wolsey, and in John Proctor's account of Wyatt's rebellion. Cavendish's work, it is true, was not published until 1640, and then in a truncated version, but it was known to Stow, Holinshed, and Speed. Cavendish was a man of good family and some education, but though he was, through his second wife, connected to Sir Thomas More, he seems to have acquired no tincture of the new learning. Certainly there is no evidence of humanism in his life of Wolsey, and Cavendish, although he remained pro-Catholic, had no especial reason to honor the man who succeeded his master as Lord Chancellor. Indeed the principal impression of the man, as one sees him through his writing, is that of a conservative, loving the old ways in all their grandeur and, after Wolsey's fall, retiring to his estates to live out his life as a country squire, separating himself as far as he could from the rapid changes that he so much disliked.[26]

Granting so much about Cavendish's character, the reasons for his writing about the Cardinal are not far to seek. In the first place, Wolsey had to be defended from the charge that he was responsible for the Reformation, that it was his ambition which had led Henry to divorce Katherine and take up Anne Boleyn. That view was prevalent even among the Catholics; if it had been merely another bit of Protestant propaganda, it is likely that Cavendish would not have been interested enough to write a counterattack. Even so, Cavendish felt that he had to go still further: it was the Reformation itself that he had to explain. It is in these reasons that we find the explanation of his method and of his so-called deficiencies. To say that *The Life and Death of Cardinal Wolsey* is "history as seen by a gentleman-usher" is, in a way, to miss the point, for Cavendish would have disclaimed his work as history. It is the record of the rise and fall of a mighty potentate, not a history of the life and times of a statesman, and Cavendish was much more concerned with Wolsey's panoply than with the details of his negotiations for the simple reason that the first was relevant to his theme and the second was not.

Wolsey's career fitted into the *de casibus* pattern of Boccaccio and Lydgate, a neat pyramid with the high road to success leading up one side and the other a rapid plummet to failure and death. To an extent, Cavendish tailored the facts to fit the pattern, but the alterations mostly were intended to foreshorten the time sequence.

[26] On Cavendish, Richard S. Sylvester, "Cavendish's *Life of Wolsey:* The Artistry of a Tudor Biographer," *Studies in Philology*, LVII (1960), 44–71; George Cavendish, *The Life and Death of Cardinal Wolsey*, ed. Richard S. Sylvester, E.E.T.S., No. 243 (London, 1959), which has a superb introduction; and Paul L. Wiley, "Renaissance Exploitation of Cavendish's *Life of Wolsey*," *Studies in Philology*, XLIII (1946), 121–146.

Wolsey's rise had been phenomenal, but because his fall had been more phenomenal still, the first part of the biography had to be foreshortened. For it was Wolsey's fall that most interested Cavendish, the problem of how a man honored almost as if he were king, who sometimes nearly was king, who lived in a pretentious grandeur that matched his position, could so rapidly have the sword of power torn from him. To that question, two answers were possible. One was the operation of the crafty goddess:

> Therfore lett all men to whome ffortune extendythe hir grace not to trust to myche to hir fikkyll favor and plesaunt promysis under Colour wherof she Cariethe venemous galle / ffor whan she seyth hir servaunt in most highest Auctorytie And that he assuryth hyme self most assuredly in hir favour / than tournythe she hir visage And plesaunt countenaunce unto a frownyng chere And utterly forsakyth hyme / suche assuraunce is in hir inconstaunt favour and Sewgerd promyse / whos disseytfull behavour hathe not byn hyd among the wyse sort of famous Clarkes that hathe exclamed hir And written vehemently ayenst hir dissymulacion and fayned favour warnyng all men therby the lesse to regard hir / And to have hir in small estymacion of any trust or ffaythfulnes / [27]

If Wolsey's rise and fall had been due only to the turning of Fortune's wheel, then one must ask, What had the Cardinal to do with it all? Cavendish was far too aware of Wolsey's virtues to reject them in favor of Fortune. But, perhaps more relevantly, what did this leave to the operation of God? For there was no doubt in Cavendish's mind that Wolsey had sinned and was being punished for his sins. His pride had been inordinate; he had had excessive faith in himself and his own powers and had not left enough to Him that guides all men. Cavendish never really solved the problems he raised. Whether it was Fortune that felled Wolsey, or God's just retribution, or a combination of the two was an unanswerable conundrum; and in Cavendish's mind the pagan goddess and the Hebrew God probably merged more and more into one another.[28]

[27] Cavendish, *Life of Wolsey*, ed. Sylvester, p. 13.
[28] This was a general problem of "Fall of Princes" literature from Boccaccio onwards: Willard Farnham, *Medieval Heritage*, esp. pp. 275–277.

There remains the question of how Fortune accomplished the destruction of the Cardinal. Wolsey kept up his triumphant glory "untill ffortune (of whos favour no man is lenger assured than she is dysposed) began to wexe some thyng wrothe with his prosperous estate // thought she wold devyse a mean to abate his hyghe port wherfor she procured Venus the Insaciat goddesse to be hir Instrument to worke hir purpose," [29] and so Henry fell in love with Anne Boleyn, who hated Wolsey and procured his downfall. Anne Boleyn was no fault of Wolsey's, and her appearance throughout the book takes on the character of a *dea ex machina*. What made her success and Henry's possible was the infinite fickleness of the inchoate mob, ready to run where chance and the desire for novelty led it. And this perennial love of change could hardly be blamed on Wolsey. Yet at the very end Wolsey saw his own faults and resigned himself to the mercies of the Almighty.

Thus Wolsey's story, to Cavendish, was at once a moral tale about the just deserts of pride and an opportunity to exculpate the Cardinal. It was Fortune who was responsible for his dramatic collapse, Fortune who supplied Anne Boleyn to ruin him. Wolsey's attitude made his punishment inevitable but was not the cause of it. If it had been, then Cavendish would have had to acknowledge that the Reformation was part of the punishment, and that would have made the punishment far too great for the crime. Wolsey had seen what was coming and had warned Henry of the Lutherans, but by then Wolsey was powerless. The Reformation was no fault of his; at most he helped precipitate his own ruin. The medieval drama of rise and fall had always held within itself this seed of doubt about ultimate causation: in Cavendish's biography the doubt was used deliberately to save a reputation.

Where Cavendish used the idea of rise and fall, John Proctor took the form of the city chronicle and elaborated it into a moral and political tract. When in 1554 Sir Thomas Wyatt the younger had led substantial parts of Kent in a rebellion against Queen Mary, Proctor had been master of the grammar school at Tunbridge Wells. He had seen the tides of revolt sweep the area, had seen how close Wyatt came to success, and had worked out for

[29] Cavendish, *Life of Wolsey*, ed. Sylvester, pp. 28–29.

himself the causes for the uprising and for its failure. A number of
things bothered Proctor exceedingly. Why had God allowed Wyatt
even a temporary success, when the divine power should have
been on the side of the queen? It is not only that Proctor was a
Catholic, though he probably was that; the whole question of the
divine authority of monarchs was at stake. More parochially,
Proctor was concerned to defend Kent from a charge of disorderli-
ness, for it was his contention that most of the county was loyal.
Finally, the ostensible cause of the rebellion worried him: if Wyatt
had really raised the county only against Mary's Spanish marriage,
as many believed, then Wyatt had some justification for his action.
Proctor offered two alternative explanations: the root cause of the
rising was heresy, but mingled with it was greed. The only reason
there was no looting in Kent, he believed, was that the rebels had
their eye on the treasure stored in the Tower.

So Proctor wrote a moral tale in the guise of a chronicle. As the
best of the city chroniclers had done, he too included documents:
proclamations, speeches, and the like. He elaborated a pattern
found in older writers when they spoke of Wat Tyler or Jack
Cade: "The industrie of writers doth sufficiently declare in a numbre of stories, that conspiracie & treason hath alwaies turned to the
authours a wretched & miserable ende, & if their persones happen
at any tyme to escape temporal punishment, yet their names,
specially of the notorious & principal offenders, have ben alwaies
had in such vile & odible detestation in all ages & among all
nations, as for the same thei have been ever after abhorred of all
good men." [30] Wyatt's rebellion was the equal of any of them, in
seriousness and in the courage of the principals—so said Proctor
in his preface, though he changed his mind later and called Wyatt
a coward for fear of making a hero of him. In fact, Proctor
suffered from a divided mind throughout: he felt that the rebellion
had to be recorded, and accurately—so far, at least, he was a historian. But the moral lesson that rebellion taught had to be emphasized too, and so he added to the pattern of the London chronicle a
whole series of sermons addressed to the reader. That was one way
to teach the lessons, but those lessons ought to have been taught by

---

[30] The Historie of Wyate's Rebellion, in The Antiquarian Repertory, ed.
Francis Grose, Thomas Astle et al., 4 vols. (London, 1807–09), III, 67.

the narrative as well. Proctor the moralist came into conflict with Proctor the historian, and omission and inconsistency resulted: "Finallye, if thou suppose I have not fully set furth the whole case al as it was, I shal not againsai it; neither thought I it necessarie so to doe, but rather so muche as for this time might be both plausible and profitable. . . ." [31] What was to be omitted was primarily the political justification of the rebellion.

The Kentishmen were only partly relieved from guilt; not only did some join the rebellion, but large numbers stayed neutral, a position that Proctor thought tantamount to participation. Some risked their lives and possessions in fighting Wyatt, and these Proctor admired; even he had to admit they were too few. Nonetheless, since Wyatt was cowardly, the rebellion would have failed. What really made the difference was the intervention of Brett and his Londoners, those men who deserted from the royal force to join the rebels. It was Brett who kept Wyatt from fleeing overseas when things went badly, Brett who insisted on the push to London. The real troublemakers were the heretics and the Londoners—who were, perhaps, the same; the real sin of Kent was its indifference to rebellion, rather than rebellion itself. That was the lesson of the disturbances raised by Wyatt; what Englishmen had to learn was that unless they were firm, England would turn into another war-torn Bohemia. That was the lesson, too, that all the Tudors, whatever their religion, wanted learned, and Proctor taught it by combining the didactic functions of history, as he found it in the chroniclers, with the more explicit teachings that were afterward to be embodied in the Homily on Obedience.

The older traditions thus continued well into the sixteenth century. The city chronicles kept by individual London merchants gradually became the printed chronicles of the Tudors: once the innovations of Polydore Vergil and Sir Thomas More had been absorbed, Fabyan gave way to Hall and Holinshed and Stow. At the same time an increasing literacy and a continuing civic spirit brought forth abbreviated chronicles. Finally, as the medieval chronicle gave way to its Tudor counterpart, Cavendish and Proctor, by seizing on particular aspects of the old tradition and using

[31] Ibid., p. 68.

them for purposes of their own, showed how much could still be done by following the old ways. Both men limited the scope of their work, one to a biography, the other to a particular incident, and both tried to avoid mere narrative by seeking some structural principle in history. But by the end of Henry's reign other men were doing the same thing and were looking further afield for means of organizing their knowledge of the past.

II

The Advent of Humanism

A number of forces combined to break up the medieval chronicle pattern. An increased national consciousness was one; and allied to that, the new Protestantism. In the long run, however, the most important new influence was that of humanism, an import from Italy and France and Germany which combined with native elements in such a way as to become involved with nationalism and the new religion. What is known as Christian humanism began with Erasmus and John Colet in England and then spread over the northern part of the Continent, where it flourished until it was absorbed by the more intense passions of the Reformation. But the original stock of the plant was Italian, and to understand what happened in the England of Sir Thomas More it is necessary to visit the Italy of Petrarch.

A complete definition of humanism, as it was understood by Petrarch and his successors, is almost impossible to construct. Humanism inevitably involved the study of new subjects, but it also meant a new way of looking at all subjects whatsoever. Professor Kristeller has shown that the term itself derives from *studia humanitatis,* and that this meant, in practice, an interest in the "human values" of grammar, rhetoric, poetry, history, and moral philosophy.[1] But the "human values" are to a large extent inherent in the subjects themselves; and the list excludes logic and theology. *Studia humanitatis* defines an attitude but also implies a limitation of subject matter. In any event, there is more to humanism than this: there is an enthusiasm for good Latin, regardless of the matter to be treated—one reason Petrarch so disliked his scholastic predecessors and contemporaries was that they wrote vile Latin

[1] Paul O. Kristeller, *Studies in Renaissance Thought and Letters* (Rome, 1956), pp. 262, 572–574.

and compounded their sin by refusing to acknowledge it as one. Petrarch was not so much averse to logic as to logic-chopping: he berated the Aristotelians and Averroists for reading each other and not their master. Petrarch was, after all, a sufficiently energetic believer in the virtues of classical antiquity not to wish to exclude Aristotle from the pantheon. On the other hand, the sage of Vaucluse was far from blind to the weaknesses of his classical heroes. The famous letter to Cicero, in which that supreme god of the humanists was berated for his political failings, proves that Petrarch considered morality to be quite as important as style. Nor was this necessarily "medievalism" on Petrarch's part. There was, in the first place, no necessary reason why a humanist could not also be a Christian (though there might be doubt as to how good a Christian any man could be who was interested more in *scientia* than in *sapientia*); more important is the fact that in Petrarch's mind the foil to Cicero was St. Augustine, and the Bishop of Hippo was quite as much a figure of the classical past as the orator. That Augustine himself was a humanist *manqué* meant that he was a poor guide for the man who wished to revive humanism after a lapse of nearly a millennium; and Petrarch realized this, though he was unable to solve the dilemma except by ignoring it.

Petrarch was inordinately aware of his own confusions, and turning his back on a problem was for him not the same as forgetting its existence. In any case, Augustine's advice to ignore the world was more appropriate to the Italy of the barbarian invasions than to that of the rising Visconti and della Scala. A man like Petrarch could go into the world and mingle with princes, and his knowledge of antique precepts might allow him to inculcate classical ideals into the rulers of Italy. It was this possibility that explains Petrarch's anger with Cicero, for the Roman was the great exemplar of one who, capable of leading either the active or the contemplative life, had chosen activity—and who had then proceeded to act badly. But although Cicero's later career was not in Petrarch's eyes an unqualified success, the ideal of civic virtue came gradually to supplant the monastic ideal. The ancient love of the commonweal was embodied, in the generation following Petrarch's, in Coluccio Salutati and later in the succession of humanist chancellors that followed in Salutati's footsteps in Florence.[2]

By the beginning of the fifteenth century, the connection between classical studies and practical—that is, political—life was already being enshrined in the educational theories of the day. The primary purpose of education was to train rulers, not to make scholars, and to fulfill this purpose new curricula had to be devised. In essence, these centered on the liberal arts, and the fifteenth-century definition of that elusive phrase explains a good deal: "We call those studies *liberal* which are worthy of a free man; those studies by which we attain and practise virtue and wisdom; that education which calls forth, trains and develops those highest gifts of body and of mind which ennoble men, and which are rightly judged to rank next in dignity to virtue only." [3] The virtue here emphasized was an active one, active in involving the body as well as the mind, active in working in the world, not in the cloister. The subjects most needful to impart such virtue were three: history, which gave concrete examples, and which was in first place because "of its attractiveness and of its utility"; moral philosophy, which supplied the precepts that history exemplified; and eloquence, which exhibited the truth learned from history and moral philosophy.[4] Vergerius was trying to educate statesmen, not politicians; his was an attempt to deny that the world must needs corrupt, an attempt to find a place for Christian virtues in political life. To be virtuous but removed from the stream of life was not enough.

The study of history in these circumstances took on a new importance. When virtue is defined in theological terms, the study of the past (however useful) is not really necessary; it is only when practical terms are used that the experience of others becomes essential. It was, of course, precisely this that lay at the back of much classical history writing, particularly the work of Livy and Plutarch, and that was the cause of the popularity of both in the

[2] Hans Baron, "Cicero and the Roman Civic Spirit in the Middle Ages and Early Renaissance," *Bulletin of the John Rylands Library*, XXII (1938), 72–97.

[3] P. P. Vergerius, in William H. Woodward, *Vittorino da Feltre and Other Humanist Educators* (Cambridge, Eng., 1897), p. 102.

[4] Ibid., p. 106.

quattrocento. That the virtues taught by Cicero and Livy were pagan virtues was a cause for much soul-searching: Petrarch especially was bothered by this and in some of his letters to the ancients went to great lengths to point up his realization of the fact. It was this problem of pagan virtue that made it so difficult for some men to accept all the implications of humanism: a return to the world of the Greeks and the Romans was inevitably a return to a world before Christ, and that this should be thought desirable was repugnant to many. The neo-paganism of Pomponio Leto and the Romans around him was exceptional, but to his contemporaries it must have seemed as if Pomponio illustrated all the least desirable implications of the humanist position. One suspects the interest in Neoplatonism as deriving at least partially from this same distrust of the incipient paganism of the humanists: one of the effects of Ficino's Christian Platonism was, in essence, to move the boundaries of Christianity back in time.

Much of the difficulty was occasioned by the fact that men were much more conscious of the remoteness of the past. Petrarch, for all of the naïveté shown in the mere fact of his writing to Cicero and Homer, was acutely aware that these men were the inhabitants of times and places different from his own and from each other. Petrarch was capable of judging Cicero by the moral standards of the fourteenth century but nonetheless understood that the political situation in the first century B.C. was very different from anything he knew by his own experience.

It was to this sense of anachronism that the study of philology owed its origin.[5] The best illustration is Lorenzo Valla's attack on the supposed Donation of Constantine, in which Valla demonstrated quite clearly that the vocabulary and phraseology of the document were not those of the early fourth century. The same basic attitude can be found elsewhere: in Valla's own *Elegantiae,*

[5] Erwin Panofsky, *Renaissance and Renascences in Western Art* (Stockholm, 1960), pp. 84–85, 100, describes the typical medieval view of the past in terms of disjunction: "wherever in the high and later Middle Ages a work of art borrows its form from a classical model, this form is almost invariably invested with a non-classical, normally Christian, significance; wherever in the high and later Middle Ages a work of art borrows its theme from classical poetry, legend, history or mythology, this theme is quite invariably presented in a non-classical, normally contemporary, form" (p. 84). Disjunction operated in realms other than art; and becoming aware of it means a developing sense of anachronism.

establishing the canons of Latin style; even in the Ciceronians who took the view that Latin prose style had reached its peak at one particular moment, and thus elevated that style as alone worthy to be imitated. The acknowledgment of growth was implied in the Ciceronians' negative; and the idea of seizing on the best aspects of all styles, or of taking whatever at any moment seemed appropriate, was explicitly rejected, even when it became obvious that Cicero's vocabulary was not entirely adequate to fifteenth-century needs.

This, then, was the first phase of humanism. It involved a return to the classics, a preponderant enthusiasm for style (and hence for philology), and a strong moral bent. In terms of historical criticism, it meant that texts were judged by their Latinity and their moral bearing rather than by their accuracy. All of this was enshrined in the new humanist educational system. Leonardo Bruni, writing on the education of women, placed religion in the forefront but even then could not long forget the new dogmas: ". . . all sources of profitable learning will in due proportion claim your study. None have more urgent claim than the subjects and authors which treat of Religion and of our duties in the world; and it is because they assist and illustrate these supreme studies that I press upon your attention the works of the most approved poets, historians and orators of the past." [6] But in fact when it came to discussing individual historians, Bruni listed the stylists—e.g., Livy and Sallust—and praised Julius Caesar more warmly still, "the style of whose Commentaries, so elegant and so limpid, entitles them to our warm admiration." [7] The basis of this education was the ideal of public service, of worldly activity, which we have discussed. But it is also notable that the ideal was taught in only a few places, and then by teachers of genius. Vittorino da Feltre accomplished it; Guarino of Verona came close, though in his case one can already see the beginnings of a new orthodoxy. The new grammar spread from school to school; the emphasis on pure classical style became commonplace. Long before the fifteenth century ended, the shadow of style was replacing the substance of moral activity, simply because the former

[6] Woodward, *Vittorino da Feltre,* p. 133.
[7] Ibid., p. 128.

could be methodized and the latter could not. In the curricula, all
that remained of the original idea was the emphasis on history and
poetry in the advanced part of the grammar course, and of these.
two kinds of exemplars for moral philosophy, the poets came to be
preferred—again, presumably for reasons of style.[8]

It was this humanism that proved the most influential. It was to
Guarino that the earliest English visitors to Italy came, and it
ought to occasion no surprise that most of them became servants
of the state.[9] Succeeding generations of visitors were more inclined
to become scholars: it is perhaps significant that Thomas More,
whose reflections on the active life somewhat resembled
Petrarch's, never saw Italy at all. However enfeebled, the ideal of
knowledge serving life was still embodied in works such as Casti-
glione's *Courtier* and in that form penetrated northern Europe; but
the new humanist schools of the north were rather more turned
toward grammar. At the same time that the earlier ideals of humanism were spreading, the techniques of specialization were developing ever more rapidly in Italy. In relation to the writing of
history, this amounted to a turning away from the brilliantly rhetorical narrative derived, most usually, from medieval chronicles
whose style was considered unbearably bad but whose contents
were accepted without much question, to a new kind of constructive history which built up a narrative by applying to the whole
range of medieval chroniclers a type of philology similar to Valla's.[10]

Flavio Biondo, whose *Decades* exemplified the techniques used
to construct the newer narratives, was also the first to realize that
much more could be done to reconstruct a writer's milieu than
merely reading him with a proper feeling for the subtleties of
anachronism, and who thus worked out a new form of historical
writing. With sufficient diligence, one could answer historical
questions which were not narrative: What was Rome like in early

[8] R. R. Bolgar, *The Classical Heritage and Its Beneficiaries* (New York, 1964),
esp. Ch. viii.
[9] Roberto Weiss, *Humanism in England during the Fifteenth Century*, 2nd ed.
(Oxford, 1957), Chs. vi–vii.
[10] Kristeller, *Studies*, p. 572; Erna Mandowsky and Charles Mitchell, *Pirro
Ligorio's Roman Antiquities* (London, 1963), pp. 1–51.

Christian times, for instance, or what was the precise configuration of Roman Italy? [11] Later the questions became still more detailed, and as they did, the types of information which might be used to answer them increased in number. A problem on the value of ancient coinage might be solved by checking all the literary references against each other, but the solution was much aided by finding and weighing actual coins. Roman law could be illustrated by inscriptions; and the history of the Roman provinces would require all of these and more. Further, antiquarianism, using the word in Professor Momigliano's sense of non-narrative history, whether applied to Roman customs or Roman lands, evaded a difficulty that beset all humanists, an excessive veneration for the Romans. If the Romans had themselves written of a subject, then the most that a humanist might do was to compare several accounts and choose the most likely; or, in most cases, simply add one to another. The history of the classical world had been written once and for all by the ancients; the humanist could do no more than add his footnotes. Hence Biondo's constructive history began with the fall of Rome and recorded the detested medieval past; hence, too, the questions he and his successors asked of the classical past were questions the Romans themselves had failed to pose, and to whose solution it was possible to bring all one's ingenuity, unfettered by guilt.[12]

Thus, in regard to history, there were three distinct phases of the humanist movement: the stylistic, the constructive, and the antiquarian. Of these, the latter two began simultaneously and interacted in the work of Biondo, though of the two the antiquarian phase spread more slowly. One must imagine, then, three movements of humanism originating in Italy, crossing the Alps at different times, and having different effects in the countries of

[11] Denys Hay, "Flavio Biondo and the Middle Ages," *Proceedings of the British Academy*, XLV (1959), 97–128; J. C. Husslein, *Flavio Biondo als Geograph des Frühhumanismus* (Würzburg, 1901).

[12] L. Delaruelle, *Guillaume Budé* (Paris, 1907), pp. 139 ff., on coins; Arnaldo Momigliano, "Ancient History and the Antiquarian," *Journal of the Warburg and Courtauld Institutes*, XIII (1950), 285–315, makes a point of the fear of tampering with the classics, a view challenged, in part, by H. J. Erasmus, *The Origins of Rome in Historiography from Petrarch to Perizonius* (Assen, 1962), pp. 32–59.

north Europe—effects conditioned, of course, by the nature of intellectual life in each country but conditioned, too, by the varying speeds with which one shock followed another.

The English made their first contacts with Italian humanism in the fifteenth century.[13] One major humanist, Poggio, spent two unpleasant years in England but returned from what he took to be exile as quickly as possible. Somewhat later a number of English clergymen took the long road south in order to absorb the teachings of Guarino, and the fact that some were of importance at home and that others became so made humanism at least a little fashionable. On the other hand, the activities of John Tiptoft, Earl of Worcester, who seems to have studied Italian statecraft and tried to impose it on his countrymen, were less likely to shed luster on imports from the south, and Tiptoft's execution presumably demonstrated (among other things) that the uncritical acceptance of all new ideas was dangerous. Moreover, the very ideal of public service, combined with the peculiarities of pre-Reformation politics, limited the spread of the new humanism. The predominantly secular education that Guarino gave his pupils was in this case absorbed by clerics who, unlike the Italian princes and noblemen for whom the system had been designed, had no children for whom they wished to perpetuate it. The most a cleric could do was to establish himself in a position of importance and then use that position to found a school. In fact, although many of the English visitors to Italy reached positions of authority, the moment they did so, the state enrolled them into its service, usually as diplomats; and the chief reason for this was not the quality of mind of the humanist—though that was good—but the quality of his Latin. The result was that, although the temporal success of the first English humanists encouraged others to seek their training in Italy, the returning scholars occasioned no change in the subjects studied in England: the old scholasticism merely received a little surface polishing.

Toward the end of the fifteenth century, then, there were humanists in England but no humanism. The real development did not take place until the advent of Christian humanism, and that

---

[13] The following is based on Weiss, *Humanism in England*.

depended on the work of two men, the Dutchman Erasmus and the Londoner John Colet. The term Christian humanism itself deserves some prior explanation, however. The primary doubt that has been raised concerning its use is that it implies that the Italian humanists were, in some sense, not Christian. Whatever the ultimate implications of the Petrarchan classicizing ideals, in practice the Italians were good Christians: that is, they tried to find Christian equivalents for classical ideals, or at least they tried to fit both Christian and classical ideas into one framework. Not only was there no rejection of Christianity, but there was no overt dissociation between Christianity and classicism. Nevertheless, a mind as given over to the essence of Christianity as Colet's saw the danger implicit in classical humanism; at the same time, Colet was equally aware of the aridity of scholasticism, to which he objected precisely because of its concern with logic and disputation rather than with morality and love.[14] Colet thus determined to alter the course of humanism by applying its methodology to Christian classics rather than to pagan ones and to use this revitalized humanism as a weapon against the scholastics. That this involved the abandonment of the activist impulse so strong in Italian humanism was to Colet a matter of no great moment: where Vittorino had hoped to train Christian statesmen, Colet (himself an ecclesiastic) was prepared to train mere Christians.

In practice, Colet's approach to a New Testament text differed substantially from that of his contemporaries. To begin with, it was the actual biblical text that came under discussion, not Peter Lombard's Sentences. Furthermore, when Colet thought of a text, he did not have in mind a phrase torn from its context but considered the entire document. Interpreting such a document meant asking what was its spirit and its purpose at the time that it was written. If the text were St. Paul's Epistle to the Corinthians, Colet insisted that it was necessary to ask what the situation in Corinth was and what Paul intended to accomplish by writing such an epistle. It was only after one knew what the text had meant *then*

---

[14] Eugene F. Rice, Jr., "The Humanist Idea of Christian Antiquity: Lefèvre d'Étaples and His Circle," *Studies in the Renaissance*, IX (1962), 126–141, emphasizes the turning to the Fathers as classics; for the attitude toward the scholastics, Edward L. Surtz, S.J., "'Oxford Reformers' and Scholasticism," *Studies in Philology*, XLVII (1950), 547–556.

and *there* that one could begin to interpret it and find some meaning for it in late fifteenth-century Oxford. In short, a text could not be treated as a nearly random series of unconnected lessons but had to be thought of and handled as a whole.[15] Colet was doing approximately what Valla had done earlier, using the concept of anachronism to localize his text temporally and then applying the rules of humanist philology; that is, he used induction to discover the meaning of the text from the text itself (not from Lombard or some other authority) and also to analyze its grammar and language, again from the text and not from the grammar books. Meaning, grammar, and language—all of them of course interconnected—had to be derived from the text. If they were imposed from outside, then distortion was bound to arise.

This was the lesson Erasmus learned from Colet and then popularized. Colet wrote comparatively little, and most of his writings had, in any case, to wait until the nineteenth century for publication. Erasmus, on the other hand, never ceased writing, and although far from all of his enormous output is relevant to the point at issue, much of it is. It was Erasmus who edited the New Testament—from the original Greek—in Colet's manner, and who edited a number of the early Fathers as well. The editions were precisely parallel to the Italian editions of the classics, only their subjects being different—and more important. It is from his defenses of Erasmus' methods that we know how deeply they influenced Thomas More.[16] And it was from Erasmus ultimately that the reformers had the idea of applying the concept of anachronism to the whole history of the Catholic Church.

Colet was fortunate in having wealth sufficient for putting his educational theories into operation. The refounding of St. Paul's School was to be his permanent monument. In it there was to be no contrast between the image of the Christ child at one end and the grammar classroom at the other. If some of the classics were unsuitable for young Christian minds, others were to be found:

[15] P. Albert Duhamel, "The Oxford Lectures of John Colet," *Journal of the History of Ideas,* XIV (1953), 493–510; Erasmus noted this in his "life" of John Colet: J. H. Lupton, *The Lives of Jehan Vitrier . . . and John Colet* (London, 1883), p. 25.
[16] More's letter to Martin Dorp defending Erasmus is in *St. Thomas More: Selected Letters,* ed. Elizabeth F. Rogers (New Haven, 1961), pp. 8–64.

morality was a higher good than pure Latinity. William Lily, who had received the proper Italian training, was made headmaster at a comfortable salary. Not until Colet had begun to worry about the future of his foundation did he run into serious difficulties: the English church could not be trusted to operate the school in the way Colet had envisioned, with the result that its future was handed over to the leadership of the Mercers' Company, of which Colet's father had been a member. But this meant that an enterprise essentially religious, both in its history and in Colet's own intentions, had been turned over to a secular body; and while Colet certainly intended to train laymen, he wished to make good Christians of them, and it was open to doubt whether any secular authority would altogether forego its own ends. Whatever the intention, his example (together with the destruction of the chantries) meant that the profusion of new schools built in the sixteenth and early seventeenth centuries came under secular guidance and control.

Colet's St. Paul's served as a model for a humanist school, and with variations the model was widely copied. It is almost impertinent to ask why this should be, yet the theory of the usefulness of a humanist education and the reality were sometimes so widely separated that there appeared to be no connection at all. To be sure, Queen Elizabeth, who thought that learning advanced both personal and social morality, informed the students of Cambridge "That there will be no directer, no fitter course, either to make your fortunes, or to procure the favour of your prince, than, as you have begun, to ply your studies diligently." [17] But while it is true to say that humanist studies were necessary to advancement, citing the cases of Sir William Cecil or Sir Thomas Smith, this is hardly a sufficient explanation. It is true that humanists were required merely in order to negotiate with humanists abroad. However, the moral argument is not to be ignored; and the state found no difficulty in encouraging a deep study of the Roman virtues, among which patriotism ranked high.

Colet's ideal was realized in some unexpected ways. At the time that St. Paul's was "founded," the Christianity that was to be

[17] Quoted by Mark Curtis, *Oxford and Cambridge in Transition, 1558–1642* (Oxford, 1959), p. 7.

inculcated in the pupils was still that undivided Catholicism which
was the religion of western Europe. Within a few years, making
Christians of one's pupils implied the dissemination of religious
propaganda. Not only did the state realize this—and make quite
certain that the proper things were taught by enforcing religious
uniformity on schoolmasters—but it is clear that one of the motives behind the great wave of Tudor school foundations was a
desire on the part of the merchants who gave the endowments to
propagate the truth as they saw it.[18] Then, too, one must ask for
whom the education was provided. If the principal beneficiaries
were future priests—as a substantial proportion of medieval
schoolboys had been—then the kind of education offered would
be different from that which would appeal to the sons of merchants
and gentlemen who were intended to follow in the footsteps of
their fathers. As it happened, the ruling classes—and we must
include the merchants in this classification—did more and more
send their children to school without any intention of making
clergymen of them. A semiliterate merchant was not likely to
make a fortune, and the rich citizens who founded the new schools
were more aware of this fact than anyone. Furthermore, it became
increasingly clear that the illiterate gentleman who knew only how
to wind his horn and raise his falcon was likely to be excluded
from the seats of power and would find himself in involuntary exile
on his own estates. And what was true for the merchants and the
gentry would be more true still for the sons of classes lower in the
social hierarchy. Yet if the upper classes did, on occasion, try to
monopolize the schools, they were not usually allowed to do so.[19]
For all that the recognition of the value of education for the
secular life spread rapidly, those with a more balanced view of the
needs of the state realized that the training of clergymen was not
only still necessary but was, in the context of the new Protestantism with its emphasis on learned preaching, more necessary than
ever. The result was that the new school curricula had to be

[18] W. K. Jordan, *Philanthropy in England, 1480–1660* (London, 1959),
pp. 279–297, esp. pp. 281–282.
[19] J. H. Hexter, "The Education of the Aristocracy in the Renaissance," in
Reappraisals in History (Evanston, 1962), pp. 45–70; Fritz Caspari, *Humanism
and the Social Order in Tudor England* (Chicago, 1954), esp. Ch. vi.

shaped to meet the requirements of classes whose interests, in terms of education, were very different.

The almost inevitable compromise was found in an emphasis on grammar and rhetoric. On this point all the great theorists— Erasmus, Vives, Elyot—agreed, and the practice of the time is confirmation of their judgment. After these subjects had been mastered—and the mastery of them was considerably delayed by the gradual introduction of an additional language, Greek, into the curriculum—then the student might turn his attention to higher studies or utilitarian ones. History, it was thought, needed some practical experience before it could be fully comprehended; moral philosophy was too difficult for schoolchildren. In any event, it was simply easier to teach grammar and rhetoric, since these subjects were more susceptible to systematization, though neither history nor moral philosophy was altogether excluded from the classroom, for any teacher could and was expected to draw them out of the texts that were studied. Nonetheless, it remains true that these subjects were secondary, not in terms of intrinsic importance but in terms of pedagogical technique. Erasmus, whose views were extremely influential in England, considered history worth study for its own sake; but he thought it important as a teaching tool because from it the students could learn the art of Latin oration, and because a knowledge of history was necessary to explain the illustrations and identify the references in the strictly literary works which were the core of the curriculum. To turn the matter around, in his *Modus conscribendi epistolae,* which was actually used at Eton around 1530, Erasmus recommended some study of history because it offered examples which could be used for moralization, and because it supplied the background necessary for the composition of historical epistles. Presumably history for its own sake was to be studied later.[20]

Practice exactly followed theory. The surviving curricula almost all contain some Roman historians, but it is unusual to find any evidence that these were studied in an effort to learn Roman

[20] William H. Woodward, *Desiderius Erasmus concerning the Aim and Method of Education* (Cambridge, Eng., 1904), pp. 128 ff., 168; T. W. Baldwin, *William Shakspere's Small Latine & Lesse Greeke* (Urbana, 1944), II, 241–242.

history. Sallust and Caesar appear most commonly, Livy and Justin less often. At Westminster, for example, Sallust was paired with Terence, Justin with Cicero, Caesar and Livy with Demosthenes and Homer. Any illusions about a history sequence should be dispelled when it is observed that the school's statutes laid down that "From these lessons the boys shall gather the flowers . . . ," that is, the phrases of use to a student of rhetoric.[21] St. Paul's, with Sallust and Caesar in the sixth form (of eight), seems to have offered less history than most of the schools; Shrewsbury, where Sallust, Livy, and Caesar (and quite possibly others) were studied, perhaps exceeded the average a little.[22] The relative popularity of the compiler Justin, whose style is virtually his only recommendation, offers additional evidence of the same point: history was subservient to rhetoric. Nor is this surprising: rhetoric was of use to all those who attended the schools, the study of history as, say, a guide to politics, to only a few.

Some lights might, however, be discerned in the general gloom. A schoolmaster whose interests ran along historical lines could take advantage of the opportunities offered him by the inclusion of historians on the reading list. There survive notes by Camden, who taught generations of Westminster boys, of classical place names, each coupled with a descriptive phrase: the list was undoubtedly made to teach rhetoric, but the mere fact of its independent existence, separated from notes on any particular Latin text, at least suggests the idea that it might have served as the basis for a lesson on historical geography.[23] This obvious way of evading the spirit of the rules might teach the students history in spite of themselves; it is also possible to argue that obedience to the rules might lead to similar results. Rhetoric was taught by the principle of imitation, and it is legitimate to assume that attempts were made to imitate the historical texts as well as the literary ones. A successful imitation of historical style does, however, imply some grasp of substance and even of historical technique: writing in Livy's vein, "in a vacuum," is virtually impossible. Moreover, such lessons as those

---

[21] Arthur F. Leach, *Educational Charters and Documents, 598 to 1909* (Cambridge, Eng., 1911), pp. 509–511.

[22] Baldwin, *William Shakspere's Small Latine & Lesse Greeke*, I, 125, 388–391.

[23] British Museum, Cotton MSS, Vespasian E. viii, foll. 108ʳ–112ʳ.

suggested by Erasmus, in which the students were told to compose letters that might have been written by some figure of the Roman past, again imply a substantial grasp of history. Indeed, it would be difficult to imagine an exercise better suited to inculcate the concept of anachronism in the minds of the students. Erasmus called it decorum, and he recommended the study of history because such study prevented one from saying "unsuitable" things. Granted that this is, once again, history in the service of rhetoric, it is history just the same.

The situation at the two universities, on the whole, closely paralleled that of the schools.[24] The sons of gentlemen gathered there in ever-increasing numbers, even if the old and rather staid universities were not entirely suitable to the humanists' purpose of advancing individual virtue and social morality. More so even than the schools, the universities had been—and continued to be—seminaries for intending clergy, and a theological course, no matter how much was done to rearrange it, was never quite adequate for men whose aims and interests were entirely secular. Logic was deposed from its former position of ruler of undergraduate studies and was replaced by rhetoric and grammar. But the decline of logic can be overstated: for theological degrees the subject remained essential, and anyone acquainted with Reformation controversy can attest to the thoroughness of the training. It is, of course, likely that the worldly-minded did not attend the logic lessons—or the disputations that were an integral part of the course—with any degree of assiduity, but then a goodly number of these left the university without taking any degree anyway.

The sixteenth century saw the foundation of a substantial number of new colleges, and if the later ones had a Puritan purpose, the earlier were strongly tinged with humanism. Bishop Fox's Oxford College of Corpus Christi (1517) made arrangements for a whole series of lectures on ancient authors, both Latin and Greek; but the authors included in, for instance, the Latin sequence—Cicero, Sallust, Valerius Maximus, Suetonius, and some

[24] Most of this is drawn from Curtis, *Oxford and Cambridge in Transition.* See also William T. Costello, S.J., *The Scholastic Curriculum at Early Seventeenth-Century Cambridge* (Cambridge, Mass., 1958).

of the poets—demonstrate that the primary purpose of the teaching was grammatical and rhetorical, with moral philosophy and history limping along behind. Trinity College, founded at the same university in 1555, differed in detail but not in principle.[25] And St. John's, Cambridge, which in the days of Cheke, Ascham, and Sir Thomas Smith was a veritable forcing house of humanists, offered virtually no history at all. In spite of the formal curricula, however, history was taught, though whether the beneficiaries of the teaching were the students or the fellows themselves is an open question. Roger Ascham undoubtedly read Thucydides and Xenophon with John Cheke and shared his enthusiasm for Herodotus—whom, in his own turn, he taught to his friend Richard Morison.[26] A group of young dons at Oxford in the early 1580's developed a passion for Tacitus, and their leaders included the French immigrant Jean Hotman, the Greek professor Henry Cuffe, and that Thomas Savile whose elder brother, Sir Henry, later produced the first English translation of the annalist.[27]

The sixteenth-century evidence is, unfortunately, rather tenuous, and it is not until the first half of the succeeding century that any concrete evidence of actual history teaching emerges. Of the two pieces of evidence on the tutorial side, one—the account books of John Mead of Christ's, Cambridge—is not as helpful as it might be.[28] Mead seems to have purchased books for his charges and kept a record of what he bought, and among the purchases were a number of classical historians, some works of geography and cosmography, and some travel literature. As it happens, however, most of the books are not histories (he bought Heliodorus, della Casa's *Galateo*, and the pseudohistorical Dictys Cretensis as well), and we lack information as to who bought the books and in what combinations. The "Directions" which Richard Holdsworth wrote out for his students are altogether more satisfactory.[29] One

[25] John Archer Gee, *The Life and Works of Thomas Lupset* (New Haven, 1928), pp. 88–89; Baldwin, *William Shakspere's Small Latine & Lesse Greeke*, I, 104–105.

[26] Lawrence V. Ryan, *Roger Ascham* (Stanford, 1963), pp. 19–21.

[27] F. J. Levy, "The Making of Camden's *Britannia*," *Bibliothèque d'Humanisme et Renaissance*, XXVI (1964), 84–85.

[28] Harris Francis Fletcher, *The Intellectual Development of John Milton* (Urbana, 1956–61), II, Chs. xvii–xviii.

[29] Ibid., II, Appendix II.

of his typical undergraduates would have worked up a good deal of logic and rhetoric along with some ethics, metaphysics, and theology, but would also have studied the rather elementary text on Roman Antiquities by Thomas Godwin, as well as Justin, Florus, Sallust, Quintus Curtius, Livy, and Suetonius; besides that, he was expected to master the general history of Philip Cluver, who was, indeed, considered rather more important than Livy and Suetonius. In general, Holdsworth assigned serious reading (Aristotle and philosophy, theology and the like) to the mornings and lighter reading (history, oratory, poetry) to the afternoons, though he does seem to have thought the afternoon's work as important as the morning's—without it the student's "other Learning though never so eminent, is in a manner voide & useless." [30] But the emphasis on rhetoric was as palpable in Holdsworth as it had been in his predecessors a century earlier, and historians such as Plutarch, Herodotus, Thucydides, and Tacitus were relegated to an appendix significantly labeled "Libri post Gradum susceptum Legendi," and more recent English historians—Samuel Daniel, William Martyn, John Speed, and William Camden—were intermingled with the *Magia naturalis* of Baptista Porta, the *Characters* of Sir Thomas Overbury, and the poems of George Herbert in another appendix headed "Studia Leviora." [31] Nonetheless, one has the impression that the study of history was more likely to be taken seriously in the 1630's than it had been even fifty years earlier, and one is inclined to feel that the influx of the sons of gentlemen—for whom much of Holdsworth's more formal program would have been irrelevant—had a good deal to do with it.

One other portent marked the changing times. Immediately before his death in 1623, William Camden founded a professorship of history at Oxford, and the terms of the bequest made it quite clear that the lecturer appointed should limit himself to civil history and avoid touching on matters either ecclesiastical or controversial. Camden suggested that Florus might serve as a text; one must be grateful that Degory Wheare, the first professor, chose a somewhat larger theme and, before he finished, had given a course

[30] Ibid., II, 637.
[31] Ibid., II, 647–648.

in European historiography.[32] Fulke Greville followed Camden's
example and endowed Cambridge similarly. Again the emphasis
was to be on civil history, though in this case the donor recognized
the usefulness of cosmography and languages. Greville's foundation was less fortunate in its first professor: Isaac Dorislaus,
while sufficiently learned, was tactless and lectured on Tacitus,
and some of his comments seemed, at least to prejudiced auditors,
to apply as much to the English monarchy as to the Roman.
Official pressure silenced the professor, and in the civil war which
followed not long after, the professorship vanished.[33] But whatever
the results, for a time at least the study of history had established a
recognized and respectable foothold in the universities.

A survey of the history teaching in Tudor England is, then,
something of a disappointment. Humanist schools had been
founded, and anyone who had read the Italian treatises on education on which those schools ultimately were based would have expected rather more than there was. At least one of the principal
reasons for including history in the curriculum—its obvious utility
to future governors—was as appropriate in England as in Italy.
But because English schools catered to a relatively wide public
with very disparate interests, and because grammar and rhetoric
were not only relatively easy to teach but were the common de-
nominator among those interests, the emphasis always lay on
those subjects rather than on history. It is only in a few theoretical
plans for educating the gentry—such as Sir Humphrey Gilbert's
Academy for the Queen's wards—that the balance is ever tilted a
little more in the direction of history.[34] Certainly the study of
history was recommended: but frequently on the excuse that it was
best understood after one had had some experience of the world, it

---

[32] William H. Allison, "The First Endowed Professorship and Its First Incum-
bent," *American Historical Review*, XXVII (1922), 733–737; H. Stuart Jones,
"The Foundation and History of the Camden Chair," *Oxoniensia*, VIII–IX
(1943–44), 169–192.

[33] James Bass Mullinger, *The University of Cambridge* (Cambridge, Eng.,
1873–1911), III, 81–90, 674–677; see also the letter from Dr. Samuel Ward to
Archbishop Ussher in *The Whole Works of the Most Rev. James Ussher, D.D.*,
ed. C. R. Elrington and J. H. Todd (Dublin, 1847–64), XV, 402–404.

[34] Sir Humphrey Gilbert, *Queene Elizabethes Achademy*, in *A Booke of
Precedence &c.*, ed. F. J. Furnivall, E.E.T.S., Extra Series, No. 8 (London,
1869), pp. 1–12.

was relegated to a later stage of a student's career.[35] Inevitably the rhetorical training of the schools helped one to understand the histories once they were approached; just as inevitably the association of history and rhetoric became fixed.

There was no danger that history writing would become an academic subject, since neither its authors nor its readers ever received any formal training in it. The association with rhetoric did, however, produce some odd results. Thomas Norton, who, it is thought, translated some of Pompeius Trogus and published it around 1570 specifically as a warning to his own contemporaries, still could not resist pointing out the value of his text to students of rhetoric.[36] Moreover, the temptation to judge the quality of a historian's work by the excellence of his style remained strong. For all that, some humanist history was written, and though its influence spread more slowly than it might have done had the subject received the recognition of the schools, spread it nevertheless did.

Some comparison to the authors of the fifteenth century illustrates the gradual change. Caxton told his readers that the object of history was to teach men what they should do and, contrariwise, what they should eschew. Thus, a volume of history stood as a record of good deeds and bad, setting out the politic and noble acts of all the world as if it were one city. A history was Nestor bound in vellum, as good or better than the counsel of the learned and the old. For the man bound irrevocably to his own fireside it provided experience of divers places. Thus reading history brought home the whole world (from as far as the furthest provinces), even to those men who lacked the internationalism of Latin and had to remain content with a knowledge of only their own poor tongue. And it helped them in the exercise of their limited resources, for Caxton knew as well as his humanist successors that history improved rhetoric.[37] To this formula a writer such as Lord Berners (the translator of Froissart) could add but little, even if

---

[35] E.g., Sir Thomas Elyot, *The Boke Named the Governour,* ed. H. H. S. Croft (London, 1883), I, 86.

[36] *Orations, of Arsanes* (London, n.d.), foll. A.iiii^v–A.v^r.

[37] W. J. B. Crotch, ed. *The Prologues and Epilogues of William Caxton,* E.E.T.S., O.S., No. 176 (London, 1928), pp. 64–66.

he found history more pleasurable than had Caxton and took a delight in the pageants of chivalry and the grandeur of battles that the sober-minded merchant-printer only imperfectly shared. On the other hand, Lord Berners was more inclined to identify romantic history with romantic fiction, while Caxton, who himself separated those categories imperfectly, nonetheless thought of history as more effective than poetry simply because it added the virtue of verity to those other virtues that poetry and history shared.[38]

The earliest translations of the classics follow this pattern rather than any newer one. Alexander Barclay almost certainly rendered Sallust's *Jugurtha* as a trot, presumably to be used by schoolboys (or their masters?) in one of those newly re-edified schools which were appearing all over England. In spite of this, and in spite of quotations from Cicero and Livy in defense of history, Barclay nonetheless saw the principal value of history in its role as a moral teacher, particularly for gentlemen. A book such as Sallust's, because it contained a warning for princes, was fit for a priest to translate and for a nobleman to read. But the moral coating was applied thinly, for while Sallust might be useful for anyone, he was particularly appropriate for gentlemen "apt to attayne to glorious fame & honour / by fayt of chyvalry"; and that description seems somehow more relevant for readers of Froissart.[39] However unlikely Barclay's conclusion may sound, it did not stand by itself: the printer, Thomas Berthelet, informed the readers of Sir Anthony Cope's *Anniball and Scipio* (a work which is primarily if not entirely a translation of Livy) that that story, too, should be read in terms of chivalry.[40] Thus the chivalric history which during the heyday of chivalry itself had never achieved any popularity in England was belatedly recommended to the subjects of Henry VIII, who would surely have found it difficult to discover how to put the ideals into practice.

[38] *The Chronicle of Froissart,* ed. W. P. Ker, Tudor Trans. (London, 1901–03), I, 3–5.
[39] *Here Begynneth the Famous Cronycle of the Warre . . . agaynst Jugurth . . . by . . . Salust,* trans. Alexander Barclay, 2nd ed. (London, [1525?]), "An extract declaryng the boke following," esp. fol. iiiᵛ.
[40] *The Historie of Two the Moste Noble Capitaines . . . Anniball and Scipio* (London, 1544), fol. [a.iᵛ].

As Barclay penned his introduction, Sir Thomas More had already written his account of the reign of Richard III, and Polydore Vergil was engaged in writing his *Anglica historia;* both works were in print before Berthelet wrote his introductory verses. That More and Polydore were well acquainted with each other is clear, and the two were at work on their manuscripts at the same time. There is, however, no evidence that either borrowed from the other, and the chief similarity between their works is the fact that each differs so radically from the sort of writing that had gone before, though their respective versions of Richard III's reign differ enormously from each other. Moreover, since it is fair to argue that the difference lies in More's biography being a bravura set piece while Polydore's is one of a series which encompasses all the rulers of England, it is best to consider the works of the two men entirely separately.

Polydore Vergil, for all that he spent more than half a century in England, remained in spirit an Italian. [41] Born in Urbino, educated at Padua and Bologna, Vergil was nearly thirty before he arrived in England to help in the collection of Peter's pence; and although he received ecclesiastical preferment in the island, eventually becoming archdeacon of Wells, nevertheless he continued to visit his own country when he could, eventually returning to Urbino in 1553 as a very old man. His closest approach to a venture into English politics led to a spell in prison: when Vergil emerged in 1515, he brought with him a detestation of Wolsey which long survived the Cardinal himself and which, when enshrined in the pages of the *Anglica historia,* did much to damage Wolsey's posthumous reputation. Thereafter, through all the changes that the Reformation brought about, Vergil lived a life of literary retirement, always conforming sufficiently to guarantee his own safety and quiet. There is nothing to suggest that Vergil was especially timorous; but he understood Reformation England sufficiently well to realize that if he thrust himself into the limelight it could only result in a call for a formal and public statement of his views, and he seems to have been unwilling to make the choice between apostasy and possible poverty-stricken exile or death. Somehow he

[41] The section on Polydore which follows is heavily indebted to Denys Hay, *Polydore Vergil: Renaissance Historian and Man of Letters* (Oxford, 1952).

survived Edward's reign unscathed, and not until it was almost ended did he return to Urbino and Catholicism. Considering that he was already well past sixty before Elizabeth was born, his taste for uninterrupted quiet is not difficult to understand, but it is revealing just the same.

One must then imagine Polydore Vergil as a cleric and a scholar, not as a man of affairs. He took his duties seriously enough, and the fact that they did not include permanent residence in the backwater of Wells must have pleased him. Instead he spent most of his time in London in the company of learned friends, sometimes at Doctors' Commons, then a kind of club for the literary as well as the legal-minded, sometimes perhaps in the homes of the wealthy and well-educated Italian merchants who plied their trade in England without allowing their intellects to atrophy. At the same time he attended to his correspondence with the company of learned men of all Europe—Erasmus, the jurist Alciati, the antiquarian Budé. He continued to write, not only on his English history but on revisions of the two books which had already given him a European reputation. For Polydore Vergil was by no means a man of one book. Indeed, his ability to recognize what would become popular was almost uncanny. As early as 1498 he published a collection of adages, very similar to the one that Erasmus issued at the same time. The two men quarreled briefly over the question of priority; then, because Polydore could see no sense in such a literary squabble, they became firm friends. Polydore's own *Adagia* had more than one edition, and the number that Erasmus' book had only confirms the indispensability of the reference tool the two men created independently. In the following year appeared *De inventoribus rerum,* an account of the origins of every sort of ceremony, custom, and object. Like the *Adagia,* the new book appealed to all those who were intent on becoming humanists or at least wished to adopt the trappings of the style. For years Polydore labored to increase the volume in size and usefulness, and in his own time it was the work for which he was best known.

The *Adagia* and the *De inventoribus rerum* were successful in gaining for Polydore both money and reputation; history writing must have seemed a profitable field as well. "Nationalistic" history,

written in the best humanist style and intended to gratify the
present holders of a state, had had a substantial vogue in Italy and
was beginning to take hold north of the Alps. Robert Gaguin had
tried, not very successfully, to write such a book about France,
and the Veronese Paulus Aemilius was working on a more literate
version. Conrad Celtis and his friends were thinking about a
similar work for Germany. Why should not England, too, have her
history, enshrined in the new noble fashion? Moreover, the project
held the promise of official patronage, which in Polydore's case
might mean continuance in his post of collector of Peter's pence
and an appointment to something such as the archdeaconry of
Wells. How soon after his arrival Polydore began to collect materials for his work there is no means of knowing, but he had
interested Henry VII in the work by around 1506–1507 and had
already begun the manuscript. Presumably Polydore began his
collections almost at once, first perhaps in a desultory way, then,
as he realized the potentialities of the project, more and more
eagerly. Henry VII, and after him Henry VIII, must have understood the advantages such a work could have for them. Much of
Henry VII's foreign policy was concerned with his need to gain
European recognition for his dynasty; a history written in the best
and newest style could help, primarily by proving the legitimacy of
the new rulers. For all the furor that Polydore's history caused
among the native English historians, it is worth recollecting that,
at least in its origins, the work was intended primarily for con-
sumption on the Continent.

The construction of a new history of England required above all
patience. Merely rewriting the *Polychronicon* would not do: Polydore soon learned that better sources were available if one looked
far enough, and it was more sensible to apply the logic of the
historian to those than to the summary of Ranulph Higden. Polydore himself tells us something of his labors:

> I first began to spend the hours of my night and day in search-
> ing the pages of English and foreign histories . . . I spent six
> whole years in reading those annals and histories, during which,
> imitating the bees which laboriously gather their honey from every
> flower, I collected with discretion material proper for a true
> history. When, on approaching our own times, I could find no

such annals (for indeed by the careless spirit of our age none such exist), I betook myself to every man of age who was pointed out to me as having been formerly occupied in important and public affairs, and from all such I obtained information about events up to the year 1500. From that time—since I came to England immediately after that date—I have myself noted down, day by day, everything of importance.[42]

The long search was productive. The only source for pre-Roman history was, unfortunately, Geoffrey of Monmouth, concerning whom Polydore was more than a little skeptical. The classical sources were easy enough to come by: Caesar, Tacitus, Suetonius, the omniscient Pliny, the geographers Strabo and Ptolemy. So much was easy; but what could be done with the Anglo-Saxon invasions? Polydore discovered Gildas, and so enthralled was he with finding a counterweight to Geoffrey that he published Gildas separately. After that there was Bede, and William of Malmesbury and Henry of Huntingdon; there was William of Newburgh and Roger Hoveden and the inimitable Matthew Paris. That all were not equally valuable was obvious; and the standard of value was fullness and intelligence:

I consider that of the various annals those written by the monks William of Malmesbury and Matthew Paris should be accounted true histories. I call those which were composed of old by monks who were wont to engage in such writing in English monasteries mere annals, and in such records bald statements of events are sometimes made inconsistent with other statements and not unfrequently mingled with obvious errors. Reports of things that have taken place, as they were talked about on the highways, were noted down by the monks in their solitudes from the descriptions of travellers and from popular rumour which reached them. Such annals, long neglected and dust-covered, William of Malmesbury and Matthew Paris have utilized and called their own. Still, from their own histories and from those of foreign countries that have had relations with England any one who did not mind the labour could get material for a proper history.[43]

[42] C. L. Kingsford, *English Historical Literature in the Fifteenth Century* (Oxford, 1913), pp. 256–257.
[43] Ibid., p. 256.

For the most recent two centuries, there was no William of Malmesbury, no Matthew Paris, and it was necessary to eke out the information from the continuations of the *Polychronicon* and the *Brut,* from Fabyan and Tito Livio, from foreign accounts such as those of Monstrelet, Froissart, and Gaguin. Besides the chroniclers, Polydore could make use of the statutes and of other documents; of direct observation, of legend and oral tradition; and of the reports of the survivors of great affairs.

The list is an impressive one, and not many of Polydore's English predecessors could have matched it. Nor was the citation of so many sources merely window dressing. Simply because he was determined to rewrite English history completely, Polydore had to go back beyond such immediately accessible works as the *Polychronicon.* Higden had sometimes pointed out discrepancies in his own account, but Polydore wished to demolish Geoffrey of Monmouth (whom Higden had accepted), and for that he had to do his own work.

Whereas previous historians had, with almost no exceptions, adopted a structure somehow related to the old Augustinian notion of one book for each of the seven days of creation (even if, on occasion, the divisions corresponded with English rather than universal history), Polydore, after allotting eight books to the period before 1066, gave each king after William I his own. Thus, in essence, his history consisted of a series of lives, and while Polydore did not go to the lengths of Suetonius, the aspect of biography remained. Thus he resembled William of Malmesbury in his emphasis on royal personality; it is interesting to note that Malmesbury, too, may have had in mind the thought of bolstering a new dynasty. In any case, Polydore's arrangement allowed him to impose order on the flux of events, and his grouping of related topics within a year reinforced the pattern. The emphasis was thus on rulers, on men, not on discrete events; on causes, rather than on happenstance.

To Polydore's readers, the opening eight books were the most revolutionary part of the volume. The *Anglica historia* began in traditional fashion: a description of names and places essential in an age when maps were still quite scarce. Even here, Polydore started to doubt: the origin of many English place names was shrouded in legend, and accepting the old derivation implied accepting the Galfridian lore from which they originated. The doubt was expressed blandly enough: Polydore merely stated a reluctance to guess too much about such obscure points, and where controversy existed, he would put down both sides—a position he continued to take up throughout the work. He disliked taking sides even on so important a matter as the origin of the Britons themselves, so he told the Brutus story for all its inherent improbabilities. Polydore naturally realized that the Britons required ancestors, and he understood that the Brutus story was no longer a recent innovation, dating back as it did to the twelfth century. But for all his distaste at taking sides, Polydore refused to accept Brutus without qualifications: for one thing it was difficult to imagine that the island could have gone so long untenanted when, as everyone knew, it could be seen from France on a clear day.[44] Moreover, the later parts of Geoffrey's tale were even harder to swallow: Caesar and Tacitus told different stories, and Polydore, like any other humanist, preferred to believe the Romans. Even without that, his own Gildas made no mention of Geoffrey's fabulous heroes. And, of course, there was the matter of the novelty of Geoffrey's history: whatever the truth behind his statement that he was merely adapting an old "British" history, Geoffrey's tales did not make their appearance before the twelfth century, and however far back that was, the age of Gildas lay in a more remote past, that of Caesar and Tacitus in one still more remote. So Polydore decided to print the "new" history, as he was fond of calling it, but with substantial and oft-repeated warnings. As he went along, he pointed out the inconsistencies: for instance that Geoffrey placed Brennus, the Celtic conqueror of Rome, too early in the list of British kings by three hundred years. But having done so much, Polydore was content to replace Brennus in his proper spot, and then continued with the old (or, as he saw them, new) stories.

What Polydore had introduced into the writing of English history was the exercise of logic. Earlier, Higden had been skeptical of some stories too, but while he realized that the British History and the ancient Roman historians clashed on some points, he

[44] *Polydore Vergil's English History*, ed. Sir Henry Ellis, Camden Soc. (London, 1846), pp. 31–32.

preferred to believe both. Higden felt that something had gone wrong, that some readily explicable error lay behind the conflict of sources; Polydore was quite prepared to jettison the British History. Obviously the Romans could not be wrong; and if Geoffrey was doubtful in one case, he might be in another. Nonetheless, Polydore was inclined to test a story by its inherent plausibility rather than by searching for new material. If such material could readily be found, well and good; if not, then logic would have to do. If one was concerned with times so remote that there was no other evidence—the days of Brutus, for instance—logical analysis was the only possible approach; for later periods it was a method that was still needful, but dangerous in its use:

> Here was an evident token of the negligence of writers, which, having noe regarde of times passed, affirmed the names of townes to be geaven of the ould British kings, which indeade were after invented bie the Englishemenne, Danes, and Normanns. For whoe hathe redde in Caesar, Tacitus, Strabo, Ptolomei, or Plinie, Caunterburie, Bathe, Caerliel, Lecester, or enie such like names of townes, of which sorte if there hadd ben enie at that time, undowbtedlie thei cowlde not have ben obscure and unknowne to them. Whearfore thei made especiallie mention of those which were then extant, which are now soe entered into the blacke booke of oblivion that nowe wee are not able to say for a certayntee, whoe in olde time were called Brigantes, whoe Trinobantes, who Iceni, or whoe Silures, or what places they did inhabite.[45]

Polydore had obviously checked the ancient sources and then applied his own rigorous logic to them—with results that were exactly wrong.

In later parts of the history the problems to be faced were different: constructing a narrative from a mass of detailed chronicles rather than determining which of two flatly contradictory sources was correct. The real difficulty, granting Polydore's scheme of one book for each king, was to find some means of bridging the reigns, some connective, super-arching theme which might provide continuity. A fairly obvious Lancastrian bias had the advantage of producing dramatic situations which could be exploited—and of course one who favored Henry VII and his son

[45] Ibid., p. 48.

had at least to be anti-Yorkist. But this left the awkward problem of what to say about Richard II. If he were to be considered a good king, then Henry IV had perforce to be a usurper. Even if he were a bad king, still Henry had revolted against him, and no Tudor—least of all the first two—wanted revolution justified. In the end, Polydore blamed the Wars of the Roses on Richard's lack of a male heir, which missed the point entirely—probably deliberately. Beyond this, the succession of monarchs had to be explained. Why, for example, did Henry VI suffer so many troubles? If he was not a good king, he was certainly a good man, and it could only be the pleasure of an inscrutable God that such a man should be so afflicted. A signal accident—Henry's crown falling off his head at a session of Parliament, where the King sat in full panoply—was taken by the populace as a prognostication of future trouble, and although Polydore did not say so, one feels that he believed the people were right. Conversely, Polydore had to explain the good fortune of Edward IV: it could be attributed either to Fortune herself, whose ways were by their very nature unknowable, or to the righteousness of God, acting to punish the Lancastrian line because of Henry IV's seizure of the crown. Even so, Edward did not escape altogether: his line too was punished, in the persons of his two young sons, for Edward's perjury before York, where on his return from exile the former king falsely swore that he only wished to recover the Yorkist properties and had no designs on the crown. Thus the workings of God, frequently spread over three generations, supplied the motive power for the rapid changes that overwhelmed fifteenth-century England. Moreover, what applied to kings applied to lesser men as well. The death of Lord Hastings served as an illustration of the rule of "do unto others," for Hastings, who had assisted in the murder of Henry VI's son, Prince Edward, now was himself killed. So God taught us lessons through the workings of history. Similarly, the execution of Buckingham was a wonderful punishment from God, emphasizing the fact that those who helped an evil man, such as Richard III, themselves received an ill return.

It might be inferred from this that Polydore's theory of causation was largely theological, but he was capable of offering different explanations. Richard III's horrible dreams on the eve of Bosworth might have been explained as an omen; instead, Polydore suggested that they were the result of a guilty conscience and a decline in courage. By and large, however, Polydore's ideas of human motivation were rudimentary. The motives of men were forever the same, and the only certain thing in the human mind was its frailty and love of change. It was these two facts that allowed Fortune to play her game, and a sensible man accepted her decisions quietly. Occasionally, God took a hand in the proceedings—though how one distinguished between the operations of God and those of Fortune Polydore does not tell us. One suspects that the differentiating factor was moral: if, as in the cases of Hastings and Buckingham, it was clear that the intervention of the supernatural was on the side of morality, then it was God's doing; if the case was less clear—one remembers Polydore's uncertainty as to why Edward IV was successful—then perhaps Fortune was at work.

From all this, it comes as no surprise to find that Polydore was willing to believe miracles, prognostications, and the like. If divine intervention was possible at the level of direct actions, then it was equally possible that God foreshadowed His decisions. Certainly Polydore expressed some skepticism and attempted to find rational explanations for irrational happenings—but, partially as a sop to the commonalty, who believed in such things, and partially because the untoward events were registered in otherwise reliable sources, he included the portents in his work as well: "At that verie time divers prodigius wonders weare shewed, whearebie men openlie avowched that the chaunge of the kingdom [to Canute] was prognosticate and signified; emonge other thingges, the unaccustomed sowrge of the ocean was especiallie noted, which withowte enie apparent cause (which might seeme to abate the admiration therof) didd flowe into suche great heyght, that it drowned manie menne and theyre villages." [46] The statement was unaccompanied by any gloss save that Polydore obviously sought out an "apparent cause" before he accepted the story. He had, however, earlier delivered himself of a general dictum on the subject:

> These and suche like things, whether thei were donn bie the illusion of menn or devells, or whether indeed there bee enie force in the nature of things, which the baser sorte doe som time

[46] Ibid., p. 260.

superstitiouslie note as signes and woonders, I would gladlie have
lett passe, lest wee showld seeme to bringe inconvenience to that
relligion which, teachinge all thinges to be ordered bie the Divine
providence of Godde, dothe rejecte suche vaine southesaings of
thinges to comme, if the nature of an historie wowlde soe per-
mitte, which will that all thinges trulie donne showld bee faythe-
fullie written. Wherfore nothing shalbee opprobrius unto us, ether
in this place or elsewheare, declaring suche thingges but to the
follie of menne, whoe like olde wiches have gonne abowte with
suche fore tokens to attaine the knowledge of things ensewinge;
and this have I said partlie to thentent that noe manne should to
farre welter in suche fanatike and fond observations; therefore
even from the beginninge I thought goodd to speake of suche
matters beefor hande, bi cause wee ernestlie minde that the reader
shoulde incurre noe error: but now to the matter.[47]

That the manifestations of the underworld should be rejected was
obvious enough; but no one, least of all Polydore, could ever be
sure which these were, and which were the signs of God's providence. As usual, Polydore included the doubtful material with a
warning.

It is possible to say that Polydore, like any true humanist,
considered history as educative, and that what it taught was, primarily, virtuous behavior. That he emphasized morality more as a
personal, active virtue, while his predecessors emphasized pious
edification, is true; but this truth is a matter of degree, not one of
strict dichotomy. Polydore was quite as prepared as Caxton to
speak of history as a repository of praise and reproach, of encouragement or discouragement. The difference between them came
not in the definition of history but in the conception of the work of
the historian:

The fyrst office of an historiographer is to write no lye, the
seconde that he shall conʒel no trueth, for favoure, displeasure, or
feare. The perfection of an historie resteth in matter and wordes.
The order of the matter requyreth, observaunce of tymes, discrip-
cions of places, the maners, lyves of men, theyr behavoures,
purposes, occacions, dedes, saiynges, casaultes, achevynges, &
finishyng of thynges. The tenour of the wordes asketh a brefe

47 Ibid., pp. 70–71.

perspicuite and syncere trueth, with moderate and peaceable ornamentes.[48]

In short, history was the record of men and their doings, and it was the duty of the historian, himself a man, to come as close as possible to those about whom he wrote. This was a long way from a mere record of events, with personalities strait-jacketed and moving about like automata—when they moved at all.

Polydore, competent though he undoubtedly was, still did not accomplish all that he set out to do. His figures, though more recognizably human, were still rigidly bound by his own limited view of man's psychology. Moreover, he left in doubt whether the motivating force was man's psychology or the inscrutable will of God as exercised in the divine providence. Further, whatever his views of truth and falsehood, Polydore had to consider the wishes of his own age and, more specifically, of his patrons. Finally, the essential timorousness of his character also left its residue in the *Anglica historia*. Polydore's reputation as a great debunker—a reputation manufactured by his enemies—has tended to blind students to the inconclusiveness of much that he said. Polydore rarely set down a definite decision on a controversial point, even if he sometimes made it clear where he stood when he printed both of two opposing stories. When it suited him, he could be willfully blind; he was perfectly capable of emphasizing one line of argument in order to avoid discussion of another. His history of the reign of Henry VIII displayed an unwonted interest in foreign affairs, quite overshadowing his almost total lack of (public) interest in the Reformation. When he came to discuss Wolsey, he could be a great deal less than just. For all this, he left a legacy to his many, mostly unacknowledged, followers: an increased interest in the human side of history, an increased sense of the importance of the historian, and a historical method which, while not totally reliable, was still an improvement on what had gone before.

The precise nature of Polydore's influence on his contemporaries and successors will concern us later; here, it is only necessary to note the development of what might well be called "The Legend of

---

[48] *An Abridgement of the Notable Worke of Polidore Vergile*, trans. Thomas Langley (London, 1546), fol. xxᵛ.

Polydore." [49] In its more obvious manifestations, this was no more than an attack on Polydore the iconoclast, spurred on by his assumed destruction of one of the Tudor myths. In its more extreme forms, it became the story of Polydore's searching the country for material for his history and burning the priceless sources for English antiquity when they did not fit his notion of what that antiquity should have been. Combined with this was a distaste for Polydore as a foreigner: in the first place, it was unsuitable for an Italian to take liberties with the stories of the ancient British, for whom he could have felt no sympathy. Since Polydore did, to an extent, take the view that English history began with the Romans, there is some excuse for this view. But once the passions of the Reformation were aroused, the attack on him took a more ugly turn. The harmless and peace-loving Polydore was turned into a nefarious papal agent, and the documents that he burned were those proving the independence of the English church from Rome. When the story began, it is difficult to say: but by the beginning of Elizabeth's reign even the equable Archbishop Parker credited it, and Sir Henry Savile, forty years later, still repeated it.

Polydore the destroyer of legends had thus been metamorphosed into Polydore the destroyer of evidence. In later years the second story was used to authenticate the first. In the end, it was the attack on Polydore's indictment of Geoffrey's British History that proved to have the most interesting results. There is little to be gained in this connection by spending much time on such hyperpatriotic Welshmen as Arthur Kelton, who assumed that a defense of the historical importance of Wales had to be grounded in an unreasoning acceptance of Geoffrey of Monmouth. Other defenders of the traditional view had more sensible things to say. But it might be useful, first, to determine why the British History was worth defending at all.

Thanks to the work of, principally, Professors Greenlaw and Millican, and more recently of Sir Thomas Kendrick, everyone is acquainted with the odd argument known as the Tudor Battle of

[49] Hay, *Polydore Vergil*, pp. 158 ff.; *Three Books of Polydore Vergil's English History*, ed. Sir Henry Ellis, Camden Soc. (London, 1844), pp. xx–xxviii.

the Books.[50] There is a possibility, however, that the whole affair has been overblown.[51] The defense of Geoffrey might have been worth undertaking, but how much that defense had to do with bolstering the Tudor legend is arguable. Geoffrey's history owed its appeal to a variety of causes, most of them obviously in effect long before the Tudors were ever heard of. For one thing, most men disliked blank pages in their histories, and the two most obvious—the period before the coming of the Romans and that immediately after their departure—were both filled up quite brilliantly by the British History. If a historian had been able to replace Brutus and Arthur by more convincing figures, there probably would have been no debate. As it was, Polydore's skepticism left a void, and it was to be a very long time before men could accept that sort of thing with equanimity. Patriotism played its part as well: Brutus had served to authenticate the great antiquity of the Britons, an antiquity which could compare favorably with that of the rest of Europe and which was only a small way behind that of Rome—and Troy. To admirers of ancient Rome, however, a Trojan descent was less important: the net result of Polydore's insistence on the Roman "beginnings" of English history was to force England into its place in the Roman Empire. In other words, there is implied in the *Anglica historia* the first statement of the *Britannia* tradition. Polydore emphasized not gross antiquity but the antiquity of civilization in the island, and that had, perforce, to begin with the Roman occupation. As some Englishmen wished, more and more, to take their places in the European humanist movement, they came to share Polydore's view. But a contrary current was also running: the Reformation put a premium on the independence of England from Rome—not, to be sure, the Rome of Cicero but that of the popes. Still, it was clear that the two visions of Rome were connected, and from that connection derived, in the end, the view of Polydore as an agent of the Roman papacy. It is thus possible to argue that there were important, if

[50] Edwin Greenlaw, *Studies in Spenser's Historical Allegory* (Baltimore, 1932); Charles Bowie Millican, *Spenser and the Table Round* (Cambridge, Mass., 1932); T. D. Kendrick, *British Antiquity* (London, 1950).

[51] Sydney Anglo, "The *British History* in Early Tudor Propaganda," *Bulletin of the John Rylands Library*, XLIV (1961), 17–48.

not overlogical, reasons for defending Brutus, and this may help to explain why the first important English Protestant historian of the church, John Bale, not only accepted Brutus but amplified the story.

The debate over Brutus was only one of the complaints raised against Polydore Vergil, and that not the most important. Geoffrey of Monmouth, whatever one thinks of him as a historian, was an extremely shrewd judge of his countrymen: they wanted not only an antiquity comparable to that of the rest of Europe but heroes who could take their place with Charlemagne. He gave them King Arthur, a hero from the oldest British stock, who conquered most of north Europe and defeated the Romans themselves. To islanders whose lands had been swept successively by the Romans, Anglo-Saxons, Danes, and Normans, Arthur was a great consolation.[52] More than that, there was a direct connection from Arthur to the last of the British kings, Cadwallader, and from him to the Welsh Tudors. Thus, a lineage linking Henry VII to Arthur not only helped authenticate the Tudor claim but also implied a prediction of future Tudor greatness, a reenactment of the deeds of Arthur. Henry VII had named his eldest son Arthur. Some, at least, of the pageantry the Tudors were wont to enjoy was Arthurian. An attack on Arthur could be understood as an attack on the Tudors themselves. Polydore's doubts were so considered by the self-appointed custodians of Tudor glory; oddly enough the ruling family seems not to have shared their view. Henry VII realized well enough that an acceptance of his connection to the greatest of native heroes could hardly do him harm; but he was also sufficiently a realist to believe that Polydore's demonstration of the validity of the Tudor claim, in terms of fifteenth-century politics, was vastly more important. Arthur had his advantages as a symbol around which men might rally: if the Elizabethan Society of Archers kept men loyal, so much the better. But Arthur never became a necessary article of belief.

Had it been possible to defend Arthur without at the same time defending Brutus, the cause of improved historical accuracy might

[52] Gordon Hall Gerould, "King Arthur and Politics," *Speculum*, II (1927), 33–51; George Gordon, "The Trojans in Britain," in *The Discipline of Letters* (Oxford, 1946), pp. 35–58.

have made more rapid headway. Since, however, both legends depended on the same source—Geoffrey—this was none too easy. The connection of the two stories placed men such as John Leland in an awkward position, for Leland was as much in the humanist tradition as Polydore and would have been willing, one suspects, to jettison Brutus. Quite as much as Polydore, Leland accepted the implications of *Britannia*. Arthur, however, was another matter. Where Polydore was willing to tread on English susceptibilities, Leland roused himself in their defense. Now the weaknesses in Polydore's method of destructive logic could be made manifest. Against Arthur the best argument was one from silence: how could so great a hero, with so many conquests to his credit, be altogether absent from the histories of those whom he supposedly overthrew? It is a good argument but hardly a conclusive one. Leland could be quite as logical as Polydore: there might be reasons for such a silence, and the excellent historical imagination of Leland projected some of them. Having turned Polydore's argument against him, Leland now went a step further by producing evidence, documentary and archaeological, in favor of the Arthurian position. Place names were brought forward; a chronicle showed that Glastonbury Abbey had been there in Arthur's time (which Polydore had denied), and this helped authenticate the relics usually produced at the abbey church, relics Leland had himself seen.[53] Whatever we think of Leland's evidence (and some of it appeared sound to his contemporaries), he was prepared to go beyond logic to fact; unlike Polydore, Leland was not satisfied with a purely negative case but wished to put up something else in its place. Moreover, Leland—and more especially his contemporary Sir John Price—began to go behind Geoffrey of Monmouth, back first of all to Geoffrey's ostensible source, his "vetustissimus liber," to Welsh folklore, to mentions of Arthur in chronicles older than Geoffrey's, and so on. In the end, that approach allowed the problem of Arthur to be separated from the problem of Brutus and thus permitted some sort of rational solution.

[53] John Leland, *A Learned and True Assertion of . . . Arthure* (*Assertio . . . Arturii*), trans. Richard Robinson, in *The Famous Historie of Chinon of England*, ed. W. E. Mead, E.E.T.S., O.S., No. 165 (London, 1925), pp. 79–84. Kendrick's book goes into the whole matter of the British History, including the arguments used for and against.

The battle over the British History continued for the remainder
of the century and beyond, and the combatants will concern us
again on other occasions. Here it is necessary only to say that the
great debate had several important results: it made Polydore's
influence less overt than that influence might otherwise have been;
it made available Polydore's legacy of historical logic, a tool invaluable in analyzing sources and establishing dates; but it showed,
at the same time, that the writing of history required constructive
thought as well as destructive, and even if that meant a continuation of Geoffrey's vogue for another half century, in the end the
historians were the better for the struggle.

Polydore Vergil rewrote the history of England in the latest and
best humanist manner and, it will be recalled, differed from his
predecessors in his increased emphasis on human character.
Thomas More, writing at about the same time, produced a life of
Richard III whose models were not Italian but Roman. The title of
his work is almost a misnomer: *The History of King Richard III*
was, to an extent, a history of a reign, but it was much more a
biography of a monarch. Precisely this intent to concentrate on
biography, which excused More from the blame of not including
everything relating to Richard's reign, explained More's flights of
language, for the diction seems almost more appropriate to drama
than to history.[54]

If one may assume that More was working on his *Richard III*
between 1514 and 1518, a number of points about the genesis
of the book emerge. Thomas More was still at the beginning of his
career, though it had already become clear that a great future
could be his if he wished it. On the other hand, More had not yet
emerged from his humanist chrysalis and at this period was still
busy with reading histories. Of these, some, like Robert Gaguin's
and Paulus Aemilius' of France, were the new national histories;
others included the world history of Hartmann Schedel and the
rather antipapal *Vitae pontificum* of Platina. Most of all, he read

---

[54] My discussion of More's *History* is indebted to the superb new edition by
Richard S. Sylvester: *The History of King Richard III*, Vol. II of the Yale edn.
of the *Complete Works of St. Thomas More* (New Haven, 1963); A. F. Pollard,
"The Making of Sir Thomas More's *Richard III*," in *Historical Essays in Honour
of James Tait*, ed. J. G. Edwards et al. (Manchester, 1933), pp. 223–238, is still
useful.

the great classical historians, Plutarch, Thucydides, Herodotus, Sallust, Tacitus, and Suetonius, and it was these, especially the Roman writers, who most influenced him. In Thomas More, indeed, one has continually the feeling that he was engaged in his own "Renaissance"; that while he was perfectly well aware of the work of his immediate predecessors and his contemporaries, he nonetheless discovered the classical past for himself and, more especially, made his own decisions on how to use it. One result of this highly personal way of reading the past has been a good deal of confusion over the problem of which historian he took as his model. Richard has been called a Sallustian villain; the *History* has reminded scholars of Suetonius, especially in its use of anecdotes, while the narrative drive is more reminiscent of Tacitus. Moreover, there were verbal borrowings from all three. On the other hand, More's love of fine language, especially in the speeches with which the *History* is replete, has been called medieval; and one may suppose that the rapid whirling by which Fortune first raised and then lowered Richard (as well as some of the subordinate characters, such as Jane Shore) owed something to the *Fall of Princes*. The simplest solution to the problem is that More had no particular pattern but simply made use of whatever came to hand and could be made to fit an order which he worked out for himself.[55]

A more intriguing question is why he chose to write about Richard. The obvious answer, that a denunciation of Richard would be pleasing to the Tudors, may contain a shred of the truth, but the Thomas More who thwarted Henry VII's plan to collect a seemingly unnecessary tax is not a very suitable candidate for the office of royal sycophant. It is more likely that, having heard all about the troubled times of Richard from his early patron, Cardinal Morton, he was tempted to record the recent past, since this had been the way of the Roman historians he had studied, and since the kind of information that was available—personal reminiscences—was congenial to him. But one suspects there was more to it even than that. More was working on the *History* at the same time that he wrote the *Utopia* and at the same time, moreover, that

---

[55] This depends on Sylvester, ed. *History*, pp. lxv–civ.

he was resolving a personal crisis, whether or not to enter government service. Among the questions that he then posed himself, one
especially seems relevant here: What were the duties, what the
responsibilities, of a servant to a tyrant? [56] In 1518 the term
"tyrant" hardly seemed applicable to the gay and carefree young
Henry VIII; nor did it seem quite correct in reference to Henry
VII. If More wished to know how a tyrant might behave, in the
context of early sixteenth-century England, the best he could do
was to analyze the career of Richard III. There was no shortage of
men who had known that tyranny themselves and who would be
more than willing to describe it.

So More set about writing his biography, and because it was to
be a piece in classical style, he wrote it in Latin; but since it might
serve to educate Englishmen in the lore of tyranny, he wrote it in
English as well. In the *History* the classical and the native English
quite literally interacted: it is impossible to say that either version
was a translation of the other, merely that More worked on them
simultaneously, and that this in turn influenced his handling of
both. Because the Latin version was intended for foreigners, More
had to explain the English situation in some detail; because the
readers of the English version were not, presumably, highly educated, explanations had to be explicit—there could not be too
much humanist shorthand embodied in classical tags that all readers of Latin would recognize. The effect of all this on the rather
indefinite future of Latin historiography is difficult to calculate;
but the effects on English history writing were very great indeed,
because an example now existed that showed history could have
both style and coherence, that it need not be wrapped in a fog of
random events and dates.

So much emphasis on More's style should not be taken to imply
that he had no matter. The centerpiece of his design was, of
course, Richard himself, and the portrait of the tyrant was boldly
drawn. Richard, as More saw him, was a monster, not only morally but physically as well. The pervading feeling was one of
disharmony, a feeling expressed in More's frequent use of the
word "unnatural." Nothing about Richard was natural, not his

[56] J. H. Hexter, *More's Utopia: The Biography of an Idea* (New York,
1965), esp. Pt. III.

birth, nor his behavior toward Henry VI and his son, nor his acceptance of the death of his own brother Clarence (if not his actual implication in it), nor his treatment of his nephews, not even his own death. The portrait was heightened almost too much: the reader is in danger of considering Richard as supernatural. Perhaps that too was part of More's intent; perhaps a figure so awful was meant to represent the devil rather than man. "Hee was close and secrete, a deepe dissimuler, lowlye of counteynaunce, arrogant of heart, outwardly coumpinable where he inwardely hated, not letting to kisse whome he thoughte to kyll: dispitious and cruell, not for evill will alway, but ofter for ambicion, and either for the suretie or encrease of his estate." [57] The devil was a rational one, and that only served to make matters more terrible still. From this derived the aura of uncertainty that so pervaded the *History:* with a man such as Richard, so careful a dissembler, the future was always terribly uncertain. That was the point of the story of Lord Hastings, who "when he most feared, he was in good suerty: when he rekened him self surest, he lost his life, & that within two howres after," [58] and it was to emphasize this, not out of superstition, that More introduced the various omens preceding Hastings' death. It is the world disordered that More showed.

What is puzzling in all this is More's use of innuendo. One would have thought that there was a surfeit of ordinary sources of information concerning so dire a villain as Richard. Why then was it necessary for so many statements to be introduced by such phrases as "some wise men also ween," "as I have learned of them that much knew and little cause had to lie," and "as men constantly say," let alone "for I have heard by credible report, of such as were secret with his chamberers"? Partly, this came about from convention—More did not name his oral sources, although it is clear that he had information from his own father, from Cardinal Morton, and from other surviving officials. But just as important, the phrases were introduced to emphasize the underhandedness of life in a tyrant's time, where plain speaking was punishable by instant death. More, for all his minor inaccuracies, was perfectly capable of evaluating sources. When he became deliberately

[57] Sylvester, ed. *History,* p. 8.
[58] Ibid., p. 52.

vague, when whisperers began to mutter among the pages, this too was part of the total effect.

The effectiveness of it all need not be described again. More's portrait of the tyrant Richard was copied into all the major chronicles, served as the basis for Shakespeare's play, and has blackened Richard's memory until our own day. That the picture resembles a caricature is almost irrelevant, because the whole is so convincing. Richard, his hand on his dagger, his eyes whirling in his head, remains our Richard because every detail is carefully inserted to bolster such an image of him. To that end, More was willing to embody the classical portrait of tyranny as found in Tacitus' Tiberius, to use every trick of anecdote and sly innuendo that he could learn from Suetonius; he was willing to bring in God's providence and the Fortune who ruled the medieval world of the rise and fall of princes. It was this blending of every resource and of every piece of information into one central theme that became More's legacy to his successors.

The various means by which the legacies of More and Polydore came to be incorporated into the body of English historical writing will continue to concern us throughout this study. Edward Hall, who translated much of Polydore and embodied More *in toto* in his work, was one obvious channel of their influence. But Hall properly belongs to the great tradition of Tudor chroniclers. Two other men, John Rastell and Roger Ascham, can serve as examples of the same influence, and since their work is rather more isolated (at least in terms of their own successors), they may legitimately be placed with their masters. Of the two, John Rastell is the more mysterious. It is not that little is known of him: his career as coroner of Coventry, as More's brother-in-law, as printer, would-be explorer, and overenthusiastic reformer has been plentifully documented.[59] It is the inspiration of his history, *The Pastyme of People* (1529), that remains in question. That history seems to owe something to Polydore, frequently in method, sometimes in particular opinions, yet it was published five years before Polydore's work first was printed at Basel. No apparent link between the two men survives, but there is no inherent improbability in

---

[59] A. W. Reed, *Early Tudor Drama* (London, 1926), pp. 1–28, 211–216.

their having known each other—through Thomas More—and thus in their having shared an interest in the English past.

Rastell's *Pastyme of People* is an odd book, though its nineteenth-century editor—who called the arrangement "barbarous"—overstated the case. The history of the European world was given in parallel columns: England, France, Rome (and later the Empire) and so on. Most of Rastell's information came from Fabyan, but he also made use of the Roman historians and applied to this his own sense of fitness. Like Polydore, he reprinted the history derived from Geoffrey while making clear his own skepticism concerning it. His method of arranging his material helped to express his attitude toward it: one is quite likely to find two differing versions of the same event on the same page, one of Roman derivation, the other of "British." Occasionally the debate took place not between the parallel columns of text but within one of them: Rastell did, for instance, make use of the Gildas whom Polydore had published some years before. Moreover, he added to the list of sources readily available a text (with translation) of Caesar on Britain,[60] for he shared Polydore's view that British history really began with the Romans, and it was clear to him that if Geoffrey were more vulnerable in any one place than another, then that place was his account of Caesar's invasions, where good Roman texts could be compared with Geoffrey's inventions.

In his method of argument, Rastell resembled Polydore. The same negative reasoning—the Romans did not mention things they should have known—recurred, and Rastell was equally capable of using mild ridicule, though the story upon which he exercised that talent (a tale intended to explain the origins of the giants who peopled the island before Brutus) could never have seemed very plausible.[61] Against Brutus he used Polydore's argument that England was clearly visible from France and had no need to await the Trojans: Rastell was inclined to favor the inhabitants of Little

---

[60] *Julius Cesars Commentaryes . . . as Much as Concernyth . . . England* ([London], 1530). The book was published by William Rastell; John Rastell's share in the Caesar cannot be proved, but suggestive similarities between the *Pastyme* and the Caesar were pointed out by Reed, *Early Tudor Drama*, pp. 76–77.

[61] John Rastell, *The Pastime of People,* ed. T. F. Dibdin (London, 1811), pp. 4–5.

Britain (Brittany) instead. Nevertheless, he told the story he
found in Geoffrey and Fabyan, because of its moral value. When
he came to Arthur, Rastell advanced upon Polydore in that he
found a way to criticize some of the nondocumentary evidence
upon which men such as Leland leaned:

> . . . he that wyll now go to the shryne of Seynt Edward, at
> Westmynster, shall there fynd hengyng in the shryne the prynt of a
> seale in red wax, about the border wherof is wryttyn thus: 'Arthu-
> rus patricius Britannie Gallie and Dacie imperator;' which they
> affirm was the seale takyn from an old dede of some gyft or
> graunt made to the house by king Arthur, wherof the perchement
> and wryting for age is wastyd and putrefyed. But yet some men
> thynk it but a thyng faynyd of late by some man havyng effeccion
> to Arthur; and that for dyvers resons; one is, for they say the tyme
> of Arthur supposid was before that Westminster was foundid, and
> byld uppon a wyld busshy place, full of thornis, then callyd
> Thorney, which was in the tyme of Sebertus, kyng of Essex, which
> was after the deth of Arthur more than .xl. yere; so that Arthur
> coud make to that howse no such graunt. And also they say that it
> is not possyble that wax shulde last so long unto this day, which is
> almost .M. yere. And also they sey that the tyme of Arthur
> supposid, nor .v.C. yere after, they usyd to put no seale of wax to
> theyr dedis nor wrytyngys, but that use began syth the conquest of
> Wyllyam Conquerour; for at the tyme of the seyd conquest they
> usyd but only to subscrybe theyr handis to dedys, wythout any seale
> of wax, as apperyth at this day in dyvers abbeys in Englond, of
> the grauntis by dedys made by Seynt Edward, and dyvers other,
> to which ye shall never fynd seale of wax, but only subscrypcyon
> of theyr handis.[62]

The value of the arguments varied, but the best of them, based
upon Rastell's own investigations into past legal practices, is reminiscent of Lorenzo Valla and the method he evolved to attack
the validity of the Donation of Constantine. Here was the technique of anachronism used precisely and correctly—and for the
first time in England, at least in regard to purely historical matters.

If some doubt exists about Rastell's discipleship to Polydore, no
similar difficulties need trouble us about Roger Ascham, for we

[62] Ibid., p. 107.

have his own word that he was following Sir Thomas More.[63] For all that Ascham was a good Protestant, he had good reason to admire More. As one of the pioneer Greek scholars of Cambridge, a fellow of St. John's at the time that that college was the leading nursery of learned men in the kingdom, Ascham had helped fight for the new Greek pronunciation first brought in by his friend Cheke; and the battle paralleled an earlier one, between Grecians and opponents of the new language (Trojans) at Oxford, in which More had taken a decisive position in favor of the new learning. With a new Trojan arisen in the person of Stephen Gardiner, Bishop of Winchester, Ascham must have longed for similar intervention—which was not forthcoming. It was, furthermore, the case that the two men had been reading the same classical historians, even if Ascham had been more interested in the Greek than had his predecessor. The similarity must not be pushed too far— Ascham was much more the professional scholar, with an enthusiasm for coins and other mementos of the classical world, and though he may have longed for a career in the great world, he never really achieved it. It was, indeed, his one venture into the morass of European politics which led to his only historical work, the *Report of the Affaires and State of Germany,* for which he collected materials during a stay as assistant to Richard Morison between 1550 and 1553.

For such an account of Germany, Ascham turned out to be surprisingly well fitted. His training had been in classical histories: he had read Livy with the future Queen Elizabeth, had taught Herodotus to his friend and patron Morison, and had himself been instructed in Thucydides (whom he did not care for) and Xenophon by John Cheke. But because he had also read in Comines and Machiavelli and More, and because he had been in contact with the great German Reformation historian John Sleidan, he had learned what to seek out, not only in a historian but also in a historical situation. In reading Livy, he had learned "what was in

[63] On Ascham see Ryan, *Roger Ascham;* and Walter F. Staton, Jr., "Roger Ascham's Theory of History Writing," *Studies in Philology,* LVI (1959), 125–137. The reference to More is in *A Report . . . of the Affaires and State of Germany* in Roger Ascham, *English Works,* ed. W. A. Wright (Cambridge, Eng., 1904), p. 126.

our opinion to be looked for at his hand that would well and advisedly write an history":

> First, point was, to write nothyng false: next, to be bold to say any truth, wherby is avoyded two great faultes, flattery and hatred: For which two pointes *Caesar* is read to his great prayse, and *Jovius* the *Italian* to hys just reproch. Then to marke diligently the causes, counsels, actes, and issues in all great attemptes: And in causes, what is just or unjust: in counsels, what is purposed wisely or rashly: in actes, what is done couragiously or fayntly: And of every issue, to note some generall lesson of wisedome & warines, for lyke matters in time to come: wherin *Polibius* in *Greeke* and *Phillip Comines* in *French* have done the duties of wyse and worthy writers. Diligence also must be used in kepyng truly the order of tyme: and describyng lyvely, both the site of places and nature of persons not onely for the outward shape of the body: but also for the inward disposition of the mynde as *Thucidides* doth in many places very trimly. . . .[64]

And it was this, he tells us, that he admired in Thomas More.

In the fragment of German history that was ordered in Ascham's *Report,* he tried to follow his own advice. In some ways, what he attempted was much more difficult than More's task had been, simply because his Germany was a vastly more complicated political organism than the England of Richard III had been. Too strict an attention to chronology meant an utter loss of continuity, and so Ascham sensibly ordered his narrative by subject. This in turn allowed him to insert sketches of the various figures who constituted the mainsprings of German political life. Because his causation was human, and because of his insistence on drawing morals as well as giving political advice, Ascham made much of his portraits. One is inclined to wonder whether the *Report* was not intended to give its author an entree into the political post he seems to have sought, so insistent was he in analyzing the political motivations of his characters with the purpose of providing a handbook for rulers. The principal difficulty was his choice of a prime motivating factor for the troubles of Germany: "In Religion & libertie were sayd to be of many men the very causes of all these sturres: yet in myne opinion & as the matter it selfe shall well

[64] Ascham, *English Works.* ed. Wright, p. 126.

prove it, unkyndnes was the very sede, whereof all these troubles dyd grow." [65] "Unkindness" has to be interpreted as base ingratitude on the part of Charles V. Even with this meaning, the cause was insufficient. In a way, Ascham had followed his master too far. Charles was more complicated than Richard, if for no other reason than that he was less single-minded; Germany was more complicated than England. Ascham's attempt to parallel More's emphasis on the "unnatural" with his own on "unkindness" failed because the situations were too much unlike.

Nonetheless, Ascham had caught the essence of More's work. He too embodied the classics in modern history; he too made use of the rise and fall of princes as directed by Fortune, and of the power of Providence, and subordinated all of them in one grand design. More's chief legacy had been that of order, of writing history around one well-chosen theme. Ascham, though he chose his theme less well, followed More as closely as he could.

Thus the humanists, although they did not succeed in making the study of history per se a part of the curriculum at any level of the educational system, nonetheless managed to give to the subject an importance it had hitherto lacked. Once they had connected the study of the past indissolubly with the life of a good citizen in the present, the humanists naturally extolled the great classical historians as preeminently qualified to lead a ruler—or his subjects— into the paths of civic virtue. Even if the typical educated Elizabethan did not read much history in school, even if he was taught to look for style more than for content, he emerged from his schooling with a desire to read about the past. This explains the great burst of translation in the second half of the sixteenth century and helps to explain, too, the great interest in history of all kinds, and at all levels, which so marks the later Elizabethan period.

But the humanists did more than give men a taste for history; they also supplied new methods for understanding and writing it. The Italians, notably Lorenzo Valla, worked out in detail the concept of anachronism, which was to prove the decisive factor in the rewriting of the record of England's past. Furthermore, by

[65] Ibid., p. 128.

giving the subject a new importance, they made necessary the development of new methods of organization. The old bare annals, which the humanists thought barbarous, gradually gave way to a history arranged by reigns. Sir Thomas More showed how the use of psychology, and of a dominant theme, could give unity to the history of a single reign; and Polydore Vergil worked out the rudiments of how to link several reigns into a coherent whole. Polydore's hint was taken by the chronicler Edward Hall, who made the most of such linkages. More's brief essay came closer to perfection with the paradoxical result that its immediate influence was perhaps less potent: everyone copied More's Richard, but not until the time of the playwrights at the end of the century did men succeed in adapting More's tour de force. Nor is this really unexpected. The changes brought about by the influx of the new ideas were too radical to be absorbed all at once, and a great deal of experimentation was required before they became part of the common stock of English historians.

III

The Reformation and English History Writing

Of all the "reformations" of Europe, the English was, in terms of its justification, the most historical. In England, as elsewhere, most controversy was inevitably theological in nature, but the attempt to find historical antecedents for current practices began at least as early as the Act in Restraint of Appeals (1534) and continued throughout the Tudor period—as, indeed, it continues today. The primary issue was the denial of innovation, and it is best summarized by John Foxe:

> Over and besides, our adversaries yet more object agaynst us, who heaving and shoving for the antiquitie of the Romish Church for lacke of other sufficient reason to prove, are driven to fall in scanning the tunes [times] and yeares. What, say they, where was this Church of yours, before these .l. yeares? To whom briefly to aunswere, first we demaunde what they meane by this, which they call our Churche? If they meane the ordinaunce and institution of doctrine & Sacramentes now receaved of us, and differing from the Church of Rome, we affirme and say, that our Church was, when this Church of theirs was not yet hatched out of the shell, nor did yet ever see any light: that is, in the tyme of the Apostles, in the primitive age, in the time of *Gregory* the first, and the old Romaine Churche, when as yet no universall Pope was received publikely, but repelled in Rome, nor this fulnes of plenary power yet knowne, nor this doctrine, and abuse of Sacramentes yet heard of. In witnes wherof we have the old actes and histories of auncient tyme to geve testimonie with us, wherein sufficient matter we have for us, to declare the same form, usage, and institution of this our Church reformed now, not to be the begynnyng of any new

79

Churche of our owne, but to be the renewyng of the old auncient
Church of Christ: nor to be any swerving from the Churche of
Rome, but rather a reducing to the Church of Rome. Whereas
contrary the Church of Rome which now is, is nothyng but a
swervynge from the Church of Rome, as partly is declared, &
more shall appeare, Christ willing, hereafter.[1]

So the charge of novelty was rejected and, frequently, returned.
Both the Catholic question and the Protestant reply were implicit
in the very concept of Reformation: when Luther, and the other
reformers after him, claimed to be restoring the very church of
Christ and the apostles, the question of the validity of fifteen
hundred years of ecclesiastical history inevitably arose. That more
than one answer was possible is obvious, and it remains to explain
why the English chose the road they did.

Luther, at least, cannot have offered much as a model.[2] There is
no question that on the issue of Scripture versus tradition he came
down unequivocally on the side of Scripture—that is what the
Reformation was all about. The difficulty is that it is misleading to
phrase the question in terms of absolutes. To reject the Catholic
Church of the sixteenth century as the bearer of the traditions of
the ancient church was relatively simple: in its full form, the
doctrine of "tradition" was a recent innovation. Could one also
reject the words of the Fathers and of the earliest Councils? In
some of these, ancient traditions might have found a harbor.
Luther refused to seek a norm outside Scripture. The records of
the first four councils of the church might be of value as showing
the part played by the emperor in early ecclesiastical history, but
dogma derived from the Scriptures alone. Whatever Luther may
have thought about the value of history—and he considered it very
useful as an aid to teaching morality—theology had all its roots in
the self-authenticating Bible. So much might be said on the posi-

---

[1] *The First Volume of the Ecclesiasticall History* [*Actes & Monumentes*]
(London, 1576), pp. 2–3.

[2] On Luther, John M. Headley, *Luther's View of Church History* (New
Haven, 1963); other books on the Reformation view of history which I have
found useful for the discussion that follows are: Walter Nigg, *Die Kirchenge-
schichtsschreibung* (Munich, 1934), pp. 1–74; Pontien Polman, *L'Élément historique dans la controverse religieuse du XVI*° *siècle* (Gembloux, 1932); George
H. Tavard, *Holy Writ or Holy Church: The Crisis of the Protestant Reformation*
(London, 1959); Norman Sykes, *Man as Churchman* (Cambridge, Eng., 1960).

tive side. There remained the matter of degeneration. That the church of the sixteenth century differed radically from that of the Apostles was undeniable, and to Luther such change was degeneracy. The history of that progressive degeneration—the history of the workings of the Antichrist—this might be traced.

Much the same might be said of Calvin. Although, unlike Luther, the French reformer had a humanist background, he firmly resisted the temptation to see Scripture against a classical background, pagan or secular. Calvin did make use of his great store of patristic learning, but his use of it was primarily negative: certain practices might be shown to be innovations because of the silence of the Fathers, but nothing was justifiable which was found only in post-scriptural literature—unless, perhaps, all the Fathers agreed. On that point, Calvin seems to have wavered. It has been suggested that Calvin was never altogether consistent and that he allowed himself liberties of interpretation that he denied his opponents. There is surely some truth in the accusation, but the implication that Calvinism thus became more historically minded than Lutheranism does not follow.[3] Calvin was more of a humanist than Luther, and thus he was more likely to have absorbed the humanist historical spirit; but not all Lutheran theology came directly from the fountainhead, and Melanchthon, at least, was quite as much a humanist as Calvin, and vastly more interested in history. In any case, whatever the views of the founders, Calvinists were more likely than Lutherans to appeal to *sola scriptura*.

Moreover, making the use of the Fathers and the early Councils into a test to a considerable extent hides one important point. One of the great achievements of the humanists, beginning with Petrarch, had been to develop the concept of anachronism. The reformers' adoption of that idea enabled them to see the apostolic church as a separate entity, to cut it away from later church history, and, indeed, to contrast it to more recent developments. No longer did men see the whole history of the church as an unbreakable unity. Luther's idea of church history as the history of degeneracy, Matthias Flacius' concept of church history as the history of the degradation of dogma, these were attempts to save

[3] Heinrich Berger, *Calvins Geschichtsauffassung* (Zürich, 1955); Polman, *L'Élément historique*, pp. 74 ff.

the appearances—by converting Eusebius' positive view of church history as the growth of Christendom into the corresponding and appropriate negative. Nonetheless, the old, Eusebian, view of the growth of Christianity was dead beyond revival.

Thus, no matter what their intention, the reformers were bound to be somewhat historical in their outlook, and the efforts of Luther and Calvin to avoid giving the historical element much room were doomed to failure from the outset. By insisting on the apostolic, that is, the scriptural, church as a norm, the reformers managed to limit the operation of historical criticism, but they could not prevent it. Furthermore, as the Reformation progressed it became more and more difficult to adhere even to that limitation. The scriptural argument worked very successfully against the Catholics, but it was of little use against reformers further to the left. To defend church polity against the Anabaptists required more than an appeal to the Bible. Simply because Lutheran church government was more fully developed than Calvinist— because, for example, it left room for bishops if not for the pope—there was an inevitable need to call on post-scriptural documents. Matthias Flacius, who thought of himself as the true heir of Luther, nonetheless published the greatest of all Lutheran historical works.

In any case, it rapidly becomes obvious that Luther and Calvin saw more clearly than their successors the danger of adding any sort of tradition to the pure fountain of Scripture. If once the Fathers and the Councils were accepted as in any way canonical, where was one to draw the line, and how could the line, once drawn, be defended? A number of solutions to those questions were suggested, most of them involving the division of the whole Christian era into a number of periods whose value as evidence decreased as their distance from the time of the Apostles widened. The full development of this type of argument took time, and even before the task was completed, or all the problems recognized, some of the lesser reformers had already begun to indulge in a historical approach. This is especially true of the more irenic among them, presumably because by widening the historical base which might be appealed to, the degree of comprehension might be widened correspondingly. Men such as Martin Bucer and Peter

Martyr Vermigli were historically oriented before they ever arrived in England, and it may be argued further that one explanation of their influence there is that they reinforced a tendency already prominent in England, rather than that they introduced an altogether new way of thought.

The English had come to the historical method by a different route. It has been said that the Reformation in England was, essentially, an act of state.[4] Interpreted too broadly, that statement can easily be misleading. Taken in a narrow sense, as meaning that most ecclesiastical change originated in governmental activity, there is much truth in it. It is only a slight oversimplification to say that, whereas on the Continent the Reformation was begun by religious reformers and was then taken over by governments which saw advantages for themselves in it, in England the reverse was largely true. Whatever Henry VIII's motives may have been, once he proceeded to action, that action followed the normal legal formulas. English law, however, was based on the interpretation of precedents and thus was, in a very special way, historical in its nature. But finding suitable precedents for anything as radical as the Reformation acts was far from simple. As a result, the justification took two forms: a plain appeal to history such as that found in the opening section of the Act in Restraint of Appeals ("divers sundry old authentic histories and chronicles"), or a recourse to political theory, bolstering the power of the king, which in turn also ended in the use of historical evidences. Thus to call England "imperial" meant more than to declare the country exempt from the suzerainty of pope and emperor; it meant also that the position of its king vis-à-vis the English church was equivalent to that of Constantine. This to a large extent accounts for the otherwise strangely exorbitant insistence by the Tudor chroniclers on the British origin of Constantine and his mother, Helena.[5]

The lead in all this was given by William Tyndale, who, though a heretic in Henry's eyes, nonetheless earned that monarch's approval for his attack on papal power and for his concomitant

---

[4] M. Powicke, *The Reformation in England* (London, 1961), p. 1.

[5] Richard Koebner, " 'The Imperial Crown of This Realm': Henry VIII, Constantine the Great, and Polydore Vergil," *Bulletin of the Institute of Historical Research*, XXVI (1953), 29–52.

elevation of the dignity of kings.[6] Tyndale's work was historical
only incidentally: he shared Luther's position and considered history useful only to denounce evils, not to prove truths. That
theological predilection was reinforced by a profound distrust of
chronicles because so many of their authors had been monks. On
the other hand, this simplistic view of the sources enabled Tyndale
to make his point much more easily: if even the monks reported
some evil, then such a sin must have been widespread indeed.
Since the evils which concerned Tyndale most were the various
usurpations of the clergy in temporal affairs, the proof was not
very difficult. Moreover, this was precisely what Henry wished to
see proved. Where Tyndale led, others more orthodox soon followed. As early as 1534 there appeared a translation of Lorenzo
Valla's demolition of the validity of the Donation of Constantine,
a work which had been published for the first time only recently by
the German knight Ulrich von Hutten as his contribution to the
war chest of Martin Luther.[7] What this might mean in English
terms was made clear enough by Stephen Gardiner in his tract on
the execution of Bishop John Fisher. The gift of England to the
pope, purportedly made by King John, "is as true, and of as myche
authorite, as thatt gifte, which the most holy muniments, of thatt
holy see witnessyth to have byn made of Constantinus to Silves-
ter," and, Gardiner roundly declared, it was up to the pope to
prove title to his own dominions before laying claim to other
men's.[8]

Most of the responsibility for the campaign of vilifying the pope
while elevating the king has been laid at the feet of Thomas
Cromwell. It was certainly he who organized the propaganda
which included the translation of Valla and, the same year, a
version of the *Defensor pacis* of Marsiglio of Padua.[9] Even the

---

[6] Rainer Pineas, "William Tyndale's Use of History as a Weapon of Religious
Controversy," *Harvard Theological Review*, LV (1962), 121–141.

[7] Lorenzo Valla, *A Treatyse of the Donation . . . Gyven . . . unto Sylvester
Pope of Rhome by Constantyne* (London, [1534]).

[8] *Obedience in Church & State, Three Political Tracts by Stephen Gardiner*,
ed. Pierre Janelle (Cambridge, Eng., 1930), pp. 39–41.

[9] *The Defence of Peace*, trans. William Marshall (London, 1535). Cromwell's
influence on Marshall is discussed by F. LeVan Baumer, *The Early Tudor
Theory of Kingship* (New Haven, 1940), pp. 44, 215, and there is much general
information as well; see also A. G. Dickens, *Thomas Cromwell and the English
Reformation* (London, 1959), pp. 80 ff.

translation, five years later, of the book by Jean Lemaire de Belges on the councils of the church was part of the same campaign.[10] Lemaire's book had been a *livre de circonstance* a quarter of a century earlier, when Louis XII had been at odds with Pope Julius II to the point of calling a council against him. The attack on papal usurpations of regal power, the insistence on the authority of princes within the councils of the church, all this was as appropriate in 1539 as it had been in 1512. Lemaire's book differs from the others issued during Cromwell's ascendancy by being purely historical in manner. Lemaire produced a simplified version of church history which attributed all the woes of Christendom to the infection of the Church of Rome by treasure in land and money. After that, virtue resided only in the monarchs of Europe, and their efforts to purify the church, through councils, make up the rest of Lemaire's story. All in all, the message of the little book must have been very pleasing to Henry. He could take his place in a long line of reformers who, by the exercise of their regal power, reformed the abuses of the church without touching her doctrine.

This entire trend of thought was summed up in the amusing case of St. Thomas of Canterbury.[11] In the general attack on shrines, it was only to be expected that the exceedingly rich one of Thomas Becket would be seized along with the rest. But greed was far from being the only reason for the suppression of the veneration of Becket. That saint had been under attack by the Lollards for years because they were convinced that he died for the sake of the possessions of the church. In 1532 one James Bainam had denounced Becket on the grounds that "he dyed for the liberties (to do all mischief unpunished) and privileges of the Church." [12] Bainam may well have been influenced by Tyndale, who disliked St. Thomas because of the resemblance to the hated Cardinal Wolsey. To these theoretical reasons for attacking the saint, Bainam added another: that Becket began the tumult by seizing Tracy and that Becket was killed in the mêlée which ensued when

---

[10] *The Abbrevyacyon of All Generall Councellys,* trans. John Gough (London, 1539).

[11] The case has been discussed by J. F. Davis, "Lollards, Reformers and St. Thomas of Canterbury," *University of Birmingham Historical Journal,* IX (1963), 1–15; the documents are in David Wilkins, *Concilia Magnae Britanniae* (London, 1737), III, 835–836, 847–848.

[12] Davis, "Lollards, Reformers and St. Thomas of Canterbury," p. 10.

the other knights came to Tracy's assistance. A few years later, the
government adopted the whole case against Becket. In 1538 the
Council cited Becket to appear before them to answer charges of
having disturbed the realm; when he (or a representative) failed
to appear, judgment was given against him. It was announced that
his crimes were the cause of his death and that, as a result, he was
no longer to be considered a martyr. Finally, Becket's bones were
to be taken up and publicly burnt, and his shrine destroyed, with
the proceeds to go to the king. A proclamation explained the
whole proceeding to the nation; and when that proved insufficient,
and the Catholics insisted on defending Becket as a martyr for the
liberties of the realm, Henry, in a letter to the Justices of the
Peace, clarified matters further:

> for conservation whereof [i.e., of the liberties of the kingdom],
> they feign, that bishop Beket of Canterbury, which they have
> tofore called Saint Thomas, died for; where indeed there was
> never such thing done nor meant in that time nor sithense: for the
> said Beket never swarved nor contended with our progenitor, king
> Henry the Second; but only to let, that those of the clergy should
> not be punished for their offences, nor justified by the courts and
> laws of this realm; but only at the bishop's pleasure, and after the
> decrees of Rome. And the causes why he died were upon a wilful
> rescue and fray, by him made and begun at Canterbury; which
> was nevertheless afterward alleged to be for such liberties of the
> church, which he contended for, during his life, with the arch-
> bishop of Yorke; yea, and in case he should be absent, or fugitive
> out of the realm, the king should not be crowned by any other, but
> constrained to abide his return.
>
> These, and such other detestable and unlawful liberties, nothing
> concerning the common weal, but only the party of the clergy, the
> said Thomas Becket most arrogantly desired and traitorously
> sued, to have, contrary to the laws of this our realm.[13]

Thus history was pressed into the service of the state and, not for
the last time, altered in the process.

From all this, it is evident that the use of history during the early
period of the English Reformation was essentially secular, simply

---

[13] Gilbert Burnet, *The History of the Reformation of the Church of England*,
ed. N. Pocock (Oxford, 1865), VI, 220–225; the quotation is on pp. 224–225.

because, in the eyes of the government, matters of theology were not at issue. An examination even of religious documents leads to the same conclusion. The various formularies of faith resorted to historical arguments only in connection with the efforts to deny the supremacy of Rome. The universal catholic church was made up of particular churches, no one of which has or had any supremacy or preeminence over the others; and the assumption of such power by the bishop of Rome was not only contrary to Christ's word but also "clean contrary to the use and custom of the primitive church," as well as a violation of the canons of the councils and the dicta of the Fathers.[14] The first point, concerning the division of the universal catholic church into national churches, remained a basic tenet of faith, although it was expanded into the doctrine that the various churches might have their own traditions and ceremonies; the second point was extended by more detailed consideration of church councils until, eventually, it was combined with the idea already mentioned, that no council could be called without the consent of the prince and that, even so, councils were human institutions and capable of error. By this time, of course, doctrine had entered the discussion; but by this time, too, we are in the reign of Edward VI.[15] All of this was in line with the thinking of Archbishop Cranmer, a patristic scholar who nonetheless believed in the supremacy of Scripture and who, despite his "Confutation of Unwritten Verities," was willing to make whatever use he could of the history of the ancient church.[16]

There was unquestionably a historical bias in the work of the Henrician apologists which might serve as a foundation for whatever similar ideas might later be introduced. But the official doctrine was rigid and essentially secular, and innovation in method had to await changes in basic ideology. The only exception to this was in the works of two "heretics," Robert Barnes and John Bale, in whom are found the tendencies already noted on the Continent.

[14] *The Institution of a Christian Man,* in *Formularies of Faith,* ed. Charles Lloyd (Oxford, 1825), p. 117.

[15] *Two Liturgies,* ed. Joseph Ketley, Parker Soc. (Cambridge, Eng., 1844), pp. 531–532, 535.

[16] G. W. Bromiley, *Thomas Cranmer Theologian* (London, 1956), pp. 12–27, 98–99; Thomas Cranmer, "A Confutation of Unwritten Verities," in *Miscellaneous Writings and Letters of Thomas Cranmer,* ed. John Edmund Cox, Parker Soc. (Cambridge, Eng., 1846), pp. 1–67, 514–516.

Barnes was the first Englishman to write polemical history rather
than polemics with more or less of an admixture of history.[17] That
Barnes was somewhat under the influence of Tyndale seems likely:
there was, for example, the same emphasis on the relation of
church and state. But where Tyndale was skeptical of all his
historical sources, Barnes was inclined to accept what he read,
regardless of its origin. Considering the polemical purpose of
Barnes's work, the list of sources prefixed to his *Vitae Romanorum
pontificum* is surprising: the early historians Eusebius and Isidore
found a place on it, but they rubbed elbows with writers who were
virtually Barnes's contemporaries: Sabellicus, Pius II, Platina,
Crantzius, Carion—and of these only the last had a definite Protestant bias, even if some of the others, for various reasons, were
not always loyally pro-Roman. Moreover, Barnes used these writers without any thought of historical criticism. Whatever there was
in any of them that seemed appropriate was taken over, with no
questions asked concerning accuracy or original source.

Of Barnes's two works, one followed the pattern of the Henrician
apologists, the other that of the Lutherans. *A Supplycacion unto
. . . Henry VIII* began as nonhistorical, and the references to the
past were not added until the second edition. The primary purpose
of the book was to demonstrate the subversiveness of the clergy
and the manipulations of the pope against the temporal rulers of
Christendom, using the clergy of each country as a kind of fifth
column. When historical evidence was used, it consisted of stories
such as King John's difficulties in collecting money, where the
pope found the same chore easy.[18] There was in this first work of
Barnes's little that could not have found a place in Tyndale's
writings. The *Vitae Romanorum pontificum,*[19] however, attempted
to prove a rather different point: that numerous practices of
the contemporary Roman church were innovations that could not
be found in the pure church of ancient Christendom. Martin
Luther contributed a preface on the superiority of the primitive
church, and then Barnes showed precisely when each practice was

---

[17] Rainer Pineas, "Robert Barnes's Polemical Use of History," *Bibliothèque
d'Humanisme et Renaissance,* XXVI (1964), 55–69.

[18] *The Whole Workes of W. Tyndall, John Frith, and Doct. Barnes* (London,
1573), Pt. II, p. 189.

[19] Wittenberg, 1536.

first introduced. The text was tendentious, the marginal notes vitriolic. Nor was the text very full: Barnes did not intend to write a history of the church. If one takes this fact in conjunction with Barnes's totally uncritical use of sources, only one conclusion is possible: Barnes was simply no historian.

Thus although John Bale used Barnes's work, it was nonetheless Bale who was the first of the English church historians.[20] The essential difference between the two men lay in the fact that Bale had a conceptualization of what church history ought to be and where it fitted into the general province of theology, and that Barnes wrote only *ad hoc*. The list of Bale's writings was very diverse, ranging from collections on the Carmelites through bibliographical works to plays and pure controversy, but in all of them, wherever historical material appeared, the subordination to a general scheme is evident. The key to that scheme was to be found in the book of Revelation: the mysteries of the text were illustrated by the chronicles, though the chronicles did not supply explanations. Theology came first: "Yet is the text a light to the chronicles, and not the chronicles to the text." [21] What Revelation, properly interpreted, made clear, and what the history of the church, seen in the light of Revelation, strongly reinforced, was a continuous decline of virtue in the church, slow at first, then increasing headlong until at last, in Bale's own time, a reaction toward purity set in. In detail, Bale's view of the past saw perfection only in the beginning: corruption began in the age immediately following that of the Apostles, though the early bishops of Rome were, on the whole, faithful shepherds and busy preachers. Soon the wrong turning of the church became evident,

---

[20] On Bale, Rainer Pineas, "John Bale's Nondramatic Works of Religious Controversy," *Studies in the Renaissance*, IX (1962), 218–233; the same author's "Some Polemical Techniques in the Nondramatic Works of John Bale," *Bibliothèque d'Humanisme et Renaissance*, XXIV (1962), 583–588; and his "William Tyndale's Influence on John Bale's Polemical Use of History," *Archiv für Reformationsgeschichte*, LIII (1962), 79–96. Also, W. T. Davies, "A Bibliography of John Bale," *Oxford Bibliographical Society Proceedings and Papers*, V (1939), 201–279; Jesse W. Harris, *John Bale, A Study in the Minor Literature of the Reformation*, publ. separately and as No. 4 of Vol. XXV of *Illinois Studies in Language and Literature* (Urbana, 1940); Honor McCusker, *John Bale, Dramatist and Antiquary* (Bryn Mawr, 1942).

[21] John Bale, *The Image of Both Churches* in *Select Works of John Bale, D.D.*, ed. Henry Christmas, Parker Soc. (Cambridge, Eng., 1849), p. 253.

as the papacy usurped a gradually widening jurisdiction. The fatal year of the beast, 666, saw this trend confirmed, and from that point on matters grew worse at an ever-increasing speed. The year 1000, it was clear from St. John, would mark the coming of the Antichrist, and the event was heralded by the necromancy of Pope Sylvester and the introduction of clerical celibacy by Pope Gregory.[22] Gregory, indeed, was the *bête noir* of all the reformers, for he introduced into the church, in their most extreme forms, the twin evils of enforced chastity for priests and interference in the business of the secular state.

Meanwhile the truth, though persecuted, somehow survived. Most of the martyrs claimed by the Roman church had lost their lives in defense of property, but a few men in each generation had died for the gospel. For these few to accomplish anything was extraordinarily difficult, because the increasing subversion of the state by the pope and his agents meant that supporters of the Word came under attack as traitors. Nevertheless, in spite of all difficulties, a tradition of learned opposition to the errors of Rome continued: Berengarius, who attacked the doctrine of the mass, Marsiglio of Padua, who opposed the Roman claims to secular dominion, Petrarch (seemingly for his denunciation of Aristotle and the Schoolmen), Wyclif, Hus, Luther, and the other reformers. So mighty had the clarion call become in recent days that hope at last replaced desperation: "So merciful is the Lord to his people in this latter end of the world, that by these and such other the antichrist is clearly uttered, and all his hypocrisy disclosed. I doubt not but within few days the mighty breath of his mouth, which is his living gospel, shall utterly destroy him with his whole generation of shavelings by their faithful administration in the word." [23]

The history of the church in England exactly paralleled the history of the church at large. To begin with, the English church was virtually apostolic in its origins, since it had been founded by Joseph of Arimathea. In those early days the control of the church had rested entirely in the hands of the laity; when, in the second century, King Lucius had allowed that problem to bother him

---

[22] Ibid., pp. 394–395, 561 ff.; *The Pageant of Popes*, trans. John Studley (London, 1574), done from *Acta Romanorum pontificum* (n.p., 1559).

[23] Bale, *Image of Both Churches*, p. 564.

(unnecessarily), he had sent to the bishop of Rome for assistance and had received two Italians who brought with them the proper authority. The English church, having been put in contact with Rome, was now susceptible to all the evils which accrued as the bishop of Rome gradually converted himself into the pope of Christendom. When monasteries entered the realm, heresy entered with them, and the result was the erroneous doctrine of Pelagius. Somehow—Bale was a bit vague on this—England nonetheless managed to keep Christianity purer than did Rome, and the final corruption of the faith had to wait for the arrival of St. Augustine:

> Gregorye . . . sent . . . into Englande in the yeare from Christes in carnacyon CCCCC.xcvi. a Romyshe monke called Augustyne, not of the ordre of Christ as was peter, but of the superstycyouse secte of Benet, there to sprede abrode the Romyshe faythe and relygyon, for Christes faythe was there longe afore. With hym entered *Melitus,* . . . and a great sort more to the nombre of .xl. all monkes & Italyanes. Wele armed were they with Aristotles artylerye, as with logyck, Phylosophye, and other crafty scyences, but of the sacred scripturs, they knew lyttle or nothynge.[24]

The story thereafter continued much as one would expect. Lanfranc and Anselm brought into England the vicious novelties of Popes Sylvester and Gregory. For Bale, Anselm became a type of the new Roman clergy, partly because of his insistence on celibacy, more especially because of his disputes with William Rufus and Henry I. The "relygyon of the clergy was none other in those dayes, than a very treason or utter betrayeng of the worldely governers," and Anselm's behavior proved the point beyond cavil.[25] The dispute between Henry II and Becket was merely a continuation of the now perennial conflict between monarchy and papacy, and indeed most of the church history of England from the time of Anselm to Henry VIII's Reformation could be seen in the same light. As on the Continent, some few brave men strove for the true Word of God, and the church moved ecclesiastical and secular governments alike in its efforts to suppress them. Wyclif,

[24] Bale, *The Actes of Englysh Votaryes* (Wesel [possibly a false imprint for London], 1546), fol. 23ᵛ.
[25] Bale, *The First Two Partes of the Actes . . . of the Englyshe Votaryes* (London, [1560]), II, fol. [H.viᵛ].

Oldcastle, and the Lollards had at all costs to be stopped, and
Thomas Arundel, the Archbishop of Canterbury, had no hesitation in arranging the deposition of Richard II and the promotion
of Henry IV in order to secure the passage of the act *De haeretico
comburendo.*

Tyndale's idea that the Reformation was necessary in order to
get the church out of politics (with its shrewd corollary that this
was precisely the point which would most appeal to power-hungry
monarchs) thus was elaborated by Bale, who, without removing
matters from the realm of polemics, nevertheless fitted the
church-state controversy into a general concept of church history.
At the same time, Bale laid down guidelines for future work on
ecclesiastical history, lines which would at once show the relationship of any detailed research to the general problems raised by the
Reformation view of the church. Bale's own writings, however
polemical some of them seem, fitted neatly into the pattern. The
Actes of Englysh Votaryes took the special problem of monastic
life and traced the evil results of enforced clerical celibacy, results
which included sexual malpractices and an increase of sin on the
moral side and an extension of the power of the popes over the
clergy on the political. In the course of the argument, Bale found it
necessary to trace the history of the idea of celibacy, for it was
certain that no such idea had existed in the apostolic church or, for
that matter, in the period immediately following—even St. Patrick
was the son of a priest. Similarly, in the *Pageant of Popes,* after a
passage relating the history of the papacy to the Apocalypse of St.
John—an idea which was elaborated in *The Image of Both
Churches*—Bale proceeded to show that St. Peter had never been
bishop of Rome at all, and then went on to make the usual points
concerning the influence of property on the church and the interference of popes in secular affairs. Bale's insistence on including
in both books all the scandal he could find—and as a diligent
researcher he found a great deal—ought not to obscure the main
lines of his argument. It was the fact that monks and popes were
lecherous, that popes were ever guilty of pride, that helped prove
both institutions uncanonical, although, of course (since the
chronicles illustrated the biblical texts and not the other way
about), the crucial point could be proved from Scripture. If any-

one doubted Bale's interpretation of the scriptural passages, that doubt should be removed by a perusal of the fate of the institutions under attack.

Even Bale's popular works may be considered in the same way. In *King Johan,* the only one of the surviving plays with any sort of historical motif, all of Bale's usual equations appear: Sedition was to be found in all monkish orders, and as the abstractions in the play gradually took on historical flesh, Sedition became Pandulph, the papal legate. Similarly, Dissimulation was gradually metamorphosed into Archbishop Langton, and it was that prelate who was responsible for England's invasion by the Dauphin Louis. That the ending of the play showed Nobility, Clergy, and Civil Order all bowing before Imperial Majesty and rejecting the pope might be a trifle anachronistic but was to be expected from Bale. King John, who of all the medieval kings resisted the papacy most strongly, was bound to become a hero of the Protestants, especially since his eventual discomfiture only emphasized further the degree to which the popes were interfering with English politics. Bale probably had the idea of using John from Tyndale but, unlike the latter, had sufficient knowledge of English history to feel a little uneasy at this interpretation: that, at least, is the obvious explanation of a passage attacking Polydore Vergil's more pro-Roman interpretation, a passage which, surprisingly in a play written for the commons, cited a substantial array of distinguished chroniclers whose evidence, Bale felt, supported his own view.[26] After this blast at Rome's temporal usurpations, to discover that Bale also wrote a play on Becket, now lost, is precisely what one would expect: and the date of the lost play, significantly, was 1538, the year of the official process against the martyr.[27]

The historical plays, coming comparatively early in Bale's career, fit into the usual pattern of Henrician propaganda. Only after Cromwell's execution, in 1540, when Bale had to flee the country, did he turn to the more extended works already mentioned and to the lives of the English martyrs Sir John Oldcastle and Anne Askew. The seemingly formidable problem of how to make mar-

[26] Bale, *King Johan,* ed. J. H. P. Pafford, Malone Soc. (London, 1931), pp. 108–109.
[27] Davies, "A Bibliography of John Bale," pp. 209–211.

tyrs out of heretics in fact presented few difficulties. Martyrs were
to be divided into two classes, those who died for the pope and
those who died for Christ. Thus the early, pre-Roman, martyrs of
the English church, such as St. Alban, were legitimate; the later,
such as St. Thomas Becket, were not. Once the Roman church
entered the island, with St. Augustine, it produced martyrs for the
true word of Christ, beginning at once with Dionothus (who
refused to preach or baptize in the Roman manner, and whose
death was caused by Augustine)—it was in this line that Wyclif,
Oldcastle, and Anne Askew might be found.[28] It followed from
Bale's general view of church history that a series of English
martyrs ought to exist, paralleling the similar series who suffered
for the Word on the Continent. A full history of those martyrs had
to wait until Bale's friend John Foxe penned it, but the lives of
Oldcastle and Anne Askew demonstrated what could be done and
what it meant.

If in the course of reading Bale's diatribes it is often forgotten
that they fit into a well-ordered plan, readers revolted by Bale's
vituperation are equally inclined to overlook the evident signs of
his scholarly industry. Indeed, Bale's interest in historical materials long antedated his involvement in Reformation polemics: at
some date between the time he left Cambridge and his conversion
in 1533, he had begun to collect notes toward a biographical
history of his own Carmelite order. Encouraged by John Leland,
he finished that work—never published—in 1536, though by that
date Bale was already in difficulties for overzealous Protestantism. Presumably the materials collected for the history of the
Carmelites later were also used for the *Actes of Englysh Votaryes*
as well as forming a fragment of his greatly extended biographical
dictionary of British authors, the *Illustrium maioris Britanniae
scriptorum . . . summarium* (1548). By the time that the *Summarium* was published, Bale had formed his views on the course of
church history, and even a biographical dictionary was forced into
the mold. But however the dictionary ended, it began as a nonpo-
lemical biobibliographical work under the influence and with the

---

[28] Bale, "The Second Examination of . . . Mistress Anne Askewe," in *Select
Works,* esp. pp. 187–189; his "A Brief Chronicle concerning . . . Sir John
Oldcastle" is reprinted in the same volume.

collaboration of John Leland. To judge by his notes, Bale not only ransacked the manuscripts of Leland and John Boston of Bury but also looked into the libraries of such of his friends as collected books.[29] Quite as much as Leland, Bale wanted to save what he could of the monastic libraries, and however intemperate he at times became when confronted with the sins of the monks, he never adopted the view that their myriad productions were best rooted out altogether. In the end, when all other attempts to save the literary spoils of the monasteries failed, Bale used his own very limited resources to purchase the manuscripts for himself, and in a career whose course was far from smooth the event which pained him most was the loss of his library in Ireland.[30]

Thus when one comes to examine Bale's career on the Continent, it is best to recollect that one reason for the high respect in which he was held was his ability to help the German church historians, working under the direction of Matthias Flacius, with vast quantities of bibliographical information. Whereas Flacius did not publish his own bibliography, the *Catalogus,* until 1556, Bale had prepared its British equivalent years earlier. Moreover, the evident similarity of Flacius' view of the course of church history to Bale's is as likely to be due to Bale's influence on the Germans as the other way about. The much greater prominence of the *Magdeburg Centuries* has obscured the fact that Flacius was less historically minded than Bale. To suggest that Bale's writings were the model for Flacius would probably be an exaggeration: there is certainly no proof. It is certain, however, that the peculiarities of Henrician apologetics forced their authors into a historical mold and that, under the influence of Tyndale and Barnes, Bale applied the techniques of history to theological polemics. Unlike his predecessors, however, Bale was a historian before he was a theologian, and that he would have picked up the historical hints in Luther's writings was only to be expected. What Bale probably learned from Flacius and his associates was the

---

[29] Bale, *Index Britanniae scriptorum,* ed. Reginald Lane Poole and Mary Bateson (Oxford, 1902), passim.

[30] Bale, *The Laboryouse Journey & Serche of Johan Leylande* (London, 1549), fol. C.v [*recte* fol. C.iii]; Honor McCusker, "Books and Manuscripts Formerly in the Possession of John Bale," *The Library.* 4th Ser., XVI (1935), 144–165.

value of printing the relevant documents *in extenso*. But by his second return to England in 1559 Bale was worn out: what energy remained to him was spent in convincing Archbishop Parker to take up that project in his stead. For that purpose he composed a long list of manuscripts, divided by headings according to their particular usefulness, and dispatched it to Parker. That letter constituted Bale's testament. In it, among much other useful information, he told the archbishop of the chronicle of Matthew Paris: "Thys chronycle remayneth in the custodye of my lorde of Arundell, beynge a fayre boke, and written in an olde Latyne lettre. . . . It were muche pytie that that noble storye shulde perish in one coppye—for no chronycle paynteth out the byshopp of Rome in more lively colours, nor more lyvely declareth hys execrable procedynges, than it doth." [31] Within a decade of Bale's death Matthew Paris appeared, and the irascible old man's last request was granted.

Bale's stylistic peculiarities and his position in the history of the English drama have overshadowed his originality as a historian. The case ought not to be overstated. His use of historical evidence was far from impeccable, and he followed Leland in attributing some value to Geoffrey of Monmouth. Indeed, he further confused the history of early Britain by adding to Geoffrey's account a bevy of early inhabitants drawn from the imaginative pages of Annius of Viterbo's Berosus. [32] Nonetheless, Bale saw the need for a good chronicle history of England and, late in his life, took it in hand himself. That nothing came of the project was due to the loss of his superb library of medieval chroniclers, and the task of reassembling a similar collection, which strained the combined strengths of her majesty's archbishop and principal secretary, was too much for him. Rather than attempt it, he made available to Parker all the information which a lifetime of collecting had put at his disposal. Bale's essential fair-mindedness—and, despite his vituperativeness, one can find that virtue in him—comes through most clearly in his treatment of Polydore Vergil, whom he disliked and attacked for his treatment of Geoffrey and for his Romishness, yet

[31] H. R. Luard, "A Letter from Bishop Bale to Archbishop Parker," *Cambridge Antiquarian Communications*, III (Cambridge, Eng., 1879), 172–173.
[32] See T. D. Kendrick, *British Antiquity* (London, 1950), pp. 69–72.

admired for his learning.[33] Thus, whatever may be said against the details of his own compositions, he bequeathed to the Elizabethans a twofold legacy: a comprehensive view of the history of the Christian church in general and the position of its English branch within it in particular, and a reverence and enthusiasm for the sources of English history which transcended religious controversy. By contrast, the violence of his language fades into insignificance.

Much of Bale's work was done in flight from the theological conservatism of Henry VIII. When once the young Josias came to the throne, and the control of government rested in the hands of the liberal Somerset, ideas that had previously sent their exponents to the stake or into exile became respectable and, often, official. Bale and others of his persuasion returned home, and following on their heels came the Continental reformers who were to be befriended by an archbishop whose own theological position was already shifting rapidly leftward. Even while the invasion was in progress, the church history of Bale was being popularized. Using only a few of the obvious sources and relying principally on the old *Polychronicon,* the anonymous author of *The Olde Faythe of Greate Brittaygne* (1549?) treated as obvious that version of church history which claimed a pre-Augustinian origin for Christianity in Britain, and which attributed to Augustine and his successors all the evils which had swept the island's church along the road to complete degradation. The little book is indicative chiefly of a mood rather than of elaborated doctrine, but that mood was to infect high as well as low. Cranmer's patristic bias made him susceptible to a historical approach to theology; the irenicism of Martin Bucer and Peter Martyr Vermigli pushed them in the same direction; and, with the return of Bale, the promonarchical, antipapal view of the Henrician apologists, now fully arrayed in all its historical panoply, was added to the mixture. Edward's reign was too brief for all this to come to fruition. There were too many other things needing to be done, and at once—such as the revisions of the prayer book and of the whole theological structure of

---

[33] Bale, "Sir John Oldcastle," p. 8.

English religion—for much time to be spent on justification. But
the seed was planted—in Matthew Parker, in John Jewel, and,
most firmly, in Bale's young friend and protégé, John Foxe.

Neither a biography of Foxe nor a complete analysis of his work
is required here.[34] The books he wrote were numerous, but his
greatest subsumed them all. Like many others, he fled from England on the accession of Queen Mary; unlike most of the exiles, he
brought his work with him, and despite the trials of lack of home
and income, he somehow succeeded in finishing and publishing his
*Commentarii rerum in ecclesia gestarum, maximarumque per
totam Europam, persecutionum, à Wiclevi temporibus ad hanc
usque ætatem descriptio. Liber primus* in 1554. The original plan
thus was to begin with Wyclif as the author of the Reformation;
presumably the story was to be brought up to date with Edmund
Grindal supplying the materials for the history of the Marian
persecutions. The death of Mary intervened, and the subsequent
rush of exiles homeward deprived Foxe of his collaborators. Unde-
terred, he remained at Basel until 1559 and came home himself
only after he saw a greatly expanded *Rerum in ecclesia gestarum
. . . commentarii* into print. Foxe added nothing at the beginning
of his story, and most of the expansion concerned the Henrician
and Marian martyrs. The history of Continental martyrs was put
off until a second volume, but the mere fact that the book was
written in Latin, for a European audience, is enough to show that
Foxe intended to place the history of the English church into a
context of the sufferings of the true church everywhere. But with
Elizabeth once on the throne, it became more important to defend
a revivified English Protestant church. Martyrs, especially those of
Mary, remained vital to Foxe's plan, but Archbishop Parker and
others in authority in the English church were determined to
provide a complete genealogy for their version of Protestantism.
Since Foxe, like Parker, had come under the influence of Bale, it
must be presumed that he altered the structure of his book willingly enough. In any case, when the *Acts and Monuments* ap-

---

[34] On Foxe, J. F. Mozley, *John Foxe and His Book* (London, 1940); Helen C.
White, *Tudor Books of Saints and Martyrs* (Madison, 1963), Chs. v–vi; William
Haller, "The Tragedy of God's Englishman," in *Reason and the Imagination*, ed.
J. A. Mazzeo (New York, 1962), pp. 201–211; and especially Haller's excellent
Foxe's Book of Martyrs and the Elect Nation (London, 1963).

peared in 1563, the story went back to the earliest days of Christianity, and a martyrology had been transformed, at least partially, into a church history.

As the quotation which opened this chapter indicates, Foxe was answering the question "Where was your church before Luther?" Like Bale, whose basic scheme he adopted, Foxe's answer involved a history of the church or, to be strictly accurate, of the two churches, the false and the true. Inevitably, Foxe had to chronicle the degradation of the Roman church, a decline which was gradual at first and became more and more precipitous as time went on and the distance from the age of Christ and the Apostles widened. At the same time, it had to be shown that the true church survived all the vicissitudes of Christianity generally as well as those additional burdens imposed by the persecutions inspired by Rome. So much was easy. But some sort of periodization was necessary, and this had to be more than a mere device intended solely to make the historian's task simpler. Here again, Foxe borrowed from Bale. The solution to the problem was to be found in the Revelation of St. John. The mystical numbers to be found there were susceptible of an interpretation which led to a division of church history into five sections, each of approximately three hundred years. The first three centuries of the church were years of purity: this was the church at its best. At the same time, these were the centuries of the great Roman persecutions, a time of trial triumphantly survived. The advent of Constantine led to a period of quiet; the persecutions were ended and, moreover, the great persecutor, Satan, had been bound for a thousand years. The quiet ended with the assumption of the papal title, with the acquisition of great lands, with the spreading of the monks—and with the rise of Islam. After about 600, the church could no longer serve as a model for true Christians. Nonetheless, matters would get worse. With the necromancy of Pope Sylvester, with the greed for power of Pope Gregory, the decline accelerated. Transubstantiation became accepted doctrine, the infamy of clerical celibacy was enforced, and, perhaps worst of all, the church began its attempts to seize the secular sword. This lasted until the time of John Wyclif: then, with Satan unloosed once more, the persecutions began again in earnest. The last period thus saw the battle of the saints against the Antichrist, now revealed as residing in the papacy. Hus and Jerome were burned at Constance, the bones of Wyclif were desecrated, and the papacy tried to extirpate the true religion in Bohemia with armies and in England through its control of the machinery of the state. With the coming of Luther the saints began to triumph and the papacy to topple. Presumably the end of the trials of the persecuted was near.

The theory behind all this was essentially the theory of Bale that history and scriptural prophecy were interrelated and explained each other. There was, moreover, an underlying stratum of predestination. God had planned the whole course of human history— and especially church history—and had, furthermore, revealed the essential outlines of that plan to man through St. John. Without at all doubting the scriptural revelation, Foxe nonetheless felt that the actual course of the history of the church proved that he had read his Scriptures rightly. The history of man and of the church had a finite beginning and an equally finite end. That was the divine plan, and man, according to his small abilities, could at least comprehend the outlines. That the whole theory demonstrated the inevitability of a Protestant triumph was only to be expected. The overall theory applied with equal force to the details. The Old and New Testaments showed how immediate was God's care of his church; the martyrology served as a continuation of the record. Moreover, the history of each man paralleled the history of all men: the drama of salvation in which each individual starred was the same drama for all mankind collectively. Each martyr, similarly, was a paradigm of all church history, and each triumph over the flames was a victory for the true church. Because the history of the church was the history of the war of good against evil, of the war between the true church and the false, Foxe had to include the histories of both. The stories of the martyrs, separated from the whole history of the greatest of all human wars, made no sense. Each story was, of course, inspirational, but, more than that, it was symbolic as well. Foxe was right when he denied that his martyrology was no more than a Protestant continuation of a Roman model. There was thus a kind of grand dialectic in the *Acts and Monuments,* and it can be seen to operate in great and in little. Foxe never allowed his readers to forget his main theme.

Periodically in the book he announced it outright, though more often it can be found in his deliberate placing of events in their proper order, so that the deaths of John Hus and Jerome of Prague meant a temporary victory for the forces of darkness, while the invention of printing, immediately after, was the countervailing stroke.

In the general history of the church the history of England played the major role. One reason for this is obvious: the *Acts and Monuments* was written in English to convince Englishmen that theirs was a chosen people. But Foxe went further than this. To him there was something unique about the English: they had received a pure church early and had kept it undefiled longer than anyone else; they had given Wyclif to the world and thus had inaugurated the Reformation. Even the divisions of general church history began to take on an English aspect: much as the great medieval chroniclers had done, Foxe converted the general to the national. Did the second era end with the coming of the Saxons, the third with the Conquest? It is not easy to say. Wyclif certainly marked the dividing line between the fourth and fifth. Church history and English history gradually became inextricably mixed. Foxe did intersperse his story with the great events on the Continent: his readers could learn about the tribulations of the Emperor Frederick II at the hands of the pope; they could discover the ways of that scourge of God, the Turks; the Bohemian revolt was clarified for them and the reformations of Luther and Zwingli explained. But if these stories were perhaps drawn out longer than was strictly necessary, nonetheless they were an essential part of Foxe's grand scheme. Could the same be said about details from the Wars of the Roses? The patriot in Foxe could not be repressed. So he told the complete story of the English church, how it had been brought in by Joseph of Arimathea, strengthened by King Lucius, attacked by the heathen Saxons, and then debased by the papist Augustine. No sooner had Augustine come into the realm than the false church began to shed the blood of the true; notwithstanding, the English church was still better than most. Kings, not popes, still made ecclesiastical laws; transubstantiation was slow in making headway. When the monks took over and the church became rich, the degradation deepened. Finally, with William the

Conqueror, the new religion of Pope Gregory found its way over
the Channel, and even then the English kings had a good record of
resistance. Henry II refused to give in to the traitorous demands of
Becket; John resisted the importunities of Innocent III until it
almost cost him his kingdom. The conclusion was clear: if anyone
sought out the true church, he could find it in England. It was the
Romans who had apostasized from the church of Christ, not the
English. That was Foxe's answer to the question, "Where was your
church before Luther?"

Since Foxe was unquestionably writing a history as well as a
martyrology, some examination of his procedures is necessary.
How accurate his narratives of the martyrs are is a point which has
been much discussed by others, and it seems to me sensible to
accept J. F. Mozley's verdict that Foxe went to considerable effort
to ascertain the facts. Certainly this fits in well with the evidence of
his care in other matters. One of the reasons Foxe gave for writing
a history was his conviction that none of any value had yet been
produced. The monks had either omitted crucial passages or had
altered facts to make their stories favorable to Rome. The same
could be said of more recent historians, especially of the Italians
among them—it is obvious that he had Polydore Vergil in mind.
The emphasis on the prejudices of monks and Italians was, of
course, hardly original with Foxe. The point had been made by
Tyndale and had recurred ever after: since it meant that a Protestant could quote any antipapal comment and then say that even
the pope's hirelings admitted the charge, the opportunity was too
good to miss. The usefulness of this line of attack did not, however, prevent Foxe from taking the original charge against monks
and their like seriously. He played the game of quotations as well
as anyone, but he did not limit himself, as Barnes had done, to
such sources alone. His skepticism was pervasive: obviously he
was unlikely to accept the miracles vouched for only by his enemies; obviously he used Valla's arguments against the genuineness
of the Donation of Constantine; but he could also doubt Geoffrey
of Monmouth's accounts of King Arthur's victories on the Continent, or the chronicles which stated that King John had been
poisoned by a monk. The last-named case is indicative. Foxe
would have liked to believe the story since it fitted in so well with

his bias. It turned out, however, that the chroniclers were not in agreement on the point, and Foxe, as befitted an honest man, quoted alternative accounts. In the end, he accepted the poisoning story, but it was not without some sifting of the evidence.[35]

The emphasis on sources is evident to any reader of the *Acts and Monuments*. Foxe quotes hundreds of them, and sometimes the quotations go on for forty pages and more. Partially, this was to ensure accuracy: it was less easy to doubt the *ipsissima verba* than a Protestant summary of them. Partially, too, he must have seen his book as an armory in the still continuing war of Protestant against Catholic. Wherever necessary, he went back to the earliest account, and necessity in this case meant that a doubt of some sort had arisen. A Catholic had attacked Foxe's version of the death of Sir John Oldcastle as presented in the first edition. In defending himself Foxe pointed out that it was he, and not his opponent, who had tried to get to the bottom of the matter. Where the Catholic used Fabyan, Hall, and Polydore, Foxe pointed out that none of these were contemporaries of the action in question, and that one had to go behind them. Such writers were useful for certain things, but not for those of the greatest importance:

> in alleaging and writing of Chronicles is to be considered to what place and effect they serve. If ye wold shew out of them the order and course of tymes, what yeres were of dearth and of plenty, where kings kept their Christenmas, what condites were made, what Maiors and shirifes were in London, what battailes were fought, what triumphes and great feastes were holden, when kings began their raigne, and when they ended &c. In such vulgare and popular affaires, the narration of the Chronicler serveth to good purpose, and may have his credite, wherin the matter forceth not much, whither it be true or false, or whether any listeth to beleve them. But where as a thing is denied, and in cases of judgement, and in controversies doubtful, which are to be decided and boulted out by evidence of just demonstration: I take them neyther for Judges of the Bench not [nor] for arbiters of the cause, nor as witnesses of themselves sufficient necessarily to be sticked

---

[35] *Actes and Monuments* (London, 1563), fol. 69ʳ⁻ᵛ; this has been slightly expanded in the edition of 1576, p. 260. A large plate entitled "The description and manner of the poysoning of king John" leaves no doubt of Foxe's final opinion.

unto. Albeit I deny not but histories are taken many tymes, and so termed for witnesses of tymes, & glasses of antiquitie &c. yet not such witnesses, as whose testimony, beareth alwayes a necessary truth and bindeth beliefe.[36]

Thus Foxe insisted on the primacy of sources; and, interestingly enough, toward the end, while quoting from Cicero's great paean for history, he pointed out that such praise should be reserved either for the sources of history or for the works of those who based themselves firmly on those sources.[37] It was that foundation that made Livy and Sallust great, not their style or pretensions; and it was as much Polydore's refusal to cite his sources as his Romanism that made Foxe dislike him.

What Foxe did was to take the grand scheme evolved by John Bale and develop it into a fully articulated church history. In so doing, he absorbed his master's work, as he absorbed the products of Flacius Illyricus and his school. Foxe had no choice: if he wanted to forge an armory as well as a history and to put the whole into some form of order, then these were the writers from whom to borrow. But Foxe did more than play the jackdaw. He searched for his own sources, and while he learned something about historical criticism from the Germans and as much from Valla and the humanists, he knew how to apply the knowledge. His best pieces of critical writing have to do with English history, where he had no models. The emphasis on sources presumably came from Flacius, though Bale had published some. It was Foxe who showed men how to use them. His attack on the Henrician Six Articles is a model of the kind: for each of the articles a vast array of materials was brought forward to counter Henry's view. The documents included texts from Aelfric (in Anglo-Saxon), a complete history of the doctrine of transubstantiation (with references to Berengarius, Ratramnus, and all the other early medieval opponents of the innovation), a dissertation on clerical marriage, which included a medieval Latin treatise on the subject, and so on.[38] Foxe thus served as a model of how to combine research with

---

[36] *The First Volume* (1576), p. 556.

[37] Ibid., p. 557.

[38] *The Second Volume* (1576), pp. 1111–49; a substantial block of Aelfric's Anglo-Saxon was printed as well in this section. It does not appear in the 1563 edition.

organization and with a point of view. As we have seen, he considered only those who did so worthy of the name of historian. But Foxe limited his lesson to "important" matters—to him, theological—and excluded the obvious political ones. When these were brought under the same discipline, the days of compilation would be over. That Foxe's lesson was likely to be learned is clear from his popularity—no one interested in religion and anxious to defend Anglicanism missed reading Foxe, and in the circumstances this meant that he was read by every literate, historically minded Englishman and not just by theologians.

The fundamental question "Where was your church before Luther?" continued to worry Protestants. Some aspects of the questioning appeared immediately after Elizabeth's accession. As a preliminary to revision of the Act of Supremacy, a colloquy between Protestants and Catholics was held at Westminster. The details of the business need not here concern us: it is sufficient to know that the first proposition offered for debate read, "It is against the word of God, and the custom of the primitive church, to use a tongue unknown to the people in common-prayers and administration of the sacraments." [39] Dr. Cole, the Marian Dean of St. Paul's and, as preacher of the sermon at Cranmer's execution, not much loved of the reformers, had great difficulty in handling historical questions. Every word of John Jewel's unflattering description of Cole's performance need hardly be taken as gospel, but it is at least revealing: "The speaker, however, made no scruple of betraying, among other things, the very mysteries, and secrets, and inmost recesses of his own religion. For he did not hesitate gravely and solemnly to affirm that, even were all other things to agree, it would nevertheless be inexpedient for the people to know what was going on in religious worship: for ignorance, said he, is the mother of true piety, which he called devotion." [40] Such a view was in flagrant contradiction to those held by all reformers, of whatever shade; and Cole's bumbling must have made the historical

---

[39] Edward Cardwell, *A History of Conferences,* 3rd edn. (Oxford, 1849), p. 56.

[40] *The Works of John Jewel,* ed. John Ayre, Parker Soc. (Cambridge, Eng., 1845–50), IV, 1203.

approach, already well established, seem a most promising weapon in controversies.

Within a few months, the same Jewel had taken advantage of the opportunity by preaching his "Challenge Sermon" at Paul's Cross, a sermon which was repeated at Court, and again at Paul's, the next year.[41] In it Jewel listed a number of Roman practices, among them transubstantiation, communion in one kind, services in a strange tongue, and acknowledgment of the bishop of Rome as universal bishop, and then challenged the Catholics to prove that any or all of them were at all ancient, "either by the scriptures, or by example of the primitive church, or by the old doctors, or by the ancient general councils." [42] A rather inconclusive fliting with Cole followed, and the sermon, together with the correspondence it engendered, was published in 1560. For a time there was quiet, and it was not until after Jewel published his *Apologia ecclesiae Anglicanae,* in which the same points were elaborated and set into a more general frame, that the "Great Controversy" broke out in good earnest.

Jewel had himself come to the historical view relatively late and was still elaborating the details even while he was preaching the various versions of the challenge sermon. Originally his view seems to have been close to Calvin's, and in an Oxford sermon of Edward VI's time he wrote: "For, although very much by the judgment of all men is to be given to the fathers, yet were they men, and also might err. Truly, to speak nothing else of them, they did oftentimes very ill agree among themselves about very great and weighty matters. But the word of God is sure, and firm, and certain, and appointed for every time." [43] The change in thinking which subsequently occurred may be traced to the influence of Peter Martyr, whom Jewel much admired. It seems likely that Jewel spent much of his exile collecting the documentation for his challenge, and even then the work was far from complete. With

[41] The whole controversy is discussed in A. C. Southern, *Elizabethan Recusant Prose 1559–1582* (London, 1950), pp. 60–66, which gives a complete bibliography. On Jewel, see W. M. Southgate, *John Jewel and the Problem of Doctrinal Authority* (Cambridge, Mass., 1962), John E. Booty, *John Jewel as Apologist of the Church of England* (London, 1963), and Booty's edition of Jewel's *An Apology of the Church of England* (Ithaca, 1963).

[42] *Works,* I, 20.

[43] Ibid., II, 958.

the publication of the *Apologia,* the fight was on. That work was, of course, intended as a general handbook and thus contained only a little historical argument; but Jewel must have realized that after his sermon whatever there was would be challenged. By that time, the author had become bishop of Salisbury; and since a bishop could command a staff, collections were systematically made. Jewel read whatever he could and marked any passages of controversial importance; secretaries then copied these into notebooks according to the subject matter. By the time Harding struck his blow, Jewel was ready.

As the debate developed, it revolved around the problem of whether certain carefully selected Roman practices could be authenticated by writings previous to 600 A.D. The opposition to Jewel was formidable. The Catholics Harding, Rastell, Dorman, and Stapleton were scholars of note, quite as accustomed to patristics or history as their Protestant counterparts. Working out the import of all the arguments is less than easy, since the commonly accepted technique of theological debate was to reprint one's opponent, suitably divided into small pieces, and then refute the segments one by one. The result was an emphasis on logic, with questions of fact relegated to the background and with general considerations of method frequently omitted altogether. Hence, there is good reason to forego chronological exactitude in order to take up matters in order of importance. John Rastell came closest to the real roots of the argument, much closer than the more learned Harding, for whereas the latter tried to prove Jewel wrong in detail, Rastell concentrated on the weaknesses inherent in Jewel's willingness to allow the first six hundred years of the church as in some sense canonical while rejecting what followed. Rastell's attack was two-pronged: he pointed out the inconsistency between Jewel's epigraph, "Let old customs prevail," and the usual *sola scriptura* and, as a corollary, asked where custom ended; as his second point he noted that "it is propre to the heretikes to appeale to the scriptures onely, because they are quickly condemned by tradition, custome, and manner." [44] This added up to an indictment of the reformers generally for retreating to Scripture when it suited

[44] *A Confutation of a Sermon, Pronounced by M. Juell* (Antwerp, 1564), foll. 3ᵛ ff., 10ʳ.

them and then advancing once more to tradition when that seemed
appropriate, without allowing the same mobility to their opponents
—an indictment which, in most cases, could be supported. Moreover, Rastell pointed out that the Catholics ought not to be forced
to fight on the reformers' ground, since there was no reason to
accept that ground, be it Scripture or primitive church: ". . . we
labor to prove, not what thing was then commonlie doone, but
what maye now, and might then have ben laufullie doone." [45]
If Rastell and his colleagues had held fast to this, the "Great
Controversy" would have died for lack of communication. But
the appeal to the past was too powerful to be ignored in this
manner. Thus, even Rastell found himself arguing on the weaker
ground that six hundred years were chosen purely for the convenience of the Protestants and that that figure was otherwise indefensible. From that point Rastell's argument degenerated into typical
polemic, consisting primarily of accusations that Jewel misused his
sources. In a few instances Rastell fell victim to the inherent
weaknesses of the whole traditionalist position. If tradition can be
said to continue to the present, then the church of today remains
as sole arbiter, and criticism, even of documents, becomes both
irrelevant and impious. Jewel had raised doubts about the genuineness of a work attributed to St. Cyprian. Rastell not only did
not share those doubts but criticized Jewel for raising them at all,
for such doubts led to impiety: "For suppose it so, that being not
S. Cyprians in deede, I so love and Reade the boke, as if it were
his: what daunger hereby is cumming unto me: the Boke being
Sound and good, whyche I doe Reade?" [46] This was, in effect,
anti-intellectualism, and Rastell's argument would apply as well to
Valla on the Donation—or Polydore on Geoffrey of Monmouth. It
was too late to repeal humanist source criticism.

The final collapse of Rastell should not blind us to the essential validity of his point regarding the extent of the primitive
church. As long as the reformers used the years following upon
the church of the Apostles negatively, that is, to demonstrate

---

[45] *A Replie against an Answer (Falslie Intitled) In Defence of the Truth*
(Antwerp, 1565), fol. 126^r.
[46] *The Third Booke, Declaring . . . That It Is Time to Beware of M. Jewel*
(Antwerp, 1566), fol. 56^v.

retrogression but not as the positive basis of any article of faith, the Rastell argument was irrelevant. But with (among other things) bishops to defend, the English, and some of the Germans, did advance beyond Luther's boundary. Thus the temporal limits of the primitive church became involved in debate; and this goes far to explain the insistence on Revelation which characterized so much of the reformers' work. Here could be found the number of the beast; here was a defense of a limit in the late sixth or early seventh centuries. Bale had seen this, as had Foxe, and their successors had no choice but to follow them.

Rastell raised the fundamental issues, even if he was unable to stick to them; at the opposite extreme, the subsidiary controversy between Thomas Dorman and Alexander Nowell rapidly became no more than an exercise in academic logic-chopping. The most substantial of the controversial works, the exchange between Jewel and Harding, lay somewhere between those positions. The question as to which of the two argued most correctly does not concern us here; what is important to the development of historical thinking is argument about the authenticity of texts.[47] Jewel was a humanist in the tradition of Valla, and Harding was sufficiently interested in the problems so raised to debate on Jewel's ground. One example, of many, suffices to make the point clear. Harding had used an epistle of Anacletus as evidence, and Jewel took the opportunity to discuss epistles decretal generally. Not only was it the case that St. Jerome and others never mentioned these epistles, but the epistles themselves abounded in inconsistencies:

> Clemens informeth St James of the order and manner of St Peter's death: yet it is certain, and Clement undoubtedly knew it, that James was put to death seven years before St Peter.
>
> Antherus maketh mention of Eusebius, bishop of Alexandria, and of Felix, bishop of Ephesus: yet was neither Eusebius nor Felix neither bishop nor born all the time that Antherus lived. . . .
>
> It would be tedious and needless to open all: these few notes may suffice for a taste. . . .
>
> He maketh mention of St Peter's church: yet was there no

[47] Jewel's accuracy is assessed by Booty, *John Jewel as Apologist*, pp. 104–125.

church built in the name of Peter within three hundred years after Anacletus.

Again, he allegeth the decrees and canons of the old fathers: his words be these: *Hæc ab antiquis apostolis et patribus accepimus:* "These things have we received of the old apostles and ancient fathers." As if the apostles had been long before him: notwithstanding, St John the apostle was yet alive, and Anacletus himself was one of the oldest fathers.

Although by that I have thus shortly touched, the likelihood hereof may soon appear, yet I beseech thee, good christian reader, consider also these and other like phrases and manners of speech, which in these epistles are very familiar, and may easily be found: *Persecutiones patienter portare: Peto ut pro me orare debeas: Episcopi obediendi sunt, non insidiandi: Ab illis omnes Christiani se cavere debent.* Here is not so much as the very congruity and natural sound of the Latin tongue. And shall we think that, for the space of three hundred years and more, there was not one bishop in Rome that could speak true Latin? and specially then, when all the people there, both women and children, were able to speak it naturally, without a teacher? [48]

The concept of anachronism, in its historical and philological forms, can hardly ever have been more neatly applied. The advantage of insisting on Scripture as the primary authority meant that the Fathers (and, indeed, all post-scriptural documents) could be treated critically: if the documents survived the scrutiny, and if they were in agreement, then they might be used to illustrate or clarify a point of dubious interpretation. But there was nothing sacred about the Fathers, even for Jewel, who had studied them long and knew them well. Thus, by the nature of their theological premises, the Protestants were in a good position to use the critical weapons forged for them by the humanists, and the more they were pressed by men of Harding's quality, the better their criticism became.

The only real answer to this was to bring forward new documents: and that was done by Thomas Stapleton, who edited Bede as one part of his share in the Great Controversy. The relevance of Bede depended on the assumption that Christianity first came into England with St. Augustine; if that were granted,

[48] Jewel, *Works,* I, 342–343.

then English Christianity was papal in its origins, and many of the rites and beliefs that the Protestants rejected went back to the earliest full and circumstantial account of the religious history of the island. "Intercession off Saints protestants abhorre. The practise theroff appeareth in this history in the first booke the xx. chapter before we had the faith, and in the iiii. booke the xiiii. chap. after the faith receaved." [49] The list went on through forty-five examples. The case was sufficiently clear, and Stapleton emphasized it in his dedication to the queen:

> The matter of the History is such, that if it may stande with your Majesties pleasure to vewe and consider the same in whole or in part, your highnes shall clerely see as well the misse informations of a fewe for displacing the auncient and right Christen faith, as also the way and meane of a spedy redresse that may be had for the same, to the quietnesse of the greater part of your Majesties most loyal and lowly subjectes consciences. In this history it shall appeare in what faith your noble Realme was christened, and hath almost these thousand yeres continewed: to the glory of God, the enriching of the crowne, and great welth and quiet of the realme. In this history your highnes shall see in how many and weighty pointes the pretended refourmers of the church in your Graces dominions have departed from the patern of that sounde and catholike faith planted first among Englishemen by holy S. Augustin our Apostle. . . .[50]

The point was well taken: Stapleton had shown the antiquity of many of the practices to which the reformers objected. This was, as the Catholics discovered, "a very telling argument with the more sober sort," and Cardinal Allen's seminary at Douai, which emphasized church history, made Bede the object of careful study.[51] If all that Stapleton had intended to accomplish was to give a more accurate picture of Anglo-Saxon Christianity than could be found in Bale or Foxe, then his translation was a success. But there had, perforce, to be more. Bede stood outside Jewel's magic circle of six hundred years, and Stapleton had to add a commentary showing that Augustinian Christianity did not

---

[49] Bede, *The History of the Church of Englande,* trans. Thomas Stapleton (Antwerp, 1565), fol. ▷4ᵛ.

[50] Ibid., foll. *2ᵛ–*3ʳ.

[51] Philip Hughes, *The Reformation in England* (London, 1952–54), III, 292.

differ materially from what had gone before. To Protestants, convinced that by Pope Gregory the Great's time deterioration had already set in irremediably, this was bound to be unconvincing. Moreover, the Anglicans denied the basic premise on which the argument rested, that Christianity in England was Roman in its origin. Augustine had found Christians in the island, and had corrupted them: the faith went back to King Lucius or to Joseph of Arimathea. Nonetheless, in that historical battle in which the weapons were old chronicles newly reprinted, the Catholics had gotten in the first blow.

During the Elizabethan period the division implicit in the ranks of the church historians became more noticeable. In the early days of Protestantism, while the state of English religion was still in flux, a defense of the Reformed religion generally was to be expected; but with the acceptance of the Elizabethan settlement there was an increasing emphasis on finding an adequate history for the specifically English church. Jewel had limited himself to the early centuries of Christian history and had said little about England; Archbishop Parker, of whom we have yet to speak, was interested almost exclusively in his native country. Most writers did not draw the line very rigidly, but they may, for convenience if for nothing else, be put on one side or the other. The few theologians who wrote professedly historical works—at least those before Archbishop Ussher—tended to specialize in one aspect of church history or the other; and most of the theologians after Jewel's day were less interested in history than their predecessors. The shift away from history was due largely to a change of opponents. After the 1570's the greatest problem facing the church was Puritanism rather than Romanism, and an appeal to history was powerless to shift the Puritans from their position. Essentially, the Puritan argument rejected any authority outside Scripture: no appeal to tradition, however hallowed, was relevant. Hooker and others of their opponents could and did point out to the Puritans the inconsistencies inherent in their position: that the appeal to Scripture alone was impossible in a world far different from that of Jesus and St. Paul, especially in that the state and its ruler were now Christian. None of this made any difference. If Hooker were to have any success at converting the Puritans, the argument had to be couched in their terms. Thus, the appeal was not to history but to Scripture and to reason; if, sometimes, one of the Fathers—or some historical happenstance—was mentioned, it was in order to lend an air of verisimilitude to an argument otherwise already fully worked out. Only occasionally was the historical appeal primary: a few chapters in Hooker's defense of bishops come to mind.[52] Richard Field, although he wrote against the Catholics, followed the same method as Hooker, and it was not until he was replying to Catholic counterattacks that historical material appeared in any quantity. The plan of the unfinished second edition of his book would have had to be very different, for Field intended to include the anti-Catholic materials in the text, and this would have altered the focus radically. The Puritans were self-debarred from answering Hooker with historical references; the Catholics were under no such disability, and Field had in the end to meet them on their own terms—which he was perfectly capable of doing.[53]

Nonetheless, the eventual legacy of Jewel's writing was a strengthening of the patristic bias of English theology, used, however, with the criticism of the literature exemplified in the Great Controversy. Among serious theological writers, especially those Jacobean and Caroline divines whose concern it was to demonstrate the glory of the Church of England, the Fathers were a constant source of inspiration. Strictly historical work of the old-fashioned sort, however, was rare. Meredith Hanmer published translations of Eusebius and other early church historians in 1576–1577:[54] although Hanmer was, or became, a Puritan, the work was fair-minded, with only a rare marginal note betraying the author's bias. Occasionally, when the text became obscure, the translator broke in and took a few

---

[52] *The Works of . . . Richard Hooker,* ed. John Keble, rev. R. W. Church and F. Paget, 7th edn. (Oxford, 1888), Bk. VII, Ch. i (III, 143–144); Bk. VII, Ch. xiii (III, 216–219); there is an appendix on "Hooker's Historical Sense" in Peter Munz, *The Place of Hooker in the History of Thought* (London, 1952), pp. 195–197.

[53] See the appendixes to the various books: Richard Field, *Of the Church,* 4 vols., Ecclesiastical History Soc. (Cambridge, Eng., 1847–52).

[54] Eusebius, *The Auncient Ecclesiasticall Histories,* trans. Meredith Hanmer (London, 1577).

paragraphs or pages to explain. The analyses were chiefly textual, but that might include an examination of the authenticity of documents. The whole is a model of its kind, and that it provided ammunition for the usual Protestant attack on the Catholics—by showing the growth of ceremonies—does not alter that fact. Where Hanmer prepared the source for use, Richard Crakanthorp, a generation later, made use of these and similar materials to defend the power of the ruler in matters ecclesiastic.[55] Cardinal Baronius had declared the Emperor Justinian illiterate and malicious and had added that he had no right to legislate for the church. Crakanthorp made no attempt to write a life of the emperor in reply: that was best left to the civil lawyers. Instead, he examined Baronius' witnesses, seeking to discover what they believed, how credulous they were, and how much they valued accuracy; and to do this he checked all their works, not merely the sections at issue. That done, Crakanthorp went further and produced witnesses of his own. The whole proceeding has a slightly forensic flavor to it; but then most good arguments of the sort do. A later book on Constantine used similar methods to oppose the temporal power of the pope.[56] The influence of Valla, obviously, was more noticeable here, but in fact both of Crakanthorp's books are tributes to the efficacy of humanist source criticism.

Since the church of the Elizabethan settlement was not only Protestant but uniquely English, the effort to find a basis for it in English history specifically rather than in the general history of Christianity continued. The publication of Foxe's *Acts and Monuments* was of the greatest importance in establishing a general base for an ecclesiastical history of England, but Foxe's book only served to sharpen the point that the available factual basis for a really detailed history was lacking. The materials were shortly to be supplied by Queen Elizabeth's new Archbishop of Canterbury, Matthew Parker, who had already

[55] Richard Crakanthorp, *Justinian the Emperor Defended, against Cardinal Baronius* (London, 1616).
[56] Crakanthorp, *The Defence of Constantine: With a Treatise of the Popes Temporall Monarchie* (London, 1621).

set about collecting manuscripts even before Foxe published his first English edition. It is impossible to say why Parker turned to a historical justification of the church as a way to spend his leisure: we know too little of his intellectual interests prior to his elevation, though probably he had begun to work on such problems in Queen Mary's day, during his self-imposed exile in East Anglia. That he should be interested in English history was, however, in keeping with what is known of Parker. The man who was made primate because he had not fled the Marian persecutions, and who thus was not sullied with the Genevan taint, was precisely the one who would turn to the history of his own church and by so doing give it an aura of independence from the factional strife of the Continent. Certainly by 1560 Parker's view of the ecclesiastical history of England was clear. In a letter to the Catholic Archbishop Heath, defending his right to try the issue of deprivation in the English courts, Parker appealed not only to the general history of the church but to the specific refusal of the British bishops of Augustine's time to bow to Roman tribunals.[57] Simultaneously, he rejected Calvin's attempted interference in matters of English church government by pointing out that the institution of episcopacy in the island derived not from Gregory the Great and Augustine but from Joseph of Arimathea, and cited Gildas (in Polydore's edition) as his authority.[58] And while Parker had certainly already decided what line of attack to take against both Catholics and Calvinists, he did not neglect to seek further ammunition: Bale's letter to Parker, listing the books which might prove useful, was quite obviously a reply to a set of detailed questions. By the time that Matthias Flacius Illyricus and his collaborators appealed to Parker for assistance, the archbishop was already engaged on a similar project of his own, a fact that may help to explain his reluctance to send manuscripts out of the kingdom.[59]

Thus, long before Stapleton published his Bede, Parker had planned his project and had begun to collect the records neces-

[57] *Correspondence of Matthew Parker,* ed. John Bruce and T. T. Perowne, Parker Soc. (Cambridge, Eng., 1853), pp. 111–112.
[58] John Strype, *The Life and Acts of Matthew Parker* (Oxford, 1821), I, 139.
[59] Parker, *Correspondence,* pp. 139–141, 286–288.

sary to it.[60] The bishops were informed that the primate required old manuscripts, especially Saxon ones, and were told to search their cathedral libraries. Parker's staff was put to the same task, and one of them later claimed to have acquired 6,700 volumes for his master, though it is probable that most of these were printed.[61] Parker himself made a determined if unsuccessful attempt to find the remains of the library stolen from John Bale; and John Joscelyn, Parker's secretary, using Bale's letter, constructed a finding list of the most valuable manuscripts. If the precious books could not be bought, then they might be copied, and Joscelyn's transcripts of hundreds of pages of material survive as a monument to his industry. The archbishop did remarkably well. He acquired many of the books of the Canterbury schoolmaster John Twyne, most deriving from the suppressed house of St. Augustine's; some that had once belonged to Robert Talbot, the antiquary, also found their way to Lambeth. Once Parker's interest and intentions became known, gifts followed, such as a manuscript of Saxon homilies, given him by the Earl of Bedford "in camera stellata," and after a time Parker had to fear only the collecting instincts of men like Burghley. By gift or by loan, the necessary books were brought together.

Once the library was formed, there remained the problem of finding learned assistants. It was clear that Parker, unaided, could accomplish little—the tasks of ruling the church, fending off greedy courtiers, and forcing the queen into decisions were enough for one man. Soon the palace resembled an academy. Alexander Neville helped to digest the newly accumulated books and found time to write an account of Ket's rebellion as well—a task which gave him an opportunity to praise his patron to the skies, since the young Parker had played a heroic role

[60] On Parker as collector, see E. C. Pearce, "Matthew Parker," *The Library*, 4th Ser., VI (1925), 209–228; W. W. Greg, "Books and Bookmen in the Correspondence of Archbishop Parker," *The Library*, 4th Ser., XVI (1935), 243–279; C. E. Wright, "The Dispersal of the Monastic Libraries and the Beginnings of Anglo-Saxon Studies. Matthew Parker and His Circle: A Preliminary Study," *Transactions of the Cambridge Bibliographical Society*, I (1951), 208–237.

[61] Stephen Batman, *The Doome Warning All Men to the Judgemente* (London, 1581), p. 400.

in that uprising.[62] Stephen Batman collected books; since he was also a scholar of some note, if an extremely credulous one, he probably was engaged on the great task. Dr. George Acworth, a civil lawyer, may have helped in writing a first draft of *De antiquitate Britannicae ecclesiae*—there survives a contemporary rumor to that effect—or, more likely, he was engaged, as was another civilian, Dr. Thomas Yale, in sifting the antiquities of the see of Canterbury for legal precedents.[63] But by all odds the most important, indeed the indispensable, helper was John Joscelyn. It was he who became the real Saxon scholar of the group, who collected most of the notes, who annotated the manuscripts and, in the end, prepared the outline of *De antiquitate*.[64] For how much of Parker's actual publication Joscelyn was responsible is anybody's guess, but it seems safe to say that without Joscelyn, Parker's plans would have remained a dream.

The plans, though, were certainly Parker's. There was nothing random in them, nothing of the fortuitous. Parker intended to set the Church of England on a solid historical base, and everything was bent to that purpose. Of sources before the Anglo-Saxon period, there was only one of importance: Gildas. Polydore had edited that book in 1525, and had made good use of it in his history; the edition did not satisfy Parker, and Joscelyn re-edited Gildas in 1567. The pre-Saxon period might have been more important in Parker's scheme had there been more information; what there was he collected diligently, but nothing new was added, and there were no other texts to edit. Even so, there was plenty to do with the Saxons. The era before the Conquest was important in English church history for three reasons: the doctrine of transubstantiation had not yet been established, the clergy was not yet celibate, and the Scriptures and services were in the vernacular. The first product

---

[62] Alexander Neville, *De furoribus Norfolciensium Ketto Duce* (London, 1575), pp. [3]–4.

[63] Burnet, *History of the Reformation*, ed. Pocock, V, 538n; Strype, *Parker*, II, 48; III, 177–182.

[64] British Museum, Cotton MSS, Vitellius E.xiv, foll. 270–365, is an early draft of *De antiquitate*, ending with Lanfranc. This is in Joscelyn's hand, but a great many changes were made before publication.

of Parker's workshop made all three points clearly. *A Testimonie of Antiquitie* (1566) was a manifesto, intended to prove the usefulness of studying ancient documents and incidentally introducing its audience to the Anglo-Saxon tongue. Of all of Parker's books, this edition of Aelfric was the only one clearly intended for a "popular" audience: not only was the strange tongue of the Saxons translated but so was the Latin. As a result, Parker here explained what he was doing. Readers were told that the archbishop supplied the impetus "by whose diligent search for such writings of historye, and other monumentes of antiquitie, as might reveale unto us what hath ben the state of our church in England from tyme to tyme." [65] They were also told how to interpret the documents that such diligent search turned up. Clearly, no one wished to return the church to the state of decline it had already reached in Aelfric's day. The point was that the Catholics thought much of the later Anglo-Saxon church, or so the great number of saints would make one believe, and yet the decline of the sixteenth-century papists even from that low standard was clear enough. If the Protestants could show that Aelfric agreed with them on celibacy, transubstantiation, and the vernacular Scriptures, that was pure gain; there was no need to accept his errors as well, and these were carefully indicated. Aelfric's writings were important because by them was "revealed & made knowen, what hath beene the common taught doctrine of the church of England on this behalfe many hundreth yeares agoe, contrarye unto the unadvised writyng of some nowe a dayes." [66]

Aelfric was the first product of the new study of Anglo-Saxon, and the trumpet call for what followed. Five years later, as if to drive the nail further, there appeared an edition of the Gospels, ostensibly edited by John Foxe. Foxe's knowledge of Old English is open to some question, but the point of printing the Gospels was clear enough, and there was an advantage in getting a historian of Foxe's stature to undertake the work. The preface made clear that those who "have judged our native tounge

[65] Aelfric, *A Testimonie of Antiquitie* (London, [1566?]), fol. 3ʳ.
[66] Ibid., fol. K.iiiᵛ.

unmeete to expresse Gods high secret mysteries, being so barbarous & imperfecte a language as they say it is" were wrong,
and that the Word of God not only should be published but
traditionally had been.[67] If Foxe added nothing new to the
study of Anglo-Saxon, he did learn something, for the next
edition of *Acts and Monuments* itself had quotations from
Aelfric, and Foxe thus showed what use could be made of the
new evidence. If the edition of the Gospels merely restated an
old point, Asser's *Alfredi regis res gestae* (1574) moved a step
beyond. Printing Asser's Latin in Saxon letters was hardly
scholarly, in the modern sense, but it had a certain aptness,
especially since the book was intended, at least in part, as a
primer. There is no other explanation for the long defense of
Old English which prefaced it, especially as it was made clear
the language was useful not only to theologians but also to
practical men of affairs. Foxe had pointed out that it would
enable lawyers to read old deeds and charters as well as the
ancient laws, and his covert reference to William Lambarde's
Archaionomia, which had appeared three years before Foxe's
Gospels, in the Asser became an open recommendation. The
editor of the Asser also mentioned that a knowledge of Anglo-
Saxon would help to solve the riddle of English place names,
and in that we can see the hand of Joscelyn, who, like Lambarde's friend and teacher Laurence Nowell, had been collecting
such data for years. The preface indicated that the study of the
language had passed beyond the bounds originally intended for
it and moved from the religious to the secular; and the shift
from a sacred subject to a worldly one emphasized the same
point. Alfred, however pious, was not a churchman; instead,
he was a model king. One may see here the first shift from
King Arthur to a newer, better, more Christian—and more
believable—hero. For Alfred was a scholar; he was godly,
having caused the Scriptures to be translated; and he pursued
these arts in times of dire war rather than wait for a peace

[67] *The Gospels of the Fower Evangelistes,* ed. John Foxe (London, 1571), fol.
A.ii^v. On the whole matter of Anglo-Saxon, see Eleanor N. Adams, *Old English
Scholarship in England from 1566–1800* (New Haven, 1917).

that never came. With the publication of the *Alfredi regis res
gestae* the gap had been bridged between ecclesiastical history
and the more usual idea of history as a mirror for princes.

The appeal to history in aid of religion had always been
two-pronged, for besides establishing what had been done in
the past (as a reason for continuing to do it now) it had
also been possible to use the records of history to prove that
the Catholic Church had fallen off from what little purity it
had ever possessed. That point was made in *A Testimonie of
Antiquitie,* as a kind of by-product of the principal contentions
of the book, but it was made in much more detail in a series
of other publications. Over the course of seven years beginning
with 1567, Parker printed the chronicles of "Matthew of
Westminster," of Matthew Paris, and of Thomas Walsingham.
The idea behind this was obviously that of Tyndale: using
the Catholic writers to condemn themselves. To a silly miracle
was appended an astringent marginal comment; or a preface
might note that a chronicler illustrated papal corruption and
monkish vanities.[68] Even so, by 1574 Parker had become interested in the chroniclers for their own sakes, and at least one of
the reasons for printing Thomas Walsingham was that he continued Matthew Paris. Toward the end of his career, Parker
was anxious to provide the sources of English history, and
the theological motive, while still crucial, was joined with
patriotism.

Most of Parker's time was spent on editing, since his ambition
was to prove a point rather than state it; and in any event,
the case had been stated very well by John Foxe. One work
of church history did, however, emerge from the archbishop's
academy. What Parker had in mind in writing *De antiquitate
Britannicae ecclesiae* was simple:

> . . . because neither my health nor my quiet would suffer me to
> be a common preacher, yet I thought it not unfit for me to be
> otherwise occupied in some points of religion; for my meaning
> was, by this my poor collection thus caused to be printed . . . to
> note at what time Augustine my first predecessor came into this

[68] "Matthew of Westminster," . . . *Flores historiarum* (London, 1567), p.
184; Thomas Walsingham, *Historia brevis* (London, 1574), fol. ¶.ii^v.

land, what religion he brought in with him, and how it continued, how it was fortified and increased, which by most of my predecessors may appear, as I could gather of such rare and written authors that came to my hands, until the days of King Henry the VIIIth, when the religion began to grow better, and more agreeable to the Gospel.[69]

Thus the book began with a preface which showed how Christianity first came into the island, and which demonstrated that it did not come with Augustine: here were found the usual references to Joseph of Arimathea and to King Lucius. Once Parker arrived at the archbishops, the contradictions inherent in the book became obvious. The archbishops, as servants of the see of Rome, could not be given too much credit for the progress of Christianity—if after the time of William the Conqueror it could be called progress at all. But the privileges of Canterbury, which Parker was most concerned to protect against those who wished to abolish episcopacy altogether, were the result of the labors of generations of primates, and for this they had to be praised. The resultant confusion gave rise to a tendentious translation of the life of the seventieth archbishop— Parker himself—printed with the subtitle "This numbre off seventy is so compleat a number as it is great pitie ther shold be one more: but that as Augustin was the first/so Mathew might be the last." [70] The author of the bilious commentary on that life suggested that Parker's researches were intended more to bolster up his own position than to shore up the church, a remark that was essentially unfair but not altogether unjustified as applied to *De antiquitate*. With the archbishop's having to fight to make his authority respected by recalcitrant Calvinists while at the same time trying to protect his see against the depredations of hungry courtiers, one cannot blame him for trying to defend his office in the way he knew best, but the book nevertheless added little to his reputation as a historian.

The results of Parker's work were salutary. His enthusiasm for evidence led him to print an invaluable series of historical

[69] Parker, *Correspondence*, p. 425.
[70] [John Joscelyn], *The Life of the 70. Archbishopp of Canterbury* ([Zurich?], 1574).

documents, and even where the editing is less than perfect it was
an advantage to have the books ready to hand. Moreover,
the combined efforts of Parker's group, together with those
of Burghley's protégés Nowell and Lambarde, revived the Anglo-
Saxon language and thus gave the initial impetus to a study
which was to be more fruitful than that of trying to make
something of Geoffrey's British History. Eventually the Saxons
were to replace the Britons as the noblest ancestors of the
population of England, just as King Alfred replaced King
Arthur as a model king. In the course of this activity Parker
discovered a love for a kind of history not entirely subservient
to religious purposes and proved that a theological impulse,
when allowed to run freely, might lead to results important
outside the arena of religious disputation. But Parker had few
immediate followers. His theory of the purity of the early
English church became part of the general stock of all who
came after him, but few men did anything to alter or add
to the details. Not until William L'Isle in the early seventeenth
century was another book published in Old English, and even
L'Isle's writing was plainly derivative.[71] The true heir of Parker
was Archbishop James Ussher, who brought together again the
strands of general and English church history, and who rewrote
both in the light of the more recent researches of the antiquaries.
But with Ussher we are in another century, where both problems
and methods have altered, and the Archbishop of Armagh is
too imposing a figure to be compressed into a brief paragraph.

The combination of history and theology led, first of all,
to an increased importance for history. The Reformed churches
turned to the past for one form of evidence of their validity,
and though Scripture obviously served that purpose better, yet
history took on a value beyond that of supplying moral examples. Moreover, men like Foxe and Bale, who saw the hand
of God in everything, returned to the theological presuppositions
of the early Middle Ages, and their idea of history resembled
that of Bishop Otto of Freising or that of St. Augustine

---

[71] *A Saxon Treatise concerning the Old and New Testament* (London, 1623):
this prints certain treatises of Aelfric.

more than it did that of Matthew Paris or Thomas Walsingham. At the same time these theological views, while based on a theory of universal church history, led also to an emphasis on the history of national churches. Local autonomy was one of the legacies left by the primitive church, and it became an article of the faith in England. But this notion, taken up by Foxe, eventually came to mean that the history of England was something special. England kept her purity longer; through Wyclif, she was the first to reestablish it. No wonder, then, that Foxe himself began to explore the English secular past, for all the history of God's elect might be made to yield fruit. The end result was that the theologians, like the humanists, found history essential for their purposes and thus dignified it. But the theologians did not leave the subject as they found it. Forced by the pressure of controversy, they adopted the latest methods of source criticism and made them serve theology. Foxe and Jewel did more to spread the knowledge of that product of humanism than the schoolmasters. Men like John Stow, whose schooling was sketchy, learned their historical method from the pages of the careful Foxe. But controversy produced more than analysis. Eventually it became evident that the texts themselves had to be made available, and Stapleton and Parker, representing competing faiths, yet did the same kind of work for reasons that were nearly identical. Inevitably the editing of texts, too, came to be connected to the growth of national history, and in the next generation the task was taken over by the antiquaries. By the time the theological impulse was spent—and for our purposes this comes with the death of Parker in 1575—the church historians had done much to educate men in the newest historical techniques; but they had done more by finding a justification for those techniques and by supplying materials for those whose basic purposes were altogether different.

IV

𝔄ntiquarianism

Of the three forms of humanism that originated in Italy, the antiquarian spread most slowly. Flavio Biondo made his antiquarian tours in the mid-fifteenth century; not until the beginning of the sixteenth century were his methods adopted north of the Alps. Then, under the influence of Guillaume Budé in France and Conrad Celtis and Beatus Rhenanus in Germany, the methods spread throughout northern Europe. Gradually the corrosive of the concept of anachronism was applied to the legends of national origins inherited from the early Middle Ages; simultaneously, as men asked new questions, such as "What was the Roman province of Germania really like?" the old stories were replaced by more accurate new ones. It was not enough merely to destroy: the idea of a Trojan origin had served the purposes of patriotism as well as filling in a conspicuous gap in the ancient history of the peoples of Europe. In Germany, for example, the concept of *translatio imperii* was more than a statement of the fact that the Germans had taken over control of the Roman Empire. A justification for the transfer of authority from Rome northward was needed, since it would not do to hand over the empire to barbarians. The Trojan descent established the Germans as equal to the Romans, for the two peoples were descended from a common ancestor. *Die Deutschen sind also edel wie die Römer*: as long as that was true, there was no reason why the Germans should not follow the Romans in their possession of the imperial scepter.[1] But once the humanists turned their attention to the old story, its life ended. Men who were accustomed to seeking evidence found none. Yet Celtis and his associates were German patriots. Not only were some of them

[1] P. Joachimsohn, *Die humanistische Geschichtsschreibung in Deutschland*, I (Bonn, 1895), 15–16.

in the employ of the emperor, whose title might have been weakened by the destruction of the Trojan connection, but these men were concerned to demonstrate that the Germans could match the Italians in scholarship.[2] Moreover, like all humanists, their attention was riveted on ancient Rome, the Rome of Cicero and Livy and Caesar. The result was inevitable. Men looked to the ancient province of Germania. That meant admitting that the Germans had once been defeated by the Romans, but the bitterness of the admission was tempered by the realization that the conquerors had been the masters of the greatest of civilizations. The Germans were the heirs of these Romans, for when they in their turn captured the control of the empire, this was not the defeat of civilization by the barbarians but the destruction of decadence by Romanized Germans. The empire had been transferred from Rome across the mountains, but the civilization of Rome had preceded it. The emperor's title was sure, the *amour-propre* of the Germans satisfied.

The situation in England, while certainly not identical to that of Germany, was in many respects parallel. Involved in the Reformation arguments was the idea that England was an empire, and this implied a further, if metaphoric, *translatio imperii*. As in Germany, the "proofs" could be found in two separate lines of argument: a descent from the Trojans, which made the English at least the equal of everyone else so descended, or a connection to Rome, with the implication that on the fall of the empire, Roman imperial authority was dispersed more or less equally among her conquerors. The first of these arguments goes back, in some form, to Geoffrey of Monmouth himself and, even at the Reformation, was adopted because of convenience; the second was not fully developed until the reign of Queen Elizabeth. Since the Reformation itself depended, to a degree, upon humanist historical arguments, the same impulse to scrutinize origins which led to the developments in English theology led also to considerable doubts about Brutus and his Trojans. Thus the humanists, who were moved quite as much by motives of patriotism as their predecessors, had

---

[2] Lewis Spitz, *Conrad Celtis* (Cambridge, Mass., 1957), pp. 40–41, 100–103; Gerald Strauss, *Sixteenth-Century Germany, Its Topography and Topographers* (Madison, 1959), pp. 22 ff.

to replace the Trojans with the Romans, who were more respectable historically.

In the sense that the development of Reformation theology and the development of historical thought both were dependent on a humanist background, the two moved in parallel paths. In another sense, however, the advent of Protestantism dealt a blow just this side of mortal to the possibility of any revision of the traditional picture of the past. When Henry VIII suppressed the monasteries, when Edward VI's commissioners attacked the scholastic learning of the universities, one result was the dispersal, and sometimes the destruction, of the inherited wealth of learning of the kingdom.[3] The precise extent of the carnage has not yet been assessed, and since medieval library lists were as liable to disappearance as any other volumes, it is unlikely that the full measure of the disaster will ever be taken. In some degree the damage was selective: service books and the writings of the schoolmen were more likely to be torn up than were more innocent-seeming chronicles. But actual destruction was never the only danger. Bale tells us that shiploads of manuscripts went to the Continent; we know that the break-up of monastic libraries put hundreds of volumes into the hands of men with no idea of their value; and at the universities the depredations of the king's commissioners not only affected those books whose leaves were seen fluttering in the quadrangles but also sometimes caused the fellows, out of a variety of motives, to embezzle some of the books from their college libraries.[4] The effects, thus, were two: in some cases manuscripts vanished; but even where this was not the case, their accessibility decreased to such an extent that for a time men were content merely to compile lists locating them.

That anything was saved from the wreckage was due principally to the historical and patriotic impulses of a few men. John Leland did his best to describe the manuscripts he saw and then persuaded

[3] C. E. Wright, "The Dispersal of the Monastic Libraries and the Beginnings of Anglo-Saxon Studies," *Transactions of the Cambridge Bibliographical Society*, I (1951), 208–237; Francis Wormald and C. E. Wright, *The English Library before 1700* (London, 1958), Ch. viii. For more detail, the catalogs of various manuscript collections are useful.

[4] Wright, "The Dispersal," p. 211, quoting Bale; Neil R. Ker, "Oxford College Libraries in the Sixteenth Century," *Bodleian Library Record*, VI (1959), 459–515.

King Henry to find a home for some of them in the royal library; where that was impossible, Leland acquired the manuscripts for himself. Even so, his perambulations uncovered considerable numbers which have since disappeared. John Bale, for all his detestation of the monks, nonetheless labored to rescue their works, and it was he who first suggested that the only solution to the problem was to establish a national library. Sir John Price, himself one of the monastic visitors who were the actual engineers of the suppression, but also a historian of Wales, searched the West Country to uncover what he could. Nor were these collectors the only ones. Robert Talbot, who later was to solve a part of the mystery of the Antonine Itineraries, scoured East Anglia and got a substantial part of the manuscripts of Norwich Priory onto his shelves: the historians included William of Malmesbury and Matthew Paris. Robert Recorde collected scientific works but did not disdain Gildas, Giraldus Cambrensis, and (probably) Roger Hoveden. Two printers, Reyner Wolfe and Richard Grafton, were especially active: Grafton, who rescued the library of the Grey Friars of London, built up a very large collection of works of all kinds, including in it Bede, Geoffrey of Monmouth, and Trevisa's translation of Higden's *Polychronicon*. John Twyne, the schoolmaster of Canterbury, acquired a substantial bloc of the treasures of the monasteries of Christ Church and St. Augustine's. But as the first generation of collectors died, their accumulations once more were dispersed, and the work had to be redone.[5]

It was not until Archbishop Parker began to gather the materials for his defense of English Protestantism that one of the collections became permanent. The same could not be said even of the library of his rival Lord Burghley, whose heirs, years later, sold the books at auction. Thomas Allen, who formed his substantial collection at Oxford and acquired a good part of it from the booksellers who had profited from the Edwardian visitations, gave

[5] John Bale, *The Laboryouse Journey & Serche of Johan Leylande* (London, 1549), foll. [C.vi^r] ff.; Neil R. Ker, "Sir John Prise," *The Library*, 5th Ser., X (1955), 1–24; Ker, "Medieval Manuscripts from Norwich Cathedral Priory," *Transactions of the Cambridge Bibliographical Society*, I (1949), 1–28; John Bale, *Index Britanniae scriptorum*, ed. Reginald Lane Poole and Mary Bateson (Oxford, 1902), passim; M. R. James, *The Ancient Libraries of Canterbury and Dover* (Cambridge, Eng., 1903), p. lxxxii.

some of his books to the Bodleian in his own lifetime; but the rest
had to pass through other hands before they rejoined their fellows.
The dispersal of John Dee's books, like that of Bale's, was brought
about by the hands of his enemies. And it was Dee who, in his
generation, once more suggested that a national library was necessary: [6] there is a tragic coincidence in the fact that that idea
originated two separate times in the minds of men who, through no
fault of their own, were later to suffer the loss of their own books.

As the sixteenth century ended, the problem of creating permanent collections gradually was resolved. Some members of the
Society of Antiquaries, with Sir Robert Bruce Cotton as their
leader, again petitioned for a national library; and again nothing
came of the idea, perhaps, in this case, because the library was to
be joined with an Academy, on the Continental model.[7] This
looked altogether too much like competition with the universities;
and by 1600 the university libraries themselves were being revived. Bodley's donation came only a few years later; at Cambridge the university and the colleges vied for books. The Royal
collection, too, grew once more, especially when the Lumley-
Arundel collection, originally purchased for Prince Henry, was
merged into it. And Cotton's own library became so large that
although it remained in the hands of the family until the eighteenth century, nonetheless it was rapidly becoming regarded as a
national treasure. By the end of the first quarter of the seventeenth
century the location of manuscripts had taken on some stability;
but meanwhile the antiquaries of previous years had endured considerable difficulty in finding what they wanted, and it was only
because their number was so small, and because most of them
knew each other, that they were able to accomplish anything. The
extraordinarily fluid conditions that prevailed until Elizabeth's
reign was well advanced help to explain the relatively slow progress of antiquarianism during the early part of the century; and the
more rapid advances that came about after the 1580's may be
explained, at least in part, by the rapidly increasing ease of access
to the necessary materials.

[6] *The Autobiographical Tracts of Dr. John Dee,* ed. James Crossley, Chetham
Society Miscellanies, I (Manchester, 1851), 46–49.
[7] Ewald Flügel, "Die älteste englische Akademie," *Anglia,* XXXII (1909),
261–268.

In this sense the march of events in England affected the tempo with which the latest ideas of Continental humanism could be absorbed. John Leland had the advantage of seeing the monastic libraries *in situ,* and even after the overthrow of the monasteries he must have known what happened to most of the important books. Thus Leland had the opportunity to perform whatever task he set for himself—provided he could first decide what that task might be. But humanism was too new; there were too many things that needed doing. Leland tried to do all of them; moreover, he tried to do them all at once. Even the first decision, that between the forms of humanism, escaped him: he never quite made up his mind whether to be a poet or an antiquary. That his poetry has been judged artistically negligible is not really relevant: throughout his career Leland thought of himself as a poet. The model of Petrarch and his successors was ever before him; but so was the model of his remarkable contemporary, Beatus Rhenanus, who did so much to discover the origins of the German tribes:

> Quantum Rhenano debet Germania docto,
> Tantum debebit terra Britanna mihi.[8]

So was a prose career celebrated in verse.

Moreover, Leland had the intention of doing for England what generations of antiquaries had done for Italy. His plan would have taxed the energies of a whole team of scholars. A general topography of Britain was an obvious first essential; this would be followed by an inventory of the British names in the classical authors, and each of the names would have to be identified. Once that had been accomplished, a chorography of Britain would be possible— the history and geography of the country could be described, county by county; the islands needed a volume of their own; and the royal and noble families of England had to be traced and their history fitted into the more general picture.[9] That the plan was in its essentials the correct one can be deduced from the fact that almost all the antiquarian research of the sixteenth century followed it; that it was visionary is obvious when we consider the

---

[8] John Leland, *Principum, Ac illustrium aliquot & eruditorum in Anglia virorum, Encomia,* ed. Thomas Newton (London, 1589), p. 52.

[9] John Bale, *The Laboryouse Journey,* passim; T. C. Skeat, "Two 'Lost' Works by John Leland," *English Historical Review,* LXV (1950), 505–508. On Leland generally, T. D. Kendrick, *British Antiquity* (London, 1950), pp. 45–64.

number of men necessary to elaborate it. As late as 1586, Camden's *Britannia* still fits the plan exactly.

Leland himself never produced any of the works he promised. It rapidly became clear that a number of preliminary studies had first of all to be prepared, and before even these could be organized and published, their author sank into insanity. The description of England, based on Leland's personal observations, remained in manuscript until the eighteenth century; but the manuscript stayed in friendly hands and virtually everyone who had cause to examine it seems to have been able to do so. Whether the miscellaneous notes eventually printed as *Collectanea* were equally accessible is doubtful, but their importance, vis-à-vis Leland's outline of what was needed, was comparatively small. Leland's own contribution to the program he had elaborated remained limited to the manuscript *Itineraries,* but those notes were immensely influential, and more than one subsequent scholar used them even in preference to his own observations. As for the influence of Leland's plan, that was immeasurable: it was the *fons et origo* for most of what follows.

Unfortunately, much of what Leland actually published concerned the veracity of Geoffrey of Monmouth. Polydore Vergil had cast doubts on Brutus and on Arthur; because of patriotism, because of the potentially useful dynastic implications of both stories, Leland felt compelled to defend them. In order to do so, however, he made use of new weapons. Leland at once admitted that there were absurdities in the Arthur story; he had no intention of allowing his whole enterprise to founder by defending the indefensible. Still, a few faults were no good reason for rejecting the whole, especially since the existence of Arthur had been admitted on all sides for generations.[10] Overthrowing Arthur meant overthrowing the entire Arthurian tradition, and this Leland was reluctant to do. The negative evidence of Gildas was an insufficient reason for denying Arthur: the Gildas that Polydore had published was only a fragment of the man's whole work, and in any case the polemical nature of Gildas' work supplied ample reason why Ar-

---

[10] John Leland, *A Learned and True Assertion of . . . Arthure* (*Assertio . . . Arturii*), trans. Richard Robinson, in *The Famous History of Chinon of England,* ed. W. E. Mead, E.E.T.S., O.S., No. 165 (London, 1925), pp. 27–28.

thur should not appear in it.[11] That no Roman writers mentioned Arthur was hardly cause for surprise: the state of Roman prose in Arthur's day was not very flourishing, and the Romans had sufficient troubles dealing with their invaders without worrying excessively about one corner of their vast and crumbling empire. It was much more logical to expect a mention of Arthur in the surviving British material, and that was embodied in Geoffrey.[12] In short, Leland examined the nature of the works and the motives of the authors of Polydore's negative authorities and came to the conclusion that their authority was insufficient.

The situation is strange and more than a little misleading. Polydore is acclaimed because in the end he proved to be right and Leland wrong. Yet an examination of their respective methods demonstrates that Leland's was that of the humanist critics of sources, of Valla and his followers, and was essentially the better of the two. Polydore demolished Arthur on logical grounds, but the argument was a negative one. Leland defended Arthur by showing that a negative argument was fruitless and made his point by a careful examination of the surviving sources. Leland's conclusion proved incorrect because he accepted as genuine materials now suspect: place names, which he was unable to date very accurately, the story of the finding of Arthur's burial place in the days of Henry II, the remains preserved at Glastonbury. Quite rightly, Leland sought the oldest evidence he could find; his error lay in refusing to believe that the men of the twelfth century might have forged that evidence. If Leland's defense had been entirely absurd, Arthur might well have been buried once and for all; since it was not, the story remained to haunt historians for the rest of the century and beyond.[13]

Of Brutus little has been said. There is no question that Leland believed the story: having decided that Geoffrey was basically trustworthy, there was no reason why he should not do so. Moreover, if Geoffrey were notably false in one direction, then his word would become dubious in others, and most believers in Arthur found themselves defending Brutus as well. There was a further

[11] Ibid., p. 79.
[12] Ibid., pp. 83–84.
[13] Kendrick, *British Antiquity*, pp. 88–98.

reason why Brutus could not be readily dismissed: his absence, and that of his progeny, from the story of Britain would leave an enormous void, and most men were as yet unprepared to accept the idea that a substantial part of their history was unknown and probably unknowable. Man had, after all, been on earth for a relatively brief period, and his history for much of that could be found in Holy Writ. Later the Greeks and the Romans recorded the story. It was excessively galling that the period between the Flood and the invasion of the island by Caesar should stand unpeopled. Thus for a time, instead of ridding the island of Brutus and his descendants, antiquaries elaborated the story: John Bale, otherwise a sensible enough historian, found a biblical descent for Brutus himself.[14] In addition, the stories found in the British History were good ones, and Shakespeare was by no means the only person who thought so. Henry Lyte was altogether enthralled by the early history of the Britons, and even the somewhat more down-to-earth Richard Harvey defended the British History principally for its moral value.[15] As for the Welsh, who claimed an uninterrupted descent from the earliest inhabitants of the island, their enthusiasm surpassed all bounds. From Arthur Kelton, who sang the praises of the Welsh in sorry poetry, from Sir John Price, who carried the methods of Leland yet further, through Humphrey Lhuyd, and on past the end of the century, patriotic Welshmen treasured the old stories.[16] In the face of all this, a historian required extraordinary courage if he were to nerve himself to challenge Geoffrey. Even the skeptical found themselves reprinting the legend, and frequently the only way in which their doubts can be discovered is by examining how much the tale had been curtailed and by collecting the occasional asides.

It is not even true that everyone who defended Geoffrey was a poor scholar. Humphrey Lhuyd, the Welsh physician, seems never to have had any doubts concerning the British History, yet the

[14] Ibid., pp. 69–72.
[15] Henry Lyte, *The Light of Britayne* (London, 1588; repr. London, 1814); R[ichard]. H[arvey]., *Philadelphus, or A Defence of Brutes* (London, 1593).
[16] Arthur Kelton, *A Chronycle with a Genealogie Declaryng That the Brittons and Welshemen Are Lineallye Dyscended from Brute* (London, 1547); Arthur Kelton, *A Commendacion of Welchemen* (London, 1546), foll. d.ii^v, [d.vii^r]; Sir John Price, *Historiae Brytannicae defensio* (London, 1573); Humphrey Lhuyd, *The Breviary of Britayne,* trans. Thomas Twyne (London, 1573).

sober Flemish geographer Ortelius chose him as a likely person to write the long-needed new history of the early days of the island. Lhuyd's *Breviary of Britayne,* which he finished just before his death, was indeed written for the Belgian, and it was Lhuyd who supplied the information for Ortelius' map of Wales.[17] For all his defamation of Polydore, Lhuyd was far from being an obscurantist: he was perfectly aware of, and used, the latest and best of Continental scholarship. Moreover, his work on British (i.e., Welsh) place names formed the basis for most of the later work on the subject, and it was Lhuyd who first showed that a knowledge of Welsh was essential for anyone who wanted to use the place-name evidence, not only for Wales but for England itself. Unfortunately, both the *Breviary* and its author are difficult to judge. The work is fragmentary, and Lhuyd's sudden and early death makes it impossible to discover what he intended eventually to do. There is no question, however, about his enthusiasm for Brutus, and it is likely that he considered some sort of defense of Geoffrey necessary as a prerequisite for his use of Welsh place names. Merely to state that the Britons were at some point in possession of the whole island, without at the same time finding a history for them, was impossible.

Just because the British History supplied explanations precisely where it was felt that they were most needed, it lived on into the seventeenth century; and other attempts to destroy its authority will from time to time have to be examined. Meanwhile, work was going forward in areas where Geoffrey's influence was less pervasive. The religious background of Archbishop Parker's writings has been explored already, but two aspects of his accomplishment bear repetition here. Not only did the archbishop collect materials relating to the history of the English church—and this meant, essentially, the history of England—and make them permanently available by enshrining them in the library of Corpus Christi College, Cambridge; he also published a surprising number of them. A Catholic publication campaign of about the same time at

---

[17] *Ecclesiae Londino-Batavae Archivum,* Vol. I: *Abrahami Ortelii . . . epistulae,* ed. J. H. Hessels (Cambridge, Eng., 1887), pp. 63–64, 77–78, 100–103; Theodore Max Chotzen, "Some Sidelights on Cambro-Dutch Relations," *Transactions of the Society of Cymmrodorion: Session 1937* (London, 1938), pp. 102–144.

least added a translation of Bede to the list. During the 1580's attention was shifted to "British" materials, principally the history of Caradoc and the works of Giraldus Cambrensis. In the 1590's there was a return to the publication of the ordinary chroniclers of the Middle Ages, which included Sir Henry Savile's collection of Malmesbury, Hoveden, Henry of Huntingdon, etc., and which included as well Lord William Howard's edition of Florence of Worcester. William Camden's reprinting of some of Parker's editions, with the addition of Thomas de la More and William of Jumièges, falls really into the same grouping, and after that the business of editing never stopped. The culmination of the Elizabethan tradition was the work of John Selden: editions of Sir John Fortescue, of Eadmer, and finally, with Roger Twysden, the publication of *Historiae Anglicanae scriptores X* (1652).[18] Meanwhile, interest had been generated among the printers abroad. Sylvius had issued William of Newburgh as early as 1567, with a dedication to Queen Elizabeth, and a decade later was still trying to claim some reward from Lord Burghley for it.[19] Commeline, twenty years after Sylvius, put out a collection of chronicles, most of which were reprints of work done earlier, but it was nonetheless convenient to have Geoffrey, Ponticus Virunnis (a summarizer of Geoffrey), Gildas, Bede, William of Newburgh, Froissart, and even a part of Malmesbury together in one volume.[20] Indeed, Savile's collection was published in Frankfort five years after its initial London appearance, and Camden's was never published in England at all but had, instead, two Frankfort editions in consecutive years.[21] Even before the queen's reign ended, a fairly substantial body of medieval source material was readily available, and it is not too much to say that most of it derived, in one way or another, from Parker.

[18] Marc Friedlaender, "Growth in the Resources for Studies in Earlier English History, 1534–1625," unpubl. diss. (University of Chicago, 1938), Ch. iv.

[19] *Rerum Anglicarum libri quinque,* . . . *Auctore Gulielmo Neubrigensi* (Antwerp: Ex officina Gulielmi Silvii, 1567); *Relations politiques des Pays-Bas et de l'Angleterre,* ed. J. M. B. C. Baron Kervyn de Lettenhove (Brussels, 1882–1900), IX, 565 (#3592).

[20] *Rerum Britannicarum,* . . . *scriptores vetustiores ac praecipui* (Heidelberg, 1587).

[21] *Rerum Anglicarum scriptores post Bedam,* ed. Sir Henry Savile (London, 1596; Frankfort, 1601); *Anglica, Normannica, Hibernica, Cambrica, a veteribus scripta,* ed. William Camden (Frankfort, 1602; 1603).

Parker's own example is sufficient to indicate that the motives for such publication were not always purely scholarly. An examination of the editions of Gildas—and there were more of these than of any other old chronicler except possibly Geoffrey of Monmouth himself—serves to make the point more clearly still. Polydore Vergil was the first to realize that Gildas might prove a crucial document, and his edition of 1525 was intended to show that the earliest available records did not support Geoffrey's version of history. But even before the Reformation, the Italian Polydore intended his work to illustrate the antiquity of Christianity in the island: that was a matter of national pride, and his book was written for the English.[22] The reprint of Gildas in 1541, at Basel, does not here concern us: it was one work in a very miscellaneous collection.[23] In 1567, however, Gildas was re-edited, this time by John Joscelyn, who as Parker's secretary took a prominent part in the work of establishing the antiquity of the English church. Polydore's Romanism was sufficient to make his edition suspect, and Joscelyn was able to find a myriad of errors (most of them minor) which required that the job be done over. A year later, the new edition was reissued.[24] Some time around 1586, Thomas Habington, a young Catholic then imprisoned in the Tower, decided to undertake a translation with the primary purpose of emphasizing religious decline; but by 1638, when he published the translation, other motives had been superimposed. His introduction made a point of defending the Scots and a union of the two realms: in the light of the impending civil war, the differences between recusants and Protestants had evidently retreated into the background, and the lapse of over half a century between writing and printing probably played its part as well.[25] The editions of Gildas make a clear case for external motives influencing scholarship; the same

---

[22] Gildas, *De calamitate excidio, & conquestu Britanniae,* ed. Polydore Vergil (London, 1525).

[23] *Opus historiarum* (Basel, 1541). Most of the works in this collection are much more recent.

[24] *Gildae, cui cognomentum est sapientis, de excidio & conquestu Britanniae,* ed. John Joscelyn (London, 1568). See the Dedication to Parker and, for example, fol. 25^r.

[25] *The Epistle of Gildas,* trans. Thomas Habington (London, 1638), [Introduction:] "To the inhabitants of the Island of great Britaine, *Unitie and Felicity.*"

could be said of the scholar-diplomat Robert Beale's collection of
Spanish chronicles (1579), intended to attack the Spanish pretensions to Portugal.[26] Savile's work, as well as Camden's, fits less well
into such categories: by their time, the progress of English antiquarianism had developed sufficient impetus so that editing might
be intended merely to supply more materials for other men's work
(or, in Camden's case, for his own). Even so, Savile took the
opportunity to attack Polydore once more, and Camden entered
into the quarrel between Oxford and Cambridge by inserting a
passage into his Asser which proved Oxford's priority.

Parker, again for religious reasons, also promoted the revival of
Anglo-Saxon studies, and a number of his publications were intended to make the key documents available not only as evidence
but also as aids in teaching the newly acquired language. But
Parker was not the only patron of the new studies. Lord Burghley
had encouraged his protégé Laurence Nowell to pursue similar
studies, but Nowell, for all that he knew Parker and Joscelyn, was
working along the lines laid down by Leland rather than those of
the archbishop. The restoration of Old English was intended to aid
in producing a historical topography of the country: Nowell's
activities in mapping England presumably supplied the necessary
geographical information.[27] Burghley himself was Parker's great
rival in the collection of manuscripts, and the Lord Treasurer
never threw off the inclinations of his scholarly youth. He continued to read histories and as the queen's principal adviser found
good maps of the counties essential. Thus the two chief figures in
the government of Elizabeth's England were both encouraging the
revival of Anglo-Saxon, each for reasons of his own, and the men
doing the work, Joscelyn and Nowell, knew each other and coop-
erated; nor were their ends mutually exclusive.

The purposes of Parker and his associates have already been
established; it remains to be determined what moved Nowell and
his pupil William Lambarde. Historical topography was part of it,

---

[26] *Rerum Hispanicarum scriptores aliquot* (Frankfort, 1579), the publisher's
preface.
[27] Robin Flower, "Laurence Nowell and the Discovery of England in Tudor
Times," *Proceedings of the British Academy*, XXI (1935), 47–73. Friedlaender
("Growth in Resources," Ch. vi) insists that Anglo-Saxon was known by a good
many people other than those here mentioned.

but almost certainly it was not all. The difficulty comes in trying to discover precisely what Nowell was trying to do, for he published nothing and did not even complete his own manuscript collections, leaving them to Lambarde to make use of as he saw fit. Lambarde did, however, elaborate on Nowell's work, and it may be argued that all of Lambarde's early writings were, essentially, extensions of ideas whose originator was Nowell. What Lambarde added was his own legal training; and this served to give another justification to the study of Anglo-Saxon.

Just as Parker had been able to find a continuous English church going back to the time of the Anglo-Saxons, so Lambarde found a legal system which also had unbroken history dating from the same era. Both men would have liked to go further: Parker spoke of British Christianity, of Lucius, or even of St. Joseph of Arimathea; Lambarde defended Geoffrey of Monmouth and tried to fit Arthur into his history of the English law. But this enthusiasm for antiquity could not be made to produce anything useful. The sixteenth century could find no detailed propaganda advantage in Lucius or St. Joseph beside the fact that their existence demonstrated that there had been a church in England before St. Augustine; but a great deal was known about the Saxon church, and vast and specific differences could be pointed out which marked it off from the sixteenth-century church of Rome. A direct comparison was possible, and it redounded to the credit of Anglicanism. Similarly, although lawyers may like the most recent precedent best, they have no aversion to proving that such a precedent follows from a long line of similar decisions going back to the beginnings of recorded law. For England, that meant Anglo-Saxon law. It may be that Lambarde's *Archaionomia,* his collection of the earliest of Saxon (that is, of English) laws, served a purpose analogous to that served by Parker's publication of Saxon religious materials: a defense of a native English tradition against the inroads of foreign theory.

> The tenure of the prince, with all the incidents thereto, as rents, oaths, reliefs, wardships, primer seisin, livery, and the rest, is no new imposition but a most ancient right; no exaction by absolute authority but a settled duty by ordinary law, as well common as statute, [a not] unreasonable demand in itself but grounded upon

just cause and most reasonable consideration. For the creation of
tenures began with the first distribution of lands made by the
prince or head of the people amongst his subjects and followers,
so as the right of tenure is of equal antiquity in this land with any
law that we have, not only since the Conquest but long before,
even with the first government of the Germans here, from whom
both we and the Norman conquerors are descended and who be
the first authors of the laws *de feodis,* or of tenures, altogether
unknown to the ancient Romans or civil lawyers.[28]

So the theory of continuity became a form of patriotism: by
beginning with the Saxons these writers avoided the taint of Rome,
and by treating the Normans as themselves Germanic—thus enabling Lambarde to argue that the only change they made in the
English legal system was one of terminology—they could write off
the Conquest as of negligible importance.[29]

The primacy of the Saxons so established became the basis
for the remainder of Lambarde's works. His general topo-
graphical-historical notes, published finally in 1730 as *Dictionarium Angliæ topographicum & historicum,* were an elaboration of notes made originally by Nowell and were to serve as the
source for a whole series of county histories. Of these only the
Perambulation of Kent was worked up into final form; within a
few years of its publication Lambarde was involved in local government, and his interests shifted. Thereafter, Lambarde wrote on
the duties of the justice of the peace, on the structure of the
English law courts, and, in some of his charges to grand juries, on
the duties of the Elizabethan citizen. He returned to topography
only once: twenty years after the *Perambulation* first appeared, a
new and revised edition, embodying the work of Camden and
others who had written since, came from Lambarde's pen. But that
was merely touching up a recognized classic; the mantle had long
since passed to others' shoulders.

The *Dictionarium* was primarily a compendium, a source book.
The descriptions of the towns derived from Leland; the histories
were worked up from a wide variety of medieval chroniclers.

[28] *William Lambarde and Local Government,* ed. Conyers Read (Ithaca,
1962), p. 177.
[29] William Lambarde, *Archeion,* ed. Charles H. McIlwain and Paul L. Ward
(Cambridge, Mass., 1957), p. 12.

Where such information was available, the relics of Rome were introduced, and Lambarde made some attempt to identify the Roman towns.[30] In a few places—under the heading "Brytannia" for instance—Lambarde resorted to the British History. There is no doubt that he thought Geoffrey was partially correct, but it is clear that Lambarde felt no inclination to involve himself in controversies of this sort. The opening lines of his description of Gloucester indicate Lambarde's method clearly:

> Suche as have comitted to Writinge the Begynninge of this Towne, be not al of one Mynd towchinge the Foundation of the same; for *Galfride* (and with him the comon Chroniclers) sayeth, that *Claudius* themperour buylded it in Honour of the Mariage which he made in it betwene *Arvyragus* Kinge of *Brytaine,* and *Genuissa* his Daughter, and so called it *Claudia,* eyther of his owne Name, or of one *Gloio,* whome he begat in the same Place; but some other of more Learninge, and no less Credit, thinke that it was not so auncyent, but that it was named of some *Claudius* of latter Age, bycause thei finde no Mention of it before the Tyme of the *Saxons,* and *Gregory Caerguent,* that wrote the Hystorie of St. *Peters* in *Glocester,* begynneth no hygher. It is likely therfore, that the Cytie receyved his first Honour by the *Saxons.* . . .[31]

Those "of more Learninge," we are told in the margin, are Nennius and John Leland—the oldest authority that Lambarde can find and his most recent predecessor.

The imaginative etymologies of Geoffrey obviously could not be trusted; if a Roman name could be found, that was excellent, but Lambarde was not particularly interested in Roman Britain. In most cases the best source was the British or Saxon name, and to understand those it was necessary to have some knowledge of Welsh and of Old English. Too many previous historians had missed that point, and the errors they had made as a result had been perpetuated by others who knew no more: "It weare to longe, and beside my Purpose, to recite how shamfully *Polydore* and a

---

[30] Most of the identifications came from Leland; Lambarde evidently did not see Robert Talbot's identifications of the Roman towns in their entirety, though he mentioned one such in *A Perambulation of Kent* (London, 1576), p. 144.

[31] William Lambarde, *Dictionarium Angliæ topographicum & historicum* (London, 1730), p. 124. He discussed Geoffrey in *A Perambulation* as well: "A short counsell, as touching the Bryttishe hystorie" (ed. 1576), pp. 59–61.

Nombre of our Hystoriographers have missed the Marke in beat-
inge out of the Etimologies of Places, and al for want of Judgement in the *Bryttishe* and *Saxon* Languages." [32] The Saxon history
had the great advantage of safety: if one understood the language,
there was no chance of making an error. There were plenty of
documents surviving from the days of the Saxons, and it was
Lambarde's view that these should be the primary source for the
early history of the island.

The *Perambulation of Kent* adopted a similar method. The
towns were arranged geographically rather than alphabetically,
and the amount of information offered for each was much larger.
But Lambarde insisted that he was not writing a history, and in
this he was correct: the work fell into a genre which Ptolemy
called chorography, a combination of geography and history. In
practice, chorography involved even more than that. Archaeol-
ogy, law, custom, observation, geography, history—anything that
might serve to illuminate the description of an area—all were
brought into play.[33] It was entirely appropriate that Lambarde
began his book with a description of "The Estate of Kent," that he
should continue with the divisions of the county according to
matters judicial, financial, and ecclesiastical, and that the actual
description should have to wait until these preliminaries were
concluded. The purpose of a chorography went further than explaining a county to the world at large: it was intended to explain
the area to the very residents of it. Lambarde was himself a native
of London and became a Kentishman only upon inheriting a
manor from his father—a manor bought by his father out of the
profits of a career as a London draper. His case was not unusual,
and the new inhabitants of the county ought to know something of
their home. The *Perambulation* was a piece of scholarship, but it
was also practical; and this may explain why Lambarde in the

---

[32] Lambarde, *Dictionarium,* p. 213.

[33] "Chorography is most concerned with what kind of places those are which it
describes, not how large they are in extent. Its concern is to paint a true likeness,
and not merely to give exact position and size. Geography looks at the position
rather than the quality, noting the relation of distances everywhere, and emulat-
ing the art of painting only in some of its major descriptions . . ." (*Geography
of Claudius Ptolemy,* trans. and ed. Edward L. Stevenson [New York, 1932], p.
26). See also Gerald Strauss, "Topographical–Historical Method in Sixteenth-
century German Scholarship," *Studies in the Renaissance,* V (1958), 87–101.

second edition added a section on "The Customes of Kent" which explained, among other things, the peculiarly Kentish system of partible inheritance known as gavelkind. If one held land in the county, such knowledge was essential; if one were a Justice of the Peace, if one took any part in the administration of the shire—as Lambarde himself did—then it became essential to know something of Kent. The *Perambulation* was as essential for a Kentish J.P. as Lambarde's later book of instructions, the *Eirenarcha*.

From this it may be deduced how much of Lambarde's output stemmed from his own ideas and how much from Nowell's. The underlying conception and the basic material—that is, the contents of the *Dictionarium*—Lambarde owed to his teacher. The embellishments, the additions which removed the *Perambulation* from the category of antiquarianism pure and simple and made of it a book fit for a certain type of general reader—these were Lambarde's. Unlike Nowell, Lambarde was never primarily a scholar, though this is not to say that he was unscholarly; thus, except for his *Archaionomia,* which was written under Nowell's supervision and may be looked upon as the *Meisterwerk* of Lambarde's apprenticeship as a Saxonist, all the works had in common a quality of usefulness which was the product of Lambarde's own background. In one sense at least this was his principal contribution to antiquarian studies in England and constituted the first major addition to the program laid down by Leland; hereafter, the antiquaries had to consider the marketplace as well as the study.

Lambarde's works were not directly products of the school which Archbishop Parker organized, but there is no question but that there was a relationship between the men around Parker and those around Burghley. Lambarde was perfectly aware that his own Saxon studies reinforced those of the archbishop, and the two circles of scholars seem to have mixed constantly. It is no coincidence that the one work recommended in Thomas Wotton's introduction to the *Perambulation* was the *Norvicus* of Parker's assistant, Alexander Neville, nor that Neville had high praise for Lambarde's book a year before that book actually appeared. This is not to say that the two books were similar. Neville wrote his description of Norwich to please Parker: it was the patron rather than the author who was a native of the place. Moreover, Neville, whose

interests were more literary than historical, wrote in a somewhat
inflated Latin prose rather than in the down-to-earth English that
Lambarde favored. Yet despite the differences, it is a point of
considerable significance that the first two finished local studies
should both have originated among the Saxonists and that both
should have involved, in some degree, the patronage of Parker.[34]

Neville's book bore at least a superficial resemblance to Lambarde's; indeed, most of the differences can be accounted for if we
remember that while the latter considered a whole county the
former wrote about one town only. The historical sources used
were similar: both men had access to Leland, and both used the
medieval chroniclers, though Lambarde used a greater variety.
But Neville lacked sufficient material for a book and padded out
his description of Norwich with a long dissertation in favor of
Geoffrey and against Polydore Vergil; furthermore he placed
much more emphasis on ecclesiastical history than did Lambarde.
The essential difference between the two men can best be seen in
their handling of the early history of the town. Where Lambarde,
in the *Dictionarium,* was content to trace the history of Norwich
back to the Saxons with merely a reference to possible Roman
names (the contradictory suggestions of Leland and Polydore
were both cited, but no choice was made between them), Neville
took more than a dozen pages in trying to establish a prior British
history.[35] Lambarde's essential quality, that of avoiding unnecessary controversy and sticking to what could be proved, simply was
not present in Neville. To an extent, however, this is carping.
Town chronicles had existed since the Middle Ages, and indeed
Neville printed one for Norwich as a kind of appendix. A comparison of that skeleton with the fully-fleshed body presented to us in
Norvicus indicates what the newer techniques could accomplish
even when they were used by inexpert hands. Neville's Norwich
was a town, geographically placed and filled with people; it was
not a series of mayors and sheriffs and unconnected events.

[34] Lambarde submitted his *Perambulation* to Parker (*Correspondence of Matthew Parker,* ed. J. Bruce and T. T. Perowne, Parker Soc. [Cambridge, Eng.,
1853], pp. 424–425, 441).
[35] Lambarde, *Dictionarium,* s.v. Norwich, p. 228; Alexander Neville, *Norvicus,*
bound at the end of *De furoribus Norfolciensium Ketto duce* (London, 1575),
separate pagination, pp. 95 ff.

Originally, then, Saxon studies developed because here could be found a kind of certainty unavailable elsewhere. For the archbishop this meant a series of clergymen stretching back uninterruptedly, a continuous English church whose development could be compared to that of the Roman church across the Channel. For Lambarde and the antiquarian Saxonists who followed him, here was a certain beginning to English history. The point could be made that the present inhabitants of England were the descendants of the Saxons, not of Geoffrey's Britons. If the Welsh wanted to defend Geoffrey, well and good, but there was no especial reason for the English to indulge in the same amusement. Lambarde took a middle position; he accepted Geoffrey but tried to ignore him where possible. Saxonism had the advantage of reducing the British History to scenic background and meant that scholarly blood need be shed no longer in defense or in opposition. It was not long, however, before the Saxonists developed an aggressive view of their own. Richard Verstegan made much of the German connection: the Germans were the worthiest of ancestors, quite able to bear comparison with the Trojans or with the Romans. The Saxon language had an elemental purity which was superior to the more decadent Latin tongues. Partly, of course, this became a weapon in the battle over neologisms; but equally, in some hands, it became a way of attacking such old enemies as France and Spain and papal Italy. It was in the countries where the Saxons had conquered utterly that Protestantism took firmest root; where the Germanic peoples had been absorbed into the Latin culture, however debased, Catholicism remained. Obviously this was an exaggeration: South Germany and Austria remained Catholic, Geneva was the home of Calvin. Nonetheless, Saxonism helped to draw England closer to her Protestant neighbors. Moreover, Saxon culture was indigenous, a homegrown product. The two notions interacted as they had from the beginning: one derived from Parker's circle and one from Burghley's, and as the two ideas had bolstered one another in the 1570's, so they continued to do in the 1620's.[36]

---

[36] Rosemond Tuve, "Ancients, Moderns, and Saxons," *English Literary History*, VI (1939), 165–190; Richard F. Jones, *The Triumph of the English Language* (Stanford, 1953), Chs. vii–viii. Much of this derives from the second chapter of Richard Verstegan, *A Restitution of Decayed Intelligence* (Antwerp, 1605), pp. 25–54: "How the Ancient Noble Saxons, the True Anceters of English-

At the same time that Old English was being revived in England, a fresh infusion of humanism came from the Continent. The example of John Leland was still remembered, but the principal follower of Leland was the Saxonist Lambarde, who, as we have seen, elaborated on only one part of Leland's legacy and altered that. The patriotic aspects of Leland's work never fell entirely from view, but the humanist, that is, classical, aspects of his work had been generally neglected. The history of Roman Britain had still to be written, and, it turned out, the immediate impetus for that came from abroad.

The most active interest in the geography of the Roman world was evinced by the Belgian geographer Abraham Ortelius.[37] This, to be sure, was only one of his numerous interests: wherever there were blanks on maps, Ortelius was anxious to fill them, and it mattered little whether the blanks were the result of insufficient exploration or of neglected research. Thus among his friends Ortelius counted the explorers and the scholars, and the latter, at least, were quite as likely to receive requests for new information about the latest voyages as they were about their own doings. Nor was this unexpected: Richard Hakluyt and John Dee both combined scholarship of a historical sort with an intense and very active interest in the progress of geographic discovery, and both were regular correspondents of the Belgian. Moreover, in an age when decent maps were extraordinarily hard to come by, everyone was prepared to assist the Continent's foremost mapmaker in producing new and better ones. Ortelius in his turn made maps of the world of the sixteenth century, but he also made them for the great ages of the past. Since his own interest, and that of his friends Hubert Goltzius and Justus Lipsius, was concentrated on ancient Rome, filling in the large gap of Roman Britain was a matter of great urgency. So for years Ortelius encouraged one after another of English scholars to map Britannia until at last the work was done by William Camden.

---

men, were originally a people of Germanie: and how honorable it is for Englishmen to be descended from the Germans." See also William Camden, *Remaines . . . concerning Britaine* (London, 1605), pp. 13–14.

[37] On Ortelius and England, see my "The Making of Camden's *Britannia*," *Bibliothèque d'Humanisme et Renaissance*, XXVI (1964), 70–98, which examines these matters in more detail and gives full references.

Meanwhile, Ortelius had to make do with what material was available. In his *Synonymia geographica,* an encyclopedic list of the place names of the ancient world (with their modern equivalents), he was able to make use of the works of Neville, Lhuyd, and Leland; he had access to the unpublished identifications of the stations of the Antonine Itineraries which had been drawn up by Leland's friend and contemporary Robert Talbot; and his cousin, the English diplomat Daniel Rogers, discovered what he could. The English, for their part, eagerly awaited the publication of the *Synonymia:* not only did Ortelius collect together more information about Roman Britain than anyone had before him, but he also included vast quantities of data about the other cities of the Empire. Thus the work of Beatus Rhenanus, as absorbed by Ortelius, was made known to everyone; and so were the works of myriad other, less-known, scholars.

It was Ortelius who, even before Lambarde, reintroduced into English scholarship the geographic emphasis. His insistence on exploring the details of Roman Britain encouraged a whole generation of scholars to work out the details of the map of Britannia; and his insistence on going to look at the actual scene forced them to repeat the travels of Leland and at the same time demonstrated to them that it was possible to carry the geographic history of the island up to the present. Historical chorography, on the basis of Roman Britain, thus became the major line of antiquarian research from the mid-1570's until past the end of the century, and if one adds to this the type of chorography practiced by Lambarde, then the trend continued for some centuries more.

There was, furthermore, one other advantage to the study of Roman Britain. Ortelius and his followers were more than a little skeptical of the British History. The two crucial points of debate, Brutus and Arthur, were not very susceptible to direct attack. The evidence against them was quite as bad as that for them, and as we have seen, the attack had followed the laws of logic rather than those of historical evidence. If, however, one moved to another point in Geoffrey's account of the history of the island, then a full-scale attack could be launched. The early history of Roman Britain could be written from either of two sets of sources, the British or the Roman. If they agreed, then the authority of Geoffrey's account would be bolstered; if they disagreed on so obvious a point, Geoffrey's reputation would be at a discount. So much had been obvious to John Rastell, who questioned the British History and may have been responsible for the publication of an edition of as much of Caesar as was relevant to the argument. Polydore Vergil had pointed out that Geoffrey's account of the invasion of Claudius was in flat opposition to the known facts of Roman history. By the time Ortelius and his disciples began to write, the attack on Geoffrey's Roman history had been going on for some time, but it lacked system. Men still had nothing to go on but the works of the Roman authors themselves; it remained to discover whether the methods of critical chorography, that is of antiquarianism, could add to the fund of information.

Moreover, antiquarianism itself offered unrivaled opportunities to classical scholars. As we have already pointed out, most scholars felt that the works of the classical historians were, in a sense, sacrosanct. It might be possible to add to them, it might be possible to use them in a way that the author had not intended, but it was impossible to rewrite them.[38] Thus a subject such as Roman Britain had immense appeal. The Romans themselves had written very little about it; much of what was known to have been written had vanished; and what remained was encapsulated in writings about something else. Because there was in fact no Roman history of Roman Britain, the field was clear for any humanist scholar to write one, untrammeled by doubts as to whether he was committing sacrilege. Moreover, once the new techniques pioneered by the collectors of coins and inscriptions were adopted, a historian could use materials other than the merely literary. He could take the ancient "map" of the Roman territories, the Antonine Itineraries, and attempt to locate the places mentioned—this was one pursuit that Ortelius encouraged. He could follow the Roman roads in person and examine what he found on the way. Statues, ruined buildings, coins, inscriptions—any might be useful in determining precisely where the Romans had been, which Romans

---

[38] Arnaldo Momigliano, "Ancient History and the Antiquarian," *Journal of the Warburg and Courtauld Institutes,* XIII (1950), 285–315; this view has been modified somewhat by H. J. Erasmus, *The Origins of Rome in Historiography from Petrarch to Perizonius* (Assen, 1962), pp. 32–59.

had been there, and what they had done. Thus antiquarianism of this sort was a subject on the very frontiers of knowledge, where a great reputation could be made.[39]

So Ortelius tried to entice someone in Britain to do the work that was necessary. The Welshman Humphrey Lhuyd seemed an obvious candidate because of his interest in the British (i.e., Welsh) place names; if he could be persuaded to expand his examination to include the Roman names in the island as well, then he might accomplish what Ortelius wanted. But as we have seen, Lhuyd was too much engaged in fighting the battle of Geoffrey of Monmouth against Polydore. Since the Welsh were the descendants of the Britons, local patriotism was involved, and Lhuyd never escaped from it. Moreover, by the time he took up Ortelius' challenge, Lhuyd was already very ill, and his *Breviary of Britayne* was not sent to Antwerp until after the author's death. Lhuyd solved a good many problems relating to British place names, and everyone after him was in his debt: some knowledge of Welsh became a prerequisite for serious antiquarian study.

With the task still not done, Ortelius then tried to beguile Daniel Rogers into doing it.[40] Rogers, as an accomplished Latin poet with an interest in anything Roman, had at least some of the necessary qualifications. There is no doubt that Rogers actually began the work, but it seems never to have gotten very far. For Rogers, although he had a claim on his countrymen as the son of the first of the Marian martyrs, possessed neither wealth nor family and thus had a career to make. Years spent in working his way up in Elizabeth's diplomatic service did not leave much time for antiquarian researches. Four years spent in a German prison finally put an end to any hope that his book would be finished. All that remained of Rogers' project was a bundle of notes; the promised history of the Roman province was never written. Moreover, there is considerable doubt as to whether the finished book would have answered the need. Rogers essentially was a humanist of the old sort. His primary interest was in language, not in history; while

[39] Momigliano, "Ancient History"; Erna Mandowsky and Charles Mitchell, *Pirro Ligorio's Roman Antiquities* (London, 1963), pp. 1–51.
[40] F. J. Levy, "Daniel Rogers as Antiquary," *Bibliothèque d'Humanisme et Renaissance,* XXVII (1965), 444–462.

he knew of the most recent techniques of research, he seemed unable to make much use of them. Thus his notes and his letters make reference to coins and inscriptions, but Rogers was content to search through other men's books for them and made no attempt to locate them on his own. Furthermore, one wonders whether he would have made much use of them had he gone to the trouble of searching. His notes make clear that his approach to the problem of Roman Britain was essentially literary and that he used nonliterary materials only to shed light on the ancient writers. One of his letters to Ortelius illustrated that Rogers knew what ought to be done, that archaeological evidence should be used either to fill in what the ancient writers did not mention or to replace those ancients whose writings had since been lost. The ideal method of the later humanists was known to Rogers through Ortelius and his circle, with all of whom he was friendly, but he never proceeded from an understanding of the method to its use.

Ortelius was then forced to turn to still another scholar, William Camden, whom he met (probably through the agency of John Dee) on a visit to London in 1577.[41] The young Camden had already thought of doing precisely what Ortelius wanted and had begun his wanderings through England with a chorography in mind. But like Rogers, Camden had his living to make and as undermaster of Westminster School did not have much leisure. By 1577 Camden seems to have been ready to give up any idea of continuing his researches; then, upon meeting Ortelius, he resumed his labors and within three years had finished a preparatory draft of the work to be known as *Britannia*. Originally the *Britannia* was intended as a tour of Roman Britain, along the lines of Flavio Biondo's tour of Italy. That meant, of course, that he had first to identify the Roman roads of the province, and that in its turn required the identification of at least some of the Roman towns along the roads.

In some of this Camden had had predecessors. The names of a

[41] On Camden, my "The Making of Camden's *Britannia*" and my unpublished dissertation, "William Camden as Historian" (Harvard University, 1959); see also Stuart Piggott, "William Camden and the *Britannia*," *Proceedings of the British Academy*, XXXVII (1951), 199–217.

few of the Roman towns were known to all: London, York, Bath, and the like. A good many others had been worked out by Robert Talbot, some of whose notes may have been known to Camden. Talbot had not investigated the problem on the scene but had used a text of the Antonine Itineraries, the old Roman roadbook. Nevertheless, he had been able to solve a number of the Itineraries with a fair degree of accuracy, and his notes on the subject were the basis for all that went after. Ortelius seems to have had access to some copy of Talbot's manuscript, and so did Lambarde; whether Camden saw Talbot's work directly or whether he made use of it as transformed by others, it is impossible to tell.[42] In any case, the earlier investigation made Camden's task simpler. So did the manuscripts of Leland, the *Breviary* of Lhuyd, and the notes of Daniel Rogers. For all that, much work remained to be done. Taken together, all of Camden's predecessors in the art of divining the location of Roman towns had managed to identify no more than half of the towns mentioned in the Itineraries, and those remaining were obviously the most difficult.

Camden solved the problem in accordance with the methods of Ortelius. First of all, it was necessary to acquire a good text of the Itineraries themselves: the printed version was notoriously corrupt, especially in the distances it gave. Ortelius and Mercator helped here by sending transcripts of Continental manuscripts. Even with that done, mere walking would not help in identification. The Roman document did no more than list the stages on the road between the major cities of Britannia, together with the distances between them. How was Camden to identify the site when he arrived at it? The answer lay in a careful study of coins, inscriptions, and any other remains that might still be visible. In a few cases he could follow the actual roads, but such luck was too infrequent to be of much use. In most cases the carefully collated

---

[42] In 1599 Camden wrote to Thomas James, "lately have I happened uppon Talbots notes in *Antonini Itinerarium*" (*Letters Addressed to Thomas James, First Keeper of Bodley's Library*, ed. G. W. Wheeler [Oxford, 1933], pp. 18–19); but in 1580, Thomas Savile asked Camden to send the notes, and there are two citations to them in the first edition of *Britannia: V. Cl. Gulielmi Camdeni . . . Epistolae*, ed. Thomas Smith (London, 1691), p. 4, and William Camden, *Britannia* (London, 1586), pp. 254, 270.

information gathered from all of his predecessors, plus his estimate
of the distance from some town which could be easily identified,
was all that Camden had available. With that in hand he proceeded to seek out the places mentioned in the Itineraries and
elsewhere. When he came to a spot suspected of hiding a Roman
town, he looked for walls, for fragments of pavements, for coins,
even for cropmarks. He spoke to the inhabitants to learn what they
had discovered and to find any old legends still hanging over the
town. All of this information was sifted—on the spot, presumably,
since the next identification would depend on the one then under
investigation—and a decision as to the name made. Thus by dint
of much traveling the riddle of the Itineraries could be solved.

How many such trips Camden made prior to 1586, the year
that he published the *Britannia*, there is no way of knowing. Of
two trips there is definite evidence: in 1578 he toured the country
of the Iceni (East Anglia), and in 1582 he journeyed to York by
way of Suffolk and returned by way of Lancaster. The second was
mentioned only briefly in his diary, but the first was described in
detail in a letter to Ortelius:

> Last summer I surveyed the whole maritime coast of the Iceni
> (Ptolemy calls them wrongly Simeni), namely Norfolk and Suf-
> folk, to trace some ancient cities buried under their ruins. I found
> a large quantity of ancient coins, and send you two of them, not of
> gold, but of brass, which appear to me to be more rare and
> valuable. One bears the image of Constantinople, the other that of
> Rome; not like the one you showed me of the consular coins, for I
> believe these to be of the later emperors. The "Urbs Roma" coin
> was found near Norwich, in a place called Caster, where extensive
> ruins of walls, and many evidences of ancient times are to be seen,
> and which I think is "Venta Icenorum," namely the city which
> Ptolemy calls "Venta Simenorum" (for you must not suppose that
> Winchester is "Venta Simenorum," as it was undoubtedly "Venta
> Belgarum"). You know that we give the name "Venta Icenorum"
> to Norwich, but with the same right with which others call Basilia,
> "Augusta" and Baldach "Babilonia," as you notice yourself. The
> "Constantinopolis" coin was dug up at Colchester, which I would
> regard as the Colonia of Antoninus, but not, with Leland, as
> Camalodunum, as certain circumstances have led me to look upon

the latter place as Colonia Victricensis and the palace of king Cunobelin, now called Maldon. . . .[43]

This is but a glimpse of Camden at work, but it indicates the combination of preparation and on-the-site investigation which constituted his basic method.

One other technique was used as well. Conjecture and the similarity of the current name to the Roman name were also tools for unlocking the secret of the Itineraries. In this case, Camden's success was rather less. It was not for want of trying. Convinced that the Romans frequently altered native names only a little, or that the successors to the Romans corrupted the Latin, Camden set out to learn Welsh and Anglo-Saxon. Humphrey Lhuyd had given some guidance in these matters, and Camden followed his lead. The principle involved is not, in fact, incorrect, but the application was a great deal more complex than Camden ever guessed. A good many of his errors can be traced to just this, and it is interesting that Camden himself had some misgivings. In his preface he found it necessary to write a defense of conjecture: "There may be many who may object that I have presumed to indulge conjectures on antient names and etymologies. But if all conjectures are to be excluded, I fear a very considerable part of our polite literature, and I may add of human knowledge, must of course follow. Our understandings are generally speaking so dull, that we are obliged to recur to conjecture in every science . . . ." [44] It is easy to be satirical at Camden's expense, for some of the errors in which he involved himself seem, at this remove, ludicrous. Camden himself might have agreed: place names were to be used only when other means failed or perhaps together with them. If new evidence turned up, he was ready to abandon previous conjectures, and any collation of the various editions of the *Britannia* indicates how often he was prepared to change his mind. And, too, the method of conjecture, provided that there were checks on it, frequently worked very well:

[43] *Camdeni . . . Epistolae*, Appendix, p. 85; *Ecclesiae Londino-Batavae Archivum*, I, 181–183 (the summary translation given here is that of the editor, J. H. Hessels).

[44] *Britannia* (London, 1586), fol. A4ᵛ; translation from *Britannia* (London, 1789), I, Preface, ii.

At Falkesley bridge before mentioned, the Roman military way
so often spoken [of], and of which more hereafter, enters this
county, and crossing it almost in a strait line, runs west into
Shropshire. I have surveyed it with particular attention to find
ETOCETUM the next station in Antoninus after *Manduessedum,*
and I have now by good luck found it, and acknowledge myself to
have been totally wide of it before. For, at the same distance
which Antoninus makes between Manduessedum and Etocetum, I
stumbled upon the ruins of a small antient city by the road side,
scarce a mile to the south from Lichfield a famous episcopal see.
The common name of the place now is *Wall,* from the pieces of
walls remaining there, and including about two acres called *Castle
Croft,* q.d. *Castle field,* to which the antient city is said to have
adjoined on the other side the road destroyed before the Conquest
according to the old tradition of the inhabitants. They shew a
place where, by the great foundations they suppose stood a temple, and produce the most certain evidences of its antiquity and
Roman coins. But the strongest proof is the military way running
from hence with a fair bold and uninterrupted ridge till it comes to
the river *Penck,* which has a stone bridge at PENNOCRUCIUM,
which takes its name from the river at the same distance laid down
by Antoninus. Nor has it yet lost its name, being called instead of
Pennocrucium *Penkridge,* though only a small village famous for
its horse fair. . . .[45]

In this case, all was well: Wall, in fact, is LETOCETUM, and Penkridge is PENNOCRUCIUM. Aided by observation and by conversation
with the inhabitants, Letocetum could be found if the search continued long enough; and that done, the identification of Pennocrucium, originally worked out on the basis of place names, could
be verified.

The original *Britannia,* as we find it in the early drafts, was a
product of the inspiration of Ortelius. It was an investigation of
Roman Britain; indeed, one can go further and argue that it was
an investigation of names. The book as finally published was more
than this. For one thing, Camden was influenced by patriotism.
There was something of this even in the original plan, for one of
the purposes of the book was to show the place of Britain in the

---

[45] *Britannia* (London, 1789), II, 375–376, from *Britannia* (London, 1607), p.
439.

Roman Empire and thus connect Britain to the fountainhead of European culture. Moreover, it was patriotic even to write such a book, for its publication would demonstrate to scholars on the Continent that Britain, too, was capable of producing a work in the latest and best manner. Having gone so far, Camden went a step further: some expansion of the original design would serve the purpose of introducing modern Britain to the scholarly world. Furthermore, such an expansion was implicit even in the original structure. The investigation of names meant that the British original, if there was such, had to be found, that the Roman name had to be worked out by whatever means were available, and that the changes that had occurred in the name since Roman days had to be described. The search for names led gradually but inexorably into the history of towns, and the outline had only to be fleshed out for a more comprehensive book to appear. Camden used Leland's notes and his own observations to add the necessary detail about current appearance and devoured the medieval chroniclers to fill in the gap between the days of the Romans and his own.

Thus the structure of the first edition of the *Britannia* was somewhat complicated. Camden opened with some general matter concerning the origins of the Britons, and followed this with brief descriptions of the various peoples that had inhabited the island: the Romans, Anglo-Saxons, Danes, and Normans. The geographical section which followed had the counties of England and Wales collected into groups according to the supposed locations of the various tribes of Britons, though these tribal groupings were never allowed to cut across a shire border, and this in turn was followed by brief descriptions of Scotland, Ireland, and the islands. Within each county Camden rambled from town to town, choosing his subjects by the availability of material first of all and then by the interest of the place. If there was a Roman or some other kind of historical interest, the description might be extended; if not that, then the interest might lie in some curiosity, a story, the home of a notable, even a fair. If nothing of the sort could be found, then the place was best omitted. Once the decision was made to include the town, the etymology of the name had to be worked out, and this meant that all the resources of Camden's linguistic equipment— Latin, Welsh, Anglo-Saxon—would be brought to bear: to assist him, he once worked out a list of prefixes and suffixes which acted as a guide.[46] If the town was large and important, then the name was followed by a short history; there might be something of genealogy and heraldry, but in 1586 Camden was still unsure of those matters, and the amount of such information was limited.

Such was the first edition. Its intended audience was primarily the scholars of Europe, not the average English gentleman. The book achieved its purpose of making Europe aware of Britain, and Camden won the plaudits of Ortelius and of the whole array of northern humanists. But the *Britannia* accomplished more than that. It won a very decided interest in England itself. In 1587 another edition was called for, and more followed in 1590, 1594, 1600, and 1607, each larger than its predecessor. In 1610 Philemon Holland finally translated it into English, and that translation, augmented, reappeared in 1637. Meanwhile, further Latin editions had appeared at Frankfort. Once it became obvious that the book was popular at home, Camden proceeded to enlarge it. Originally Camden wished to bring England back into connection with the rest of Europe by showing that Britain, too, had a Roman heritage. Nor did he ever lose sight of that goal: the increase in the number of inscriptions, very noticeable in Cumberland, and his own visit to the Roman Wall, bear witness to that. But to all intents and purposes the task of explicating the geography of ancient Britain was completed in the first edition. It was possible to expand the historical information, and to some extent that was done. But Camden as a historian must have realized that if one's intention was to write the history of Britain, even the worst annals were better than history fragmented by the exigencies of a geographical framework. At the same time, the *Britannia* became more and more a collection of sources. The "Chronicon regum Manniae" had been included from the beginning. In 1607, a chronicle of Ireland was added. There is throughout, too, an impression that the *Britannia* was to be, among other things, a "Corpus inscriptionum Britanniae," and occasionally Camden tells us that he is quoting from a document at length because of its

[46] Trinity College, Cambridge, MS. R.5.20, unfoliated. The list follows a series of blanks after "f. 55."

rarity.[47] But all these things, taken together, were only a small proportion of the new material.

The major additions, the genealogy and the descriptions, were put there for the benefit of his English audience. Camden was undoubtedly aware that those same patriotic motives which in the beginning had moved him to write the *Britannia* were also at work on his English audience. There was nothing that interested the gentry and the urban middle class more than "the Discovery of England." [48] And so, though the original framework of the book remained unchanged, the purpose shifted. From 1590 onward its readers were presumed to be English, interested in the antiquities of Britain but concerned as well with its topography and with the histories of its noble families. It was for this reason that Camden, in the preface to the 1607 folio, found it necessary to defend himself against charges of slighting one or another town or family by omission. The charge would have been inconceivable in 1586.

Where did the additional material come from? Part of it came from Leland's *Itineraries,* which had been used from the beginning but which Camden continued to mine as his own focus shifted. But Leland's materials never constituted a very large fraction of Camden's work, and at least one authority has stated that the *Britannia* might have been a better book had there been more borrowing rather than less.[49] Part of it came from Camden's own travels. He had made at least two trips even before 1586, one to East Anglia and the other to York, and after the publication of the *Britannia* he continued his traveling. In 1590 he went to Wales with his old friend Francis Godwin, the future bishop of Llandaff; in 1596 he toured the west country (Salisbury and Wells), returning by way of Oxford; and in 1600, together with Sir Robert Cotton, he returned to the north. By the time of the last trip, Camden had been made Clarencieux King-at-Arms and no longer had to attend the boys at Westminster School, and so the two friends were gone from midsummer to December. I suspect that

[47] *Britannia* (London, 1789), I, ciii: a passage from Procopius copied for Camden in Paris by François Pithou.
[48] Louis B. Wright, *Middle-Class Culture in Elizabethan England* (Ithaca, 1958), pp. 297–338; A. L. Rowse, *The England of Elizabeth* (New York, 1951), pp. 31–65.
[49] T. D. Kendrick, *British Antiquity*, p. 149.

there may have been still other trips, for Camden's list of them is patently incomplete: but of so much we can be sure.[50] In sum, Camden's traveling never approached that of Leland—Leland had, after all, the advantage of being able to make a profession of it—but it sufficed to allow Camden to describe a great many of his scenes from personal observation. These travels also help to explain the increasing amounts of archaeological materials in the ever-growing *Britannia*. There was nothing aimless in Camden's wandering. Where he could, he followed the Roman roads, and along the way he explored for the monuments of Roman Britain.

There were times when finding Roman monuments turned out to be an easy matter. In the city of Bath the town clerk, Robert Chambers, had been collecting them; at Carlisle it had been Thomas Aglionby; out in the country J. Senhouse, a Cumberland gentleman, had gathered a whole group of remains. Some men went at it quite systematically. Reginald Bainbrigg, the schoolmaster of Appleby, Westmoreland, made regular trips along the Roman Wall in the hope of turning up something new, penetrating into territory that Camden and Cotton found too dangerous.[51] Nor were these the only cases. There was a whole legion of helpers available. Some must have become interested because the increasingly classical education offered Englishmen opened their eyes to the remains of ancient Rome; a few men were collecting inscriptions and the like even before Camden published his *Britannia*.[52] Others may have been made aware by the *Britannia* itself of the treasures around them, and, once alert, they preserved the old stones, made copies of them, and sent their notes on to London. Perhaps in Camden's next edition they would find their own names. Before the seventeenth century was far advanced, collec-

---

[50] *Camdeni . . . Epistolae*, Appendix, p. 85.

[51] The names come from the book itself. Bainbrigg's letters survive in British Museum, Cotton MSS, Julius F.vi. Some of the material was printed by F. Haverfield, "Cotton Iulius F. VI. Notes on Reginald Bainbrigg of Appleby, on William Camden and on Some Roman Inscriptions," *Transactions of the Cumberland & Westmorland Antiquarian & Archaeological Society*, N.S., XI (1911), 343–378.

[52] There is a puzzling, anonymous description of an antiquarian tour dated 1574 which mentions inscriptions amongst much else: "Certaine Verie Rare Observations of Cumberland, Northumberland, &c. . . ." in *Reprints of Rare Tracts & Imprints of Antient Manuscripts, &c. . . . Miscellaneous* (Newcastle, 1849).

tion had become serious. Sir Robert Cotton went to great lengths to have remains brought from the north to his house at Connington and indeed had agents looking for more on the Continent; the Earl of Arundel collected English antiquities as well as foreign ones.[53] Antiquarianism had become fashionable: some of the results may be seen in the heavily illustrated *Britannia* of 1607.

One other result of the changes in the original *Britannia* must be noted. It was the genealogical additions, most of them made in 1590 and 1594, which called forth Ralph Brooke's charges of inaccuracy.[54] Brooke, long York Herald, had become enraged when in 1597 Camden was appointed over his head to the position of Clarencieux King-at-Arms. The envy and spite in Brooke's attack are here unimportant—Brooke was noted for such behavior; and that an attack on the recently added genealogy did not in any serious way lessen the value of the book was self-evident. But it must be admitted that Brooke's charges, at least in the first instance, were accurate. He quoted Camden correctly, and the errors in question were real enough. The results were salutary. In 1600 most of the errors were corrected. Camden, not surprisingly, was far from accepting all the corrections meekly (Brooke's tone precluded that), and that he rechecked each one is borne out by the corrections even in those genealogies not under attack. Also, Camden counterattacked in the added "Ad Lectorem" of 1600, and his grudge against Brooke continued for many years. But the controversy with Brooke had another effect, more far-reaching than a mere correction of errors. Questions of such nicety could be answered only by reference to records; both sides realized this, and there was indeed nothing very new in the recognition, for some forms of records did, of course, underlie historical statements. But Camden was forced to change his technique of reference and thereby, in some degree, his way of thinking. In 1586 the only sources identified were those classical authors whose texts Camden was explicating. By the time of the last edition, in 1607, all

[53] British Museum, Cotton MSS, Julius C.iii, fol. 210 (Lord William Howard to Cotton, Aug. 13, 1608, on sending an inscription); Cotton MSS, Vespasian F.xiii, fol. 303 (another letter, Aug. 29, 1608, on the same subject); Cotton MSS, Julius C.iii, fol. 26 (William Bold to Cotton, [Paris] June 29, 1615 [new style], on France).
[54] Brooke, *A Discoverie of Certaine Errours* (London, 1723).

statements which might be questioned were supplied with sources. Augustine Vincent, Camden's disciple in the College of Heralds, writing of the dispute two decades later, told of his first disillusionment with Brooke: "I then grew bolder, and beganne to handle him neerer; labouring, by comparing their Bookes, to satisfie my selfe, whether Master *Camden* were so blacke, as hee had painted him, or not. I found for Master *Camden*, that if hee had erred, hee had erred with Authority: For *Yorke*, I saw no proofes, but *Pythagorian* proofes, in steed of *Scriptum est, Ipse dixit*, no Record, no Antiquitie, but his owne antiquitie of *fortie yeares Practise* in that Studie: this I liked not." [55] This was not entirely fair to Brooke. But indicative of the changed concept of documentation, Vincent accepted the idea of continuous references so completely that his questions, "If he have such Records, why doth he not produce them in their turnes? Why doth he not lay them downe upon the Margent?" were, in fact, complete condemnation.[56] Thus controversy, among the antiquaries quite as much as among the theologians, led to a greater demand for clearly documented fact.

Camden's *Britannia* may be looked upon as the culmination of one line of endeavor and the beginning of another. Camden accomplished what Ortelius had been demanding, but he did more. The *Britannia* is the book that Leland might have written. Its author made use of Leland's notes and of Daniel Rogers' and absorbed the truncated work of Humphrey Lhuyd. The latest scholarship of the northern humanists found a place in it; so did the Anglo-Saxon researches of Archbishop Parker and of William Lambarde. The British History of Geoffrey of Monmouth was relegated to its proper place, for while Camden avoided the controversy that a direct attack on Geoffrey would have brought on, the emphasis on the Roman and post-Roman past meant that Geoffrey's worst excesses could be reduced to relative unimportance. Bringing the scholarship of the past into focus was but one achievement, for Camden also supplied the future with questions

---

[55] Augustine Vincent, *A Discoverie of Errours* (London, 1622), "To Raphe Brooke, Yorke Herald," fol. ¶3ʳ. Vincent had Camden's help in this attack on Brooke: see Camden's notes in Bodleian Library, MS. Smith 17, pp. 146–148, 174–177, where are collected some of the errors in Brooke's *A Catalogue and Succession of the Kings, Princes . . . of This Realme* (London, 1619).
[56] On this point, T. D. Kendrick, *British Antiquity*, pp. 151–155.

and, most important, with a method for answering them. The careful checking of interpretations by using several lines of reasoning bearing on the same point, the insistence on observation, and in the end, the use of references—these were to be the way in which antiquaries in the next generation worked.

Before the first edition of *Britannia* only one county history had appeared: Lambarde's Kent. Gradually, and at least partially as a consequence of Camden's work, the writing of such local chorographies became widespread. Of the early participants in this movement, a considerable number were in communication with Camden, and he noted their names as contributors. Richard Carew was an old friend, and his *Survey of Cornwall* and Camden's section on Cornwall may both be considered as works almost of joint authorship.[57] So close a partnership was unusual, but Camden certainly benefited from the assistance of Sampson Erdeswicke, George Owen, Henry Ferrars, and St. Lo Kniveton, all of whom were at work on chorographies of their own.[58] They in turn benefited from Camden's writings, partly because he offered them a method, partly because he presented a national context for their concentration on localities. Lambarde had wanted to write "Perambulations" of all the counties and had found the task insuperable; once the *Britannia* was available, a man could attend to his own bailiwick.

By their very nature, the county topographies emphasized just those matters that Camden had been adding to his *Britannia;* only Lambarde, whose *Perambulation* of course preceded the *Britannia,* was really interested in the history of a county, in this case the Anglo-Saxon past of Kent. Most topographers wished to illustrate the history of landholding in their own shire, and so they pro-

---

[57] Carew's *Survey* circulated in MS before 1594: *Richard Carew of Antony: The Survey of Cornwall &c.,* ed. F. E. Halliday (London, 1953), p. 62; and Camden praised Carew in his *Britannia,* while some of his Cornish material emphasized features of the sort that Carew was more likely to notice than Camden. Carew, however, continued work on his *Survey,* and part of the new material added between 1594 and 1602 derived from Camden.

[58] Sampson Erdeswicke (Staffordshire and Cheshire) was called "an eminent encourager of venerable antiquity," *Britannia* (London, 1789), II, 376. The comments on the others are similar: George Owen (Pembrokeshire), ibid., II, 515; St. Lo Kniveton (Derbyshire), ibid., II, 301; and Henry Ferrars (Warwickshire), *Britannia* (London, 1586), p. 319.

ceeded manor by manor and traced the ownership of each.[59] In a few cases they went further. Robert Reyce, writing on Suffolk, was most intrigued with social history and with description: the book is a delight to read but is about the least historical of the topographies.[60] Tristram Risdon, the topographer of Devon, began with genealogy (most of which he got from his predecessor, Sir William Pole) but then spread his net wider and described the county.[61] Possibly he had come into contact with Carew's *Survey* or with a manuscript of Reyce. Most commonly, however, the genealogy was nearly unrelieved by geographical description, and the only history was that of descents of land. Only in a few cases was the pattern of Camden's book followed, and the two books which follow it most closely are both relatively minor: the *Chorographia, Or A Survey of Newcastle upon Tine,* attributed to William Grey and not published until 1649, and a perfect miniature, William Bedwell's *A Briefe Description of the Towne of Tottenham High-Crosse* (1631).[62]

What is most impressive about the topographies is their use of sources. Citations to various local records were common, and some of the authors went to the great storehouse of the Tower as well. Moreover, there was a substantial amount of cooperation among them and the exchange of information was a common-

---

[59] John Denton of Cardew, *An Accompt of the Most Considerable Estates and Families in the County of Cumberland,* ed. R. S. Ferguson, Cumberland and Westmorland Antiquarian and Archaeological Society, Tract Ser. No. 2 (Kendal, 1887); Thomas Habington, *A Survey of Worcestershire,* ed. John Amphlett, The Worcestershire Historical Society, 2 vols. (Oxford, 1895–99): Habington used Domesday and a few records, but gathered most of his data in churches; William Burton, *The Description of Leicester Shire* (London, [1622]): by manors, even though Burton owned the MSS of Leland's Itineraries—Burton had an interest in arms as well, and a love of digression, but little concern for topography; Sampson Erdeswicke, *A Survey of Staffordshire,* ed. Thomas Harwood (London, 1844): much use of Domesday but little interest in antiquities.

[60] *Suffolk in the XVIIth Century: The Breviary of Suffolk,* ed. Lord Francis Hervey (London, 1902).

[61] Sir William Pole, *Collections towards a Description of the County of Devon* (London, 1791); Tristram Risdon, *The Chorographical Description, or, Survey of the County of Devon,* 2 vols. (London, 1714).

[62] Gilbert Pilkington, *The Turnament of Tottenham* (London, 1631): Bedwell edited the title poem and then appended his treatise to it, foll. C1^r–E3^v. Thomas Gerard of Trent, *The Particular Description of the County of Somerset,* ed. E. H. Bates, Somerset Record Soc., XV (London, 1900), lies between the purely genealogical and the descriptive.

place. Nonetheless, it must be noted that the topographies were not really historical. Camden himself insisted that the *Britannia* was not a history, and apologized whenever he found himself retelling the past without some geographical connection. But Camden worked hard at getting his historical data right, and the topographers all too frequently went to very little trouble. The records were used to trace descents; and a book whose author took immense pains to straighten out a tangled genealogy might be marred by a tardy acceptance of the British History, or what little historical information it contained might have been taken from the pages of the *Polychronicon* or from the little handbooks of John Stow. Many of the topographers seem to have been intellectually isolated. They knew the *Britannia* and knew each other but were completely unaware of anything else. References to contemporary scholars such as Selden or Spelman or Ussher were rare. For these men the pattern had been set, and they had no intention of altering it.

Only one topographer can be accounted an exception to these rules. John Norden, unlike the others, was not a resident of the counties he described and thus did not suffer the compulsion of recording the landed wealth and heritage of himself and his neighbors. Instead, as a professional surveyor, he drew maps and the verbal pictures to accompany them. *Speculum Britanniae,* begun around 1591, was intended to cover all England, and at least one of its purposes was to keep its author employed. Lord Burghley, still in quest of exact geographical information, gave some assistance in the form of passes asking the local Justices of the Peace to help. Even that was not enough, and Norden eventually had to take up the writing of religious tracts in order to balance his budget.[63] Meanwhile, he had produced a *Preparative* to his project, a book which insisted on the necessity of examining the site, which pointed out the importance of history to the geographer, and which gave help to both geographer and historian by laying down a series of rules for interpreting town names. Norden was no expert on the various languages necessary, but he was less inclined than the scholars to indulge in wild etymologies, and his list of

---

[63] Alfred W. Pollard, "The Unity of John Norden: Surveyor and Religious Writer," *The Library,* 4th Ser., VII (1926), 233–252.

prefixes and suffixes was extraordinarily sensible.[64] Indeed, common sense prevailed throughout Norden's writing. He was unwilling to dismiss the British History because it solved so many problems and because nothing had been suggested to take its place: his view was that of Lambarde, that there might be some truth in Geoffrey and that it was unwise to dismiss him out of hand.[65] In his Cornwall, he was perfectly willing to believe that the land of Lionesse might have been swallowed by the sea, not only because he liked the story but because he knew of instances where the land had been devoured by the sea (and vice versa).[66] Moreover, Norden had a strong visual sense, a sense that was titillated by the vicissitudes of time as shown in ruins. Unlike almost everyone else in the sixteenth century, he went beyond describing a ruined castle merely because it was there: Norden almost automatically saw it peopled and thriving, as it must once have been.[67] His was the eye of the geographer come late to history rather than that of a historian forced into the field by the rules of his profession.

The historians of towns traveled along a road similar to that which had led to Camden's *Britannia*. Originally town histories had been little more than a frame to hold the documents necessary for governing. Such was certainly the case with John Vowell *alias* Hooker's description of Exeter. The son of a mayor of the town, Vowell had been educated at Oxford and traveled in Germany before he returned home and settled down as chamberlain of Exeter. Once the records of the town were to hand, he proceeded to arrange them in historical order, accompanying them with some explanation as he went. His massive collections were not published in his lifetime; instead, all that saw print was a short history and description of the city, drawn from his notebooks, emphasizing the heroism of the citizens when besieged by rebels in 1549 and before. Prefaced to the whole was an attempt to demonstrate the antiquity of Exeter by showing its connection to Brutus and his

[64] *Nordens Preparative to His Speculum Britanniae* (London, 1596), pp. 22–30.

[65] *Speculi Britanniae Pars: A Topographical and Historical Description of Cornwall*, ed. Christopher Bateman (London, 1728), pp. 1–3.

[66] Ibid., pp. 4–5.

[67] Ibid., pp. 79–82; see also his *Vicissitudo rerum* (1600), ed. D. C. Collins, Shakespeare Assoc. Fac. No. 4 (London, 1931), the first part of which concerns the relationships between heaven and earth; the second part, describing the effects on man, was never written.

Trojans. The total impression is one of bookishness. There is obviously no doubt that Vowell knew his town well, but, for all his acquaintance with the notes left by Leland, description did not come easily to him.[68]

By the time that John Stow followed with his *Survey of London,* almost a quarter of a century had passed. Meanwhile, Camden had written his *Britannia.* Even before that, the two men had become friends and each had aided the other. Strangely enough, there was a relationship between their books, however different their purposes and contents. Camden, at least in the beginning, was most interested in restoring the past, Stow in showing the historical antecedents of the present. Nonetheless, the structure of the *Survey* was based on that of the *Britannia.* Both books opened with general sections, in the one case of history, in the other of description mixed with history. Then they settled down to their proper business, the detailed examination of the ground. With that, it must be admitted, the similarity became less obvious. Stow knew his London better than Camden knew England, and he made much greater use of records. The reason for the first is clear enough, and the second can be attributed to the difference in purpose. That the similarity to the *Britannia* continued even here, however, can best be shown by comparing Stow to Vowell. Vowell must have known Exeter as well as Stow did London, and he probably knew the records (which were in his keeping) better. Yet a great gulf separated the two descriptions. Stow was not preserving records but using them to illuminate the history of each segment of London as he came to it. The crucial difference was one of method. Stow observed his city and then used his knowledge to broaden and deepen his observation; Vowell, when he observed at all, used present-day Exeter to expound his records. The combination of clear-sighted observation with historical material was the method of Camden—which is not a denigration of Stow, for he excelled his master.[69]

Stow had been bound to Camden by ties of friendship at a time

[68] John Vowell *alias* Hooker, *The Description of the Citie of Excester,* ed. Walter J. Harte, J. W. Schopp, and H. Tapley-Soper, Pts. II and III (Text), Devon and Cornwall Record Soc. (Exeter, 1919); *The Antique Description and Account of the City of Exeter* (Exeter, 1765).

[69] John Stow, *A Survey of London,* ed. C. L. Kingsford, 2 vols. (Oxford, 1908).

when the former had produced only small chronicles and the latter had written nothing at all. Moreover, both men had made the acquaintance of others in London with like interests: the heralds, the record keepers, the lawyers, all of whom had something of a professional motive for studying the past. Around 1586 these men formed themselves into a Society of Antiquaries.[70] They continued meeting for two decades, usually at Derby House, the home of the College of Heralds. Since most of the members were gentlemen, the meetings were held during the law terms, when men congregated in London. Attendance was compulsory, and everyone was expected to contribute (and the contributions, however brief, were to be prepared in advance). At least 198 such discourses have survived, read during 38 meetings, scattered through the years 1590–1607. Certain patterns can be traced, and it would seem that "courses" of lectures were arranged. From 1590 to 1594 there was one on the peerage; 1591–1594 saw another, running concurrently, on law; topography was the subject for 1599; and between 1601 and 1603 the history of the great officers at court was traced. At any given meeting there was, predictably, a good deal of repetition; so, for the benefit of the members, a secretary prepared a summary of the proceedings.[71]

Most of the papers shared certain characteristics. There was a great penchant for tracing the history of any subject as far back as it would go—or further. Hence, the papers were filled with conjectural identifications of names and with etymologies that were commonly overblown. On the other hand, there was a great respect for records. Historians were basing themselves more on rolls and charters, less on past chroniclers; lawyers, perhaps still feeling that the most recent precedent was the best, nonetheless wanted to go back to the earliest record they could find;[72] and some, at least, of the heralds were sufficiently skeptical of the old genealogies to

---

[70] Most of the following is based on Linda Van Norden, "The Elizabethan College of Antiquaries," unpubl. diss. (University of California at Los Angeles, 1946).

[71] One such appears to survive: *The Several Opinions of Sundry Learned Antiquaries . . . Touching the Antiquity . . . of Parliament* (London, 1658), pp. 1–27.

[72] R. J. Schoeck, "Early Anglo-Saxon Studies and Legal Scholarship in the Renaissance," *Studies in the Renaissance*, V (1958), 102--110.

wish to establish them on firmer ground. The presence of the record keepers encouraged this: it meant that the members of the Society had relatively easy access to the great storehouses of official documents, and it meant that men such as Arthur Agarde, Deputy Chamberlain of the Exchequer, forewarned of the subject of discussion, might rummage through the records in their keeping and produce something of interest to everyone. Thus the discussions took on a rather mixed tone: on the one hand, there was a rather excessive love of etymology; on the other, the latest techniques of documentation were used. Similarly, there was no set position on such matters as the British History, and no one was embarrassed to take up the cause of Brutus. In sum, the Society may be seen as an attempt to spread the doctrine of a new history, an attempt that was not entirely successful. Some of the members must have learned a great deal, and all learned something. It is nonetheless revealing that Camden, when he came to use the materials prepared for the meetings of the Society, included only a little in his *Britannia* and found room for the rest in a miscellany entitled *Remains of a Greater Worke concerning Britaine* (1605).[73]

The Society died probably because of the departure of its members. By 1607 some were dead, others had moved to their properties in the country, still others were in the service of the king. When Sir Henry Spelman tried to revive the Society in 1614, King James expressed some disapproval, and the plan fell through: by that date the political situation of the realm was reaching a point where a search into the origins of various institutions had political overtones regardless of the motives of the searchers. By that time, too, antiquarian study was being given another twist by the influx of new ideas from France.[74] Younger men, such as John Selden, were already beginning to make names for themselves along lines derived from Camden but owing some-

[73] The chapters "Epitaphs," "Allusions," etc., derived principally from Camden's addresses; some of the material came from the addresses of others.

[74] On the early seventeenth-century antiquaries, who fall outside my scope, the most important book is J. G. A. Pocock, *The Ancient Constitution and the Feudal Law* (Cambridge, Eng., 1957), pp. 1–123; see also F. Smith Fussner, *The Historical Revolution* (London, 1962), and David Douglas, *English Scholars, 1660–1730*, 2nd edn. (London, 1951). Pocock begins with French thought, and this line has been extended by Julian H. Franklin, *Jean Bodin and the Sixteenth-Century Revolution in the Methodology of Law and History* (New York, 1963).

thing as well to the legal scholarship of Bodin, Cujas, and Hotman. The comparative approach that the French had applied to law was being used to solve historical and religious problems as well. Selden investigated the history of tithes as if it were a subject no different from the history of anything else and applied to it, as to his other works, the canons of the new scholarship: records had to be used, manuscripts had to be looked at (and printed in the original language, not in translation), the authorities had to be weighed.[75] Philology, as understood by the humanists and developed by the theologians and antiquaries, had at last become the new ruler of the kingdom of scholars: "the truth is, both it [tithes] and not a few other inquiries of subjects too much unknown, fall only under a far more general study; that is, of true *Philology*. . . ."[76] The work of the sixteenth-century antiquaries had been completed and a new, more politically oriented generation was to use the tools supplied to erect buildings never dreamed of by those who first forged them.

[75] John Selden, *Opera omnia* (London, 1726), III, 1002–03 (*Titles of Honour*, on records); III, 1692–93 (Letter to Augustine Vincent, on MSS); III, 1336–37 (*A Review* [of the *History of Tythes*] on translation).
[76] Ibid., III, 1073 (*The History of Tythes*).

V

The Great Chronicle Tradition

Of all the forms of historical writing in Tudor England, the chronicle changed most slowly. The *Polychronicon* of the Middle Ages and the production of Raphael Holinshed and his associates in 1577 are clearly close relatives. What change did occur was due primarily to the influence of Polydore Vergil, and that, though pervasive, was perhaps less effective than is sometimes believed. The point may be illustrated by considering the Tudor chronicle generally and by examining the common features of those chronicles which will concern us for the remainder of the chapter, those of Hall, Grafton, Holinshed, and Stow. Speed's *History* (1611), with which we end, is sufficiently different to warrant exclusion here: by the beginning of the seventeenth century new forces were at work, though even these did not entirely erase the traces of the distant past.

Perhaps the most striking fact about any of these chronicles is the amount of random information they contain. A few reigns might have a noticeable structure (which was usually borrowed from Polydore), but even in these there was a vast quantity of miscellaneous matter which in no way contributed to the organization. The sources from which the chronicle was composed were never fully integrated, and the borrowings from the London chronicles, which were mostly of a localized nature, were inserted into a schema which might emphasize foreign affairs or internal revolution. The reason for this is not far to seek. Hall tells us of his work, "I have compiled and gathered (and not made) [it] out of diverse writers," [1] and Stow, much later, varies the statement only slightly when he informs us that his *Summarie* was put together by

---

[1] Edward Hall, *The Union of the Two Noble and Illustre Famelies of Lancastre & Yorke, . . .* (London, 1548), Dedication, fol. ii^v.

conference of "Chroniclers, out of whom I have gathered many
notable thinges, moste worthy of remembrance, whiche no man
heretofore hath noted." [2] There was no conception of history writing as selective: a historian did not remake the past in his own
image or in any other but instead reported the events of the past in
the order in which they occurred. The criterion by which a historian was judged was the quantity of information he managed to
cram between the covers of his book; if the matter of quality arose
at all, it was relevant to accuracy. Once facts could be established
as equal in authenticity, they were assumed to be equal in all other
ways as well. Thus Stow could pride himself on the amount of new
information he had found without worrying unduly about its importance. This attitude, in its turn, meant that the opening of new
sources of information was not, in itself, of particular importance.
The use of records in the Tower and of the manuscript chronicles
that kept coming to light improved the accuracy of the account to
some extent but also increased its size without in any way improving the degree of understanding of the past. What was required
was an increase in sophistication in using the new sources of
information, and that came much more slowly than the increase in
research.

Up to a point, chronicles developed by accretion. The reason
for this is evident if one considers the purposes of the authors.
John Stow's message "To the gentle Reader" was typical and has
the advantage of brevity:

Amongeste other Bookes, which are in this our learned age
published in gret nombers, there are fewe, eyther for the honestie
of the matters, or commoditie whiche they bringe to the common
wealth, or for the pleseauntnes of the studie and reading, to be
preferred before the Chronicles and Histories. what examples of
men deservinge immortalitye, of exploits worthy great renowne, of
vertuous living of the posteritie to be embraced, of wise handeling
of waighty affayres, diligently to be marked, and aptly to be
applyed: what incouragement of nobilitie to noble feates, what
discouragement of unnatural subjectes from wicked treasons, per-
nitious rebellions and damnable Doctrines: to conclude, what

[2] John Stow, *A Summarie of Englyshe Chronicles* (London, 1565), fol. a.ii[r].

perswasions to honesty, godlines, & vertue of all sort, what disswa-
sions from the contrarie is not plentifully in them to be found? [3]

Most chronicles accomplished all these ends, and some, whose
authors were theologically oriented, added to the list a demonstration of the mutability of man's fortune and of God's providence. It
proved impossible, however, to do all this and still arrange the
materials by any one principle of selection. Thus the comets were
included to show how God signaled forthcoming change; rebellions and the drastic fate that awaited rebels were included to
foster the peacefulness of Tudor England; lists of mayors, sheriffs,
and events in London had to be put in for the delectation of the
townsmen; battles were written up in great detail to encourage
nobility. Nothing could be omitted because any fact might become
the text of some historical sermon; even if the author was unable to
see its bearing, someone else might, perhaps, see further.

The same reasoning explains another common feature of the
chronicles. One of Polydore's legacies had been a heightened sense
of criticism. What is somewhat puzzling is why this criticism was
rarely brought to any sort of conclusion. Polydore himself is an
example of this peculiarity, and most of the chroniclers of the
century followed his example. If two or three inconsistent accounts
of some event existed, most likely all would be recorded, and it
was rare for the chronicler to make it clear which he favored. This
was partly due to an unwillingness to antagonize possible readers
by raising another controversy; moreover, on some issues, such as
the antiquity of Britain, considerations of patriotism supervened.
There was also, however, a deplorable lack of faith in the new
methods of criticism. Suppose the methods themselves were
wrong, or the chronicler's application of them inexpert, then some
potentially useful fact would be omitted and the inference that
might be drawn from it would be forever lost. The risk was more
than most chroniclers dared take, and so they contented themselves by leaving the final choice to the reader. The reader's choice
would presumably vary according to which of the several possible
motives for reading history had been adopted; but that was no

---

[3] *A Summarye of the Chronicles of Englande* (London, 1570), fol. [a.iv^r].

worry of the author who had done his job by providing the raw material for them all.

So much may be said about almost all of the sixteenth-century chroniclers and about their late medieval predecessors as well. Yet however great the similarities, differences arose as well, and the recurrence of the name of Polydore Vergil even in so brief a summary as this gives some indication of where to look for the origins of change. Polydore had found means to select some facts as more important than others; he had gone further and found patterns in the seeming confusion of the massed materials that constituted the English past. In his hands, for the first time, the reign became a proper unit for rearing the new edifice. To Polydore, unlike his predecessors (who had, after all, also divided their massive tomes by reigns, although that method was used as only one among several, even in one book), the reign became something more than merely a convenient means for giving dates to events. The English tradition, perhaps because of the influence of the lawyers, had always dated happenings by their regnal years. Polydore, by infusing the merely chronological reign with the personality of the particular ruler, produced not only a series of suitable divisions, differentiated by the accidents of birth and death, but blocs of time each dominated by the character of one man. By doing so, he made it inevitable that, sooner or later, those events that did not fit such a conception would be eliminated. Minor happenings in London, for instance, might be omitted if they could not be related to a greater theme. This result was not finally reached even in the work of the master, let alone in that of his immediate disciples, but it was implicit in Polydore's method, and he did move some way in that direction.

The reason for the reluctance to accept the full implication of Polydore's organization is clear from what has already been said about the confused purposes of the typical chronicler and, it may be added, even of Polydore himself. This, in turn, helps to explain another puzzling feature of the chronicles. From Hall onward, every large-scale chronicle unabashedly printed Sir Thomas More's *History of King Richard III* in its entirety, yet none of the authors seems to have been influenced by it. Some went so far as to interpolate additional matter into More's narrative, matter of the

sort they were accustomed to include in other reigns. Now what
More had done could be described as pushing Polydore's method
to its ultimate conclusion. His portrait of Richard was psychological, and it dominated the historical events entirely: the selection
was rigorous in the extreme. Everyone realized that the portrait
was brilliant and considered it unsurpassable; everyone printed it
and yet no one imitated it. The reluctance to give up the old ways
was too strong. In comparison, Polydore must have seemed rather
pedestrian and a good deal safer. If he was reluctant to face the
inevitable conclusion of his own methods, his successors could be
more reluctant still. Thus, though More's *History* was reprinted
more often than any other single piece of historical writing, its
influence was nonetheless negligible.

Presenting a reign as an entity led to other results. For one
thing, there had to be a certain amount of causation. There could
be no unity in the traditional listing of disparate and unconnected
facts. If the personality of the monarch were to be dominant, then
there was a need to show how it affected events. In Polydore's case
there was another step. However much he might have been taken
with the idea of personality, Polydore retained an abiding faith in
the direct intervention of the providence of God. The operations of
Providence had to be made clear. If one could assume that God
operated in mysterious ways only, that is, that His actions were
conditioned only by His will, there would be little to report. Man
could not presume so much. Occasionally, when Polydore reverted
to using Fortune as a causative factor, or when he was trying to
prove the mutability of man's estate, then the linkage between man
and God was broken. More usually, God acted as He did because
of the previous actions of men. King Edward IV forswore himself
before the gates of York; God saw to it that the sin was punished
by destroying Edward's young sons. Thus history remained a
moral subject in that it enshrined the woes that came to the sinner,
but it left the roots of action entirely in the hands of man. Edward
had to choose between a political decision and a moral one: his
perjury was a necessity if he were to recover his lost throne, but it
led to the loss of that throne in the next generation. A moral
decision would have lost him the throne at once but would also
have preserved the lives of his children. A man had to choose. The

intervention of God notwithstanding, the impact of personality
remained predominant as the chief cause of human history.

Thus the individual reign was unified by the causative factor of
human personality, and the principle could be applied as well to
small events as to large. By a further step, Polydore extended this
to include groups of reigns. We have already seen how Edward's
perjury affected not only his reign but that of his son; so Henry
IV's illicit seizure of the throne from Richard II meant that Henry's line would end with his own grandchild. In the end, the crown
came to Henry Tudor, a Lancastrian but so distantly related that
his own family had avoided the curse: the Tudors were justified
because they had not sinned in acquiring leadership. A later generation was to see things differently: because Henry VII extirpated
the remainder of the Yorkists, his line too did not extend beyond
his grandchildren. So the game could be played on, time without
end, though the rules were vague—who knew in what generation
the punishment would fall? However crude the method, the results
were salutary: facts had to be ordered in causative chains.

Polydore also made some attempt to improve the accuracy of
those facts. As an Italian he could feel a certain skepticism about
the grand tradition of the British History, and as a humanist he
was inclined to compare the account of Geoffrey of Monmouth to
the more familiar writings of the ancient Romans. Polydore never
quite went to the extreme of denying the old stories altogether, but
his commonsense doubts made it clear to his readers where he
stood. Thus to deprive his adopted country of a substantial and
irreplaceable part of its ancient history won Polydore few friends,
and had the same canons of intellectual doubt been applied rigorously throughout his book it is possible that he would have had
fewer disciples. In fact, Polydore loved portents and signs and
good stories, and his incisiveness was most commonly directed to
finding explanations, not to debunking his predecessors. He refused, however, to limit himself to one source, and he refused to
accept the obvious without a question. Where chronicles better
than the *Polychronicon* could be found, Polydore used them, and
his enthusiasm for Gildas alerted men to the idea that the oldest
rather than the most recent historian was best. After Polydore, it
was very nearly impossible to be unaware of the idea of anachro-

nism, and, as time went on, the whole English educational system and the very premises of the Reformation helped to reinforce the strength of that idea.

Polydore's history was brief, cut down to its essentials because of its purpose, that of explaining Englishmen and their past to the men of the Continent who were only just becoming aware of the island in the north. That is one reason why no complete translation of his book was ever published: for Englishmen the unfleshed skeleton was not enough. Instead, Polydore was published piece-meal, embodied in the work of others. In the first instance, Richard Grafton's continuation of the chronicle of John Hardyng (1543), the translation was almost verbatim. Grafton's Edward IV was pure Polydore; his Edward V was equally pure Thomas More, and this was continued as far into the reign of Richard III as possible, when Polydore took over once more; Henry VII was Polydore abridged, and it was only when Grafton reached Henry VIII that he became independent and that simply because the first edition of Polydore ended in 1509. One can hardly speak of Polydore's influence on Grafton in this instance, for there is virtually nothing of Grafton's in the book. Not until Edward Hall wrote his *Union of the Two Noble and Illustre Famelies of Lancastre & Yorke* was anything made of Polydore's new approach to the structuring of history. Hall saw in Polydore the justification of the House of Tudor; that had been one of the Italian's ostensible purposes, if not the only one. Because he saw Polydore in this limited way, Hall was able to go one step beyond him. There was no reason why the total history of England had to be retold if the emergence of the Tudors was the principal event that had to be explained. A limitation was possible, indeed necessary, and the form of that limitation was dictated by the concern at hand. Hall's history was to be that of the chaos of the Wars of the Roses, with the Tudors as saviors of the realm.

The theme of order was predominant. Hall's own life and prejudices led to that quite naturally.[4] A lawyer, a reader at Grey's Inn, common serjeant and under-sheriff of the City of London, Member of Parliament, Hall understood as well as any man the neces-

[4] On Hall, see A. F. Pollard, "Edward Hall's Will and Chronicle," *Bulletin of the Institute of Historical Research*, IX (1932), 171–177.

sity of order and knew that order came only from good kingship. Once the Reformation began and revolt once more became a reality, a good servant of the monarch had to fight with whatever weapons the situation offered. History had been used to provide a secure underpinning for the newly-arrived Tudors; it could be used as well to preserve them on the throne. Hall favored the Reformation, principally, one suspects, because it enhanced royal power. For him that was the reality. At one point he told the members of the House of Commons that "in chronicles may be found that the most part of the ceremonies now used in the church of England were by princes either first invented, or at the least were established," [5] and whatever his religious convictions, he agreed to act as one of the commissioners for the enforcement of the Act of Six Articles. Because Hall saw his own times as a kind of drama, as a morality in which chaos was the villain and order, in the person of Henry VIII, was the hero, he saw the past in the same terms. Each reign was an act in the play: Richard II's was a prologue, and then the others followed in an alternation of success and failure. Henry IV's time was "unquiet," Henry V's acts were "victorious"; Henry VI's reign was "troubleous," Edward IV's "prosperous"; the joint reigns of Edward V and Richard III were "pitifull" and "tragicall." It was not until Henry VII that relief came, and it was his "politike governaunce" that made possible the "triumphant reigne of king Henry the viii."

The scaffolding and some of the material came from Polydore, who had seen the fifteenth century in much the same way. But Polydore saw it too as only one part of the long sweep of English history, in which such alterations had occurred before, and accordingly his picture was painted in subdued colors. Hall, by concentrating on one point, heightened the effect enormously. The dispassionateness of Polydore was replaced by the boisterousness of complete involvement. Consider their reflections on the relief of Orleans by the French:

> [Upon the departure of the English] those of Orleance were sodenly replenished with all joy and mutuall gladnes, for that they had escaped so great daunger. Wherefore, referring the benefite

[5] Quoted by Mandell Creighton in the *Dictionary of National Biography*, s.v. Hall.

thereof to God, publique prayer was appoynted for sundry dayes togethers, they gave prayse to him in all holy churches, beseeching him of universall victorie. Here truly we may see that he sometimes getteth to litle who coveteth too much.[6]

Thus Polydore, who pointed only the moral that the English, by refusing to allow the town to surrender to the Burgundians, had lost it. Yet Hall, whose dislike of the French was violent, saw it differently:

After this siege thus broken up to tel you, what triumphes wer made in the citee of Orleaunce, what wood was spente in fiers, what wyne was dronke in houses, what songes wer song in the stretes, what melody was made in Tavernes, what roundes were daunced in large and brode places, what lightes were set up in the churches, what anthemes, wer song in Chapelles, and what joyc was shewed in every place, it were a long woorke and yet no necessary cause. For thei did, as we in like case would have dooen, and we beeyng in like estate, would have doen as thei did.[7]

Certainly the second passage was based on the first, for the verbal expansion was typical of Hall's treatment of Polydore. The difference lies in sympathy, for Hall was able to imagine himself in Orleans and Polydore could never leave his role of pious looker-on.

It will not do to leave the impression that Hall did no more than expand the work of another. For one thing, he had learned that other lesson of his master, to go behind his chief source to those other sources on which it too was based. Hall used the French historians; he used the obvious English materials such as the *Brut*, Trevisa, Fabyan, Hardyng, Caxton, and the chronicles of London.[8] Not all the expansions were merely verbal. Vast blocs of raw material were included—treaties, articles, and the like—and in this Hall followed the example of his English predecessors. Occasionally he added notices of natural occurrences—tempests, rains, famines. Sometimes he even outdid Polydore in his moral commentary. But in the end his debt is clear.

[6] *Three Books of Polydore Vergil's English History*, ed. Sir Henry Ellis, Camden Soc. (London, 1844), pp. 27–28.

[7] *Union*, Henry VI, fol. Cviii[r].

[8] C. L. Kingsford, *English Historical Literature in the Fifteenth Century* (Oxford, 1913), pp. 261–265.

In the matter of historical causation, much the same pattern emerges. The basic theorem, that the sins of the fathers shall be visited upon the children, Hall got from Polydore, although he made rather more of it. The same may be said of the influence of omens and prognostications, though here Hall displayed rather more skepticism: "This peace [between Louis XI and Edward IV] was said to be made, onely by the holy ghoste, because that on the daie of metyng, a white Dove satte on the very toppe, of the kyng of Englandes tent: whether she sat there to drie her, or came thether as a token, geven by God, I referre it to your judgemente." [9] On the occasion of Glendower's prophecies Hall pointed out that prognostications might be diabolical and pestiferous and that by them "many an honest man hath been begyled & destroyed." [10] In this, as elsewhere, Hall was more politically minded than Polydore; prognostications were all very well, but the faith of the French was known to be bad and no dove would make it better. The same political sense may be the cause of one other idiosyncrasy, Hall's emphasis on the uncertainty of fortune. The divine justice of God provided one form of causation, but there were times when it seemed inadequate, at least in the sense that man had no understanding of why God behaved as He did. Thus the politician Hall paradoxically found himself distrustful of politics and adopted the view that felicity comes only to those who seek to flee the world altogether:

> What trust is in this worlde, what suretie man hath of his life, & what constancie is in the mutable comonaltie, all men maie apparantly perceive by the ruyne of this noble prince [Richard II], whiche beeyng an undubitate kyng, crouned and anoynted by the spiritualtie, honored and exalted by the nobilitee, obeyed and worshipped of the comon people, was sodainly disceived by theim whiche he moste trusted, betraied by theim whom he had preferred, & slain by theim whom he had brought up and norished: so that all menne maie perceive and see, that fortune wayeth princes and pore men all in one balance.[11]

[9] *Union*, Edward IV, fol. CCxxxv^v.
[10] Ibid., Henry IV, fol. xx^v.
[11] Ibid., Henry IV, fol. xv^v.

It was not until this view was abandoned that true political history, in the sense that Sir Francis Bacon or John Hayward wrote it, could be produced; but Hall's principal purpose, the justification of the Tudors and the encouragement of order, depended less on inculcating a sense of political realism than it did on convincing men that certain forms of political activity were sinful and that political quietism was much the safest course open to them.

Hall left his work unfinished, and the task of completing it was left to his friend Richard Grafton, who had already published Hardyng with a continuation drawn from Polydore. Grafton at the end of his career himself began to compose chronicles, beginning with *An Abridgment* and concluding with the much more sizable *A Chronicle at Large*. The latter will take us back once more to Hall, but the former of these was derivative from a work which was the direct ancestor of most of the miniature chronicles of the second half of the century. There was nothing new in the idea of a compressed chronicle: several have already been considered as outgrowths of the manuscript London chronicles of the fifteenth century. *An Epitome of Cronicles* (1549), begun by Thomas Lanquet (who reached only the birth of Christ before dying at the age of twenty-four) and completed by Thomas Cooper, stemmed not from any native root but from the chronicle of Johann Carion. The German work was heavily theological: its organization centered around the idea of the Four Monarchies, and its purpose was to make the will of God more evident to man. Lanquet and Cooper adopted most of this but submerged it in a mass of additional material, much of it British. Nevertheless, the somewhat more detached attitude of a foreigner to events on the island penetrated even to those parts of the epitome which were not borrowed. Thus Lanquet, like Polydore, was much happier when he could leave the ambiguities of the British History and concentrate on the more reliable Roman narratives. The history of the early time "is full of errours, and hath in it no manifest apparance of truthe, as beyng written neither of no ancient tyme, nor yet by noo credible hystorian." Nonetheless, Lanquet and Cooper both used Geoffrey because they "wil not discent from the common opinion therof" though they compared his account with the others available.[12] These included Polydore, and thus Cooper was the first to publish the Italian's ideas about the early history of the island in English. Because of Cooper's reluctance to abandon Geoffrey entirely, a form of compromise was established, the terms of which are best illustrated in the life of King Arthur:

> Arthur, the sonne of Uter Pendragon, a strepling of xv. yeres of age, beganne his reigne over Britaine, and governed the lande .xxvi. yeres, havyng continuall warre, and mortall battaile with the Saxones. Of this Arthur be written many thynges in the englishe cronicle, of small credence, and farre discordant from other writers. But yet all agree, that he was a noble and victorious prince in all his deedes: and thei testifie, that he fought .xii. notable battailes against the Saxones, and was alwaie victour. But notwithstanding he might not clerely voyde theim out of his lande, but that they helde theyr countreys, whiche thei were possessed of.[13]

That view of Arthur was to be repeated continually.

An Epitome of Cronicles was sufficiently popular to be pirated by Robert Crowley in 1559, when it was once again safe to print a work so heavily tinged with Protestantism. Cooper, not unnaturally, resented the theft and brought out an edition of his own a year later in which he pointed out (rightly) that the piracy was slipshod work. The outrage was sufficient to make Cooper expand the last part of the book considerably; by 1565, with no such spur, Cooper himself became desultory. By that time Grafton had entered the competition. Annoyed, he tells us, by the number of errors in Cooper—one wonders if he had Crowley's edition in hand—and, as a good patriot, unwilling to see English history buried in a mass of extraneous matter, Grafton extracted what he wanted from the larger work of his despised predecessor. One finds the familiar judgment of Arthur, the little summaries of the character of each king; oddly enough, one finds no signs that he used Hall. However imperfect the performance, new editions were called for in both the succeeding years. By 1572, the competition of Stow had forced the addition of a vast heap of "almanac" information—vigils, fasts, tides, fairs, highways, and the like—but

[12] Thomas Lanquet and Thomas Cooper, *An Epitome of Cronicles* (London, 1569 [*recte* 1549]), fol. 32ʳ.
[13] Ibid., fol. 144ʳ.

little else had changed. It must be admitted that Grafton's abridgments are of little interest to the student of historiography except insofar as they illustrate an almost insatiable appetite for such fare and except for their having brought John Stow into the field.

Since it must have become evident to Grafton that he was losing the battle of the pocket-sized editions, he attempted to reestablish himself with a larger work. *A Chronicle at Large and Meere History of the Affayres of Englande and Kinges of the Same* (1569, 1568) was written from an ostensibly patriotic motive. It was to be a history of the proper size, concentrating on England and written by an Englishman because foreigners "have eyther by ignoraunce or malyce slaunderously written and erred from the manifest truth." [14] There was nothing the matter with the original idea, as the later success of Holinshed and Stow proved, and had Grafton lived up to his own promises his book might well have been a success. No one could doubt that there was interest in a book "Large ynough . . . without tediousnesse, short ynough without darknesse, meerely and onely of Englande, not mingling the same with foreyne matters impertynent to oure state, and finally true without misreporting, so farre as the following of the best Aucthors & reporters & mine awne experience (having of long time seene and purposely noted much therof) could conceave." [15] Moreover, Grafton, as editor of Hall and of Hardyng and as intimate of some of the Reformation leaders because of his printing of the English Bible and his role as King's Printer, ought to have had the knowledge of which he boasted.

Grafton lacked the imagination to put his knowledge to work. *A Chronicle at Large* was patterned after the typical histories of the fifteenth century: like them, it began with the Creation, moved on to the story of Brute, and divided the past into the usual seven ages. The sheriffs and mayors were not appended to the individual annals but appeared in a table at the end. The text was little more than an amalgamation of the obvious sources. Part I, a brief run through the period to the Norman Conquest, was compiled from Lanquet-Cooper, Fabyan, and the *Polychronicon,* and where

---

[14] Richard Grafton, *A Chronicle at Large and Meere History of the Affayres of Englande and Kinges of the Same* (London, 1569, 1568), The Epistle, fol. 2^r.
[15] Ibid., The Epistle, fol. 2^r.

these disparate sources conflicted, Grafton was content to let the
reader choose. The much fuller second part began as an amalgam
and ended as an abbreviated version of Hall. Grafton's pruning of
Hall's sometimes flamboyant prose can hardly be considered a
loss, and the omission of some documents did no real harm, but
Hall's judgments and attempts at finding causation were removed
with the rest, and the result was the conversion of Hall to an
ordinary annalist. In exchange, Grafton inserted some London
notes, which meant that Hall's shaping of his materials was buried
even deeper. Very occasionally, Grafton made an attempt to explain some mystery, but neither the mysteries nor the explanations
were political or historical: problems of coinage, why the Thames
might have an excess number of tides in one day, and so on. On
one rare occasion he seems to have gone out to investigate a
problem personally:

> And here Fabyan sayth [the occasion is the restoration of the
> liberties of London through the agency of Bishop Gravesend in
> Richard II's time], that for the great zeale and love that the
> aforesayde Bishop of London bare unto the Citie and Citizens in
> this their sute to the King for their liberties, they of theyr awne
> good willes to this day, yerely upon the feastful dayes, as the day
> that the Maior taketh his othe, which is the morowe after Simon
> and Jude, and Alhalowen day, Christmasse day, the Twelfe day,
> and Candlemasse day, when they go to Paules in theyr Livereys,
> they visite the place of his buryall, beyng in the middle Isle in the
> West ende of the Church, where the sayde Bishop is pictured and
> drawen foorth in Brasse, holdyng the Charter of the Citie of
> London, and the great seale of England in his hand. But it
> seemeth to me that this is not true, for the place of buriall in
> Paules, to the which the Maior doth resorte, is the grave where
> William, sometyme Bishop of London is buryed, of whom we
> have made mention in the first yere of William the Conqueror,
> who first obteyned the privileges for the Citie, and so it appereth
> by the inscription upon the same Gravestone.[16]

For the sake of comparison, it is interesting to see John Stow's
account of the same event:

16 Ibid., II, 383.

A fabulous booke compiled by a namelesse autor, but printed by *William Caxton* (and therefore called *Caxtons Chronicle*) reporteth these troubles to happen through a fray in Fleetestreete, about an horse loafe which was taken out of a Bakers basket, by a Yeoman of the Byshoppe of Salisburies, and that the same troubles were pacified, and their liberties were againe restored by meanes of *Richard Gravesend* Byshoppe of London, in reward whereof the Citizens repaire to the place of burial in the midle Isle of S. *Pauls* church, &c. but al that is untrue, for at this time *Robert Brabroke* was Byshop of London, and *Richard Gravesend* had bene Byshoppe, and deceased in the time of *Edward* the first, in *Anno 1303,* almost *90.* yeeres before this time. After whom succeeded. . . .

Moreover, the place of buriall in Saint *Pauls,* whereunto the Maior and Citizens of London have repayred, is of *William,* who was Bishop of London in the time of *William Conquerour,* who purchased the first Charter of the said king *William,* for the same Citie as I have before declared.[17]

Grafton, in short, was willing to check the accuracy of what was happening in his own day, while Stow took the trouble to determine the accuracy of the source; still, Grafton's later version was an improvement over that in his *Abridgment,* where the story was simply accepted.

Stow, quite rightly, pointed out that Grafton had borrowed his material without acknowledgment, and Grafton's reply, that he had himself written much of the work that passed under the name of Hall, was at best disingenuous, since it is perfectly clear that he did not understand in what way Hall was valuable.[18] It is some tribute to the Elizabethan reading public that *A Chronicle at Large* was the only history which did not have a second edition. About all that can be said in favor of Grafton is that he had judged the public appetite correctly even if he had been unable to satisfy it. There was a need for a large-scale English history, but it was not until the publication of Holinshed a decade later that one was available.

---

[17] *The Annales of England* (London, 1592), pp. 483–484; the same point was made in less detail in *A Summarye* (1570), fol. 243ʳ.

[18] The dispute is fully discussed in John Stow, *A Survey of London,* ed. C. L. Kingsford (Oxford, 1908), I, ix–xii, xlviii–liii.

The original plan for the work that came to be known as "Holinshed" resembled a kind of vastly enlarged *Polychronicon*. As its originator, the learned printer Reyner Wolfe, first conceived the project, there would be a world geography (complete with maps), to be followed by the histories of the various nations. Wolfe had hoped to be able to write it himself; gradually, as his collections increased in size, he abandoned that idea and turned the project over to his research assistant Raphael Holinshed. When Wolfe died in 1573 with the plan still nowhere near fulfillment, Holinshed had to turn elsewhere for the necessary funds. The syndicate of publishers who decided to risk supporting the project also insisted on limiting its scope: it was they who were responsible for its becoming a British history rather than a universal one. At the last moment the maps, too, were omitted. When in 1577 the chronicle finally appeared, it contained histories of England and Scotland by Holinshed, descriptions of Britain, England, and Scotland by William Harrison, and a description of Ireland, with a history, by Richard Stanyhurst, the whole illustrated with a series of delightful if not always appropriate woodcuts. It was easily the most sumptuous history published in England thus far.

To distinguish between the two editions of Holinshed is essential. Only the first was really Holinshed's in any strict sense; by the time the second appeared, a decade later, Holinshed was dead and the editorial direction had passed to John Vowell *alias* Hooker. Because most investigations of the book have been concerned with it as a source for the Elizabethan dramatists, especially Shakespeare, attention has been focused on the second edition, with perhaps an occasional glance spared for the first. The second edition was vastly the larger, but it was also much less coherent, and the notion of "Holinshed" as a badly articulated potpourri of diverse historical materials applies to Vowell's injudicious compilation rather than to the original.

Holinshed was much more aware of what was happening in the world of English scholarship than was Grafton. In the decade that had elapsed since the publication of *A Chronicle at Large,* Archbishop Parker and his associates had published a substantial number of the sources for the history of medieval England, and it became a great deal easier to go behind the volumes of Caxton, the

Polychronicon, and Polydore Vergil. Indeed, the reader of Holinshed is struck by the vast array of sources. For the earlier sections of the "Historie of Englande" there was virtually no relevant classical writer who was not at some time cited, and even in the later parts Holinshed continued to seek out new materials. Holinshed was rarely satisfied with merely one source, and he was much given to comparing the various reports of the same incident. The difficulty is that he never elaborated any method for deciding which source had priority, which should be followed. Holinshed had to the full the collecting instinct of the humanist historians —principally Polydore—but he lacked their skepticism. For him all sources were equal in value. His account of Caesar's invasion made use of Caesar himself, of Tacitus' *Agricola,* of Dio Cassius; but intermixed with these were references to Gildas, Bede, Geoffrey of Monmouth, and Fabyan. The position of the British kings during and after the Roman invasions was never clarified, and Holinshed eventually proposed a compromise:

> But where as in the common historie of Englande, the succession of Kings ought to be kepte, so ofte as it chanceth in the same, that there is not anye founde to fyll the place, then one while the Romane Emperours are placed in their steades, and another while their lieutenants, and are sayde to be created Kings of the Britaines, as though the Emperours were inferiours unto the Kings of Britaine, and that the Romane Lieutenants at their appoyntments, and not by prescripte of the Senate or Emperours administred the Province. But this may suffice here to advertise you of the contrarietie in writers, & now we will goe forth in following our histories, as we have done heretofore, saving that where the Romaine histories write of things done here by Emperours or their Lieutenants, it shall be shewed as reason requireth, sith there is a great appearance of troth oftentimes in the same, as those that be authorised and allowed in the opinion of the learned.[19]

The problem was that this solved nothing, and as the British and Roman histories were incompatible, the reader remained as confused as ever.

Obviously, none of this led to any historical scheme of selection,

[19] *The Chronicles of England, Scotlande, and Irelande* (London, 1577), I, "The Historie of Englande," 45.

and so Holinshed's *Historie* demonstrated most fully the idea that
history could be written by agglomeration. Holinshed's wide reading in the sources of English history was used not to determine the
truth in matters doubtful but merely to add more and more detail.
All the old legends were included; sometimes Holinshed expressed
a doubt, but he never made an attempt to resolve it. In any case,
many of the doubts were Polydore's, and Holinshed followed his
master in allowing the reader to make the final decision. The fear
that his selection would somehow deprive the reader of something
useful was carried by Holinshed to its ultimate conclusion, so that
in reporting the history of Scotland he followed the Scottish writers
even when he was almost positive that they were wrong, for he did
not wish, so he tells us, to deprive the Scots of any honor.[20] The
result of this accumulation was that there was virtually no attempt
to find the cause of events: without saying so, Holinshed leaves us
with the impression that establishing causality is also the task of
the reader. In a way, this made him the ideal source for the
playwrights; everything needful (and a great deal more) was included, but the "construction," the ordering of events, was left to
others, who thus could make of the multitudinous facts what they
would.

When there was any selection at all, it was not based on matters
of evidence but on morality. Holinshed shared the view that history should teach men, and especially princes, how to act. It was
this belief which allowed him, on one of the few occasions when he
came down definitively on one side of a dispute, to state that
Merlin had not conjured up a certain Welsh castle long attributed
to him: "Of the building of this Castell, and of the hinderance in
erecting the same, with the monstrous birth of Merlin and his
knowlege in prophesying, the Britishe histories tell a long processe, the whiche in Caxton, and in Galfrides bookes is also set
foorthe, as there yee may see: but for that the same seemeth not of
suche credite as deserveth to be registred in any sound historie, we
have with silence passed it over." [21] Obviously, the services of such
as Merlin should not be used by a Christian prince. One other
purpose also affected Holinshed's ordering of his materials: the

[20] Ibid., I, "The Historie of Scotlande," 32.
[21] Ibid., I, "The Historie of Englande," 122.

belief that discord was fatal to the survival of a nation. It was discord among the Saxons that allowed the Danes to conquer England; it was discord that allowed foreigners, papal and French, to wreak havoc in the England of King John. Beyond this, Holinshed offered his readers little guidance through the maze of information that he had presented them.

Holinshed's own approach to the writing of history thus left him open to the kind of editing that followed in the edition of 1587. John Vowell, and more especially his assistants Francis Thynne and Abraham Flemyng, simply carried further a method that was latent in the original work. Nonetheless, it is true that Holinshed had sufficient sense of order not to encumber his text with entirely extraneous trivia, however much he was inclined to include everything relevant to the narrative. The lists of various officers, the excursus on Exeter or on the manner of holding a Parliament, these were the additions of the later editors. Holinshed himself had not been given to the parading of that sort of out-of-the-way erudition, and his contribution to the great chronicle is best seen as a grafting of new scholarly methods onto an old root. If one could imagine a humanistically learned Ranulph Higden, writing a new *Polychronicon* in the third quarter of the sixteenth century, the book would much resemble Holinshed's.

An exception must be made of the section on Ireland. Written ostensibly by Richard Stanyhurst, both the description and the history were revisions of the earlier work of Edmund Campion. Stanyhurst, who knew Campion well, much enlarged his friend's rather hurried composition, but the tone remained Campion's. The patent lack of conviction with which the legends of the Irish were reported, the genial humor which saw the wilder antics of the natives with amused eyes, these were Campion's. So, more importantly, was Stanyhurst's account of the reign of Henry VIII basically that of Campion. This brief section, it may be argued, was the best thing in Holinshed's whole compilation, for Campion, and Stanyhurst after him, saw the history of the island as a drama played out among a number of powerful personalities, and the descriptions of the men who molded Irish politics in Henry's time are admirable. Moreover, there was a deliberate attempt to see the whole reign in this fashion, and the elaboration of how personality affected politics makes the causation in this episode the most satisfying in the volume. It is a tribute to the various editors of Holinshed that, regardless of their religious convictions, they recognized Campion's art, and their acknowledgment of a debt to a man whose name stood for the worst of treasons is honorable. But except for Stanyhurst, none of the other editors were able to match Campion's broad sympathy for things Irish, and John Vowell, who wrote the continuation of the Irish history, and who under normal circumstances was given to considering the study of history as of vast importance, was convinced that the Irish past was useful only in a negative way, by showing what happened to traitors.[22]

Holinshed was the last to attempt to write a totally comprehensive history, and the fate that befell his work in its second edition proved that the conception was unworkable just because of the continual advances in the techniques of historical research which would, in the end, increase the amount of available information past all hope of intelligibility. John Stow's history also grew by accretion because Stow never stopped seeking new information. The growth was never as great as all the new sources might have warranted, for Stow did work out some means of selection and did have criteria by which to judge his materials. The great quantity of his production—there were well over a dozen editions of his various histories—does enable one to judge how Stow learned his trade and how changes were worked in the fabric of the chronicle.

The most important fact about John Stow was his love of the past. Unlike most of his contemporaries, he saw the past and present as indissolubly linked and thus was inclined less to think of history as a pool of information whence moral examples could be dredged than as an explanation for what he saw around him. Moreover, this sense of continuity meant that—unlike those humanists who sought a link only with the classical age—he had no inclination to look upon the Middle Ages as deplorable, and that attitude was strengthened by his strong love for London and its records. It was entirely fitting that Stow should have begun his career with an edition of Chaucer, and there is some evidence that

---

[22] Holinshed, *The First and Second Volumes of Chronicles* (London, 1587), "The Conquest of Ireland," foll. A.ii^v–A.iii^r.

he edited Lydgate and Skelton as well;[23] moreover, bits of medieval verse enlivened his chronicles. John Manningham, who talked with Stow in 1602, tells a story which expresses Stow's attitude toward the past with great clarity: "He gave me this good reason why in his Survey he omittes manie newe monuments: because those men have bin the defacers of the monuments of others, and soe thinks them worthy to be deprived of that memory whereof they have injuriously robbed others."[24] That would seem to have been his attitude from the beginning, and because he felt so strongly about the matter, the poverty-stricken Merchant Taylor, ill-educated and unable even to take up his livery, set himself to school to become a historian.

A formal education could not have helped Stow with his English poets, but it might have made reading the chronicles easier, for there were rumors throughout Stow's life that his Latin was poor.[25] What precisely that meant it is difficult to say, for there is no doubt that he used Latin manuscripts. The most likely explanation is that he was unable to write good neoclassic Latin and that he read the language with more difficulty than a grammar-school boy. That, certainly, may provide a reason for his reluctance to accede to the request of Marshe, the printer, to revise Lanquet-Cooper's abridgment in competition with Grafton. Stow insisted that someone with more experience be assigned to help him, and Marshe persuaded William Baldwin, the editor of the *Mirror for Magistrates,* to do so. Unfortunately, Baldwin died soon after, and Stow was forced to work alone. The first edition of the *Summarie* (1565) was not prepossessing. Much of the early section was taken from Lanquet-Cooper almost verbatim, and only as he approached his own times did Stow make use of any new material of his own. His boast that he had gathered his materials by comparing chronicles and then setting down the most worthy things from each suggests that Stow was still unsure about how sources should

[23] William Ringler, "John Stow's Editions of Skelton's *Workes* and of *Certaine Worthye Manuscript Poems," Studies in Bibliography,* VIII (1956), 215–217.

[24] *Diary of John Manningham,* ed. John Bruce, Camden Soc. (Westminster, 1868), p. 103.

[25] Grafton said so; and so did Thomas James of Oxford: *An Apologie for John Wickliffe* (Oxford, 1608), p. 59.

be judged, and this feeling is strengthened by his admission that his principal sources were Fabyan, Hardyng, and Hall. Yet Stow insisted that he had written honestly, if crudely, and that "in hystories the chiefe thyng that is to be desyred is truthe." [26] That was to remain his motto for forty years.

Stow's entrance into the lucrative pastures of pocket histories was certain to arouse the antagonism of Richard Grafton, and although Stow claimed that he did everything possible to prevent a clash, eventually each of the antagonists publicly called the other incompetent. The details of the argument are best forgotten, nor is it of great importance to select a winner; what does matter is that Stow was forced to examine everything with great care, for any statement which was dubious was certain to be attacked. It was this attitude that led to Stow's clarification of the matter of Bishop Gravesend: in his first edition, Stow had accepted the tale as readily as Grafton, and it was not until Grafton had cast doubt on the story that Stow investigated it thoroughly. At about the same time, Stow's collection of manuscripts brought him into contact with the group around Archbishop Parker.[27] It is impossible to say whether Stow had had much previous contact with professional scholars, but within a very few years he became friendly with most of the antiquaries and historians in the kingdom. Some, such as Camden and Sir Henry Savile, were most interested in the classical past; others—Lambarde, Robert Glover the Herald, Recorder Fleetwood—in the Middle Ages. Harrison and Holinshed were busy with their own history, and Stow was able to assist them, just as he assisted Holinshed's successors a decade later.

The effects of Stow's contacts are fairly evident in the successive editions of his chronicle. By 1570 the list of authors put at the beginning of the book had grown considerably, and Stow used the opportunity presented by a few blank pages to describe some of his sources. Grafton's edition of Hardyng, he thought, was poor, and so was Polydore's of Gildas. The comment on Geoffrey of Monmouth is particularly interesting:

[26] Stow, *Summarie* (1565), fol. [a.iv^r]. The reference to Fabyan, Hardyng, and Hall is on fol. a.iii^v.
[27] He supplied some MSS for Parker's Matthew Paris, Thomas Walsingham, and *Flores historiarum*.

Galfridus Monumetensis, his Cronicle of the Britons is of some: scornefully rejected: wherein they shewe their greate unthanckfulnes, not to embrace him, who painfully for their behofe playeth onely the part of an Interpretour, litle wisedom to condemne that, which they cannot amend, or if they can, not to consider the time wherin he lyved. The true Histories may of a skilful Reader be well decerned from the false, and many things in him that seeme straunge are confirmed by the best writers of al Ages.[28]

This is a view of Geoffrey not far distant from Leland's and still closer to Lambarde's, but with the addition of one remark peculiarly Stow's—consideration of the time wherein Geoffrey lived. Stow had always had an awareness of anachronism, and the growth of this awareness was the primary factor in his development as a historian. There was nothing instantaneous in the process, and Stow was always reluctant to abandon one of the old stories. Certainly in 1570 the British History still dominated the *Summarie.* But the story of the conversion of England had been increased in size (one suspects the influence of Parker here), and there are evidences that the sources mentioned in Stow's list were being read and absorbed.

The most substantial changes occurred when Stow altered his format. Before 1580 all the editions had been small octavos or smaller sextodecimos; that is, he had worked within the framework of Lanquet-Cooper or had summarized still further, and the alterations in the text had had to be, perforce, minor. The *Chronicles of England* was a much larger book, appealing to a different market. C. L. Kingsford called the book "a sort of re-edition of the old Chronicles of London," [29] and this is true. The mayoral years, the lists of sheriffs, and the other trappings of the London chronicles were there, but a close examination of the beginning of the book indicates that substantial alterations had been made along lines far different from civil chronicling. A definite shift in favor of classical history can be noted, and for the first time Geoffrey of Monmouth was not allowed to take precedence where other materials could be found. A preliminary section, "Of the first habitation of this Islande," rejected the post-Galfridean Samothes because this story

---

[28] Stow, *Summarye* (1570), fol. [B.iv^v].
[29] *Chronicles of London,* ed. C. L. Kingsford (Oxford, 1905), p. xxxv.

derived from Annius of Viterbo's forgery of Berosus, but Albion
and Brutus remained. Nonetheless, though the early history of the
island was not omitted, it was severely compressed, and other
matters, such as the labors of the governor Agricola, were much
enlarged.

The cause of this shift seems to have been the influence of
Camden. In Harleian MS. 530, in the British Museum, there are
about a dozen leaves of material intended to be added to some
edition of the *Summarie* in order to aid its transformation into the
Chronicles of 1580.[30] The passages appeared verbatim from
1580 on, and they were in a hand which I take to be Camden's.
Among the passages was part of the section on the first inhabitants; there was a reference to an archaeological discovery made in
the Netherlands, of a lighthouse seemingly built by Caligula on his
abortive expedition to Britain; there were numerous citations, not
only to classical authors, but to humanists such as Hubert Goltzius
and Lilius Geraldus.[31] Taken together, these inserts amounted to
most of the Roman section of Stow's book, but they were arranged
in such a way as to disturb as little as possible the elements taken
from Geoffrey. Room was found for some of the British kings, but
only on the condition that they did not interfere with their Roman
overlords.

The precise relationship between Camden and Stow is difficult
to evaluate. Camden was the younger by a quarter of a century.
He had been trained at Oxford and in 1580 was undermaster at
Westminster School. By 1580, too, Camden had come into contact with Ortelius and, through him, with Continental scholarship.
Moreover, by this time his *Britannia* was already well under way.
In terms of training and in terms of what were the recognized
criteria of European scholarship, Camden was well ahead of Stow.
This may account for Camden's condescending tone, for he de-
scribed Stow to Ortelius as a man of great diligence but of uncertain judgment.[32] In a sense this was true; Stow was much less

---

[30] Foll. 79ʳ–95ᵛ, with some blanks.

[31] First inhabitants: fol. 82ʳ, *The Chronicles of England* (London, 1580),
pp. 15–16; the lighthouse: foll. 83ᵛ–84ʳ, *Chronicles*, pp. 36–37; Goltzius, fol. 83ʳ,
Chronicles, p. 35; Lilius Geraldus, fol. 82ᵛ, *Chronicles*, p. 16.

[32] *V. Cl. Gulielmi Camdeni . . . Epistolae*, ed. Thomas Smith (London,
1691), p. 12.

willing than Camden to give up the traditional—and nonhumanist—history of Britain, and it may well have cost Camden a considerable struggle to get his older friend to accept even as much of the new as he did. Yet Stow's library was essential to Camden. It was Stow who had Leland's manuscripts, a necessary component of the *Britannia*. And whatever may be said about Stow's judgment, his knowledge of the postclassical history of the island was unexcelled.

No complete list of the manuscripts that Stow owned—let alone those he read—has ever been compiled, but it is possible to get some idea of how he worked. C. L. Kingsford investigated Stow's sources for the fifteenth century and discovered that he had used Thomas Walsingham, Thomas Otterbourne, the "Translator of Livius," various of the London chronicles, the more obvious Hall, Fabyan, and Hardyng, certain French historians (Gaguin and Comines), poets (Gower and Hoccleve), and some of the official records such as the Patent Rolls, Close Rolls, and Inquisitiones post mortem.[33] To take another example: for the early part of the sixteenth century, Stow began with one manuscript chronicle (Harley 540), which constituted his principal source for Henry VIII up to the edition of 1580; then, as more and more material came to light, Stow used it to supplement and eventually replace his original manuscript.[34] Harley 540, like many another manuscript chronicle, was oriented to events in London: the material was detailed and local. In the early editions much of it had to be cut because of the limited scope of the *Summarie;* later, as Stow's own interests widened from the local to the national, much of Harley 540 became irrelevant.

It is evident from Kingsford's work that Stow copied whatever he could not purchase, and frequently the only surviving text of some chronicle or document is Stow's transcript. Substantial fragments of Stow's collections have survived, and some of these have been printed. Lambeth MS. 306 is a fifteenth-century chronicle, owned by Stow, but not much used by him because he had already

---

[33] Kingsford, *English Historical Literature,* pp. 266–271, and passim for references to MSS annotated by Stow.

[34] *Two London Chronicles from the Collections of John Stow,* ed. C. L. Kingsford, Camden Miscellany XII (London, 1910), v–vii.

found most of the material elsewhere. There were, however, blank leaves at the end, and on these Stow took notes of his own.[35] Some are transcripts: a proclamation made by Jack Cade in 1450 (plus some other documents relating to the same event), a description of the christening of King Henry VII's son Arthur, the method of making Knights of the Bath. Others of the notes described the events of Stow's own day and are in the nature of a retrospective diary. The account of the fire at St. Paul's in June of 1561 seems to be that of an eyewitness; it is certainly independent of the official story. Stow, of course, collected proclamations and the like as well, and the government's own explanation was the basis of his telling what had happened during the unfortunate withdrawal from Newhaven. Much of Stow's attention was focused on religious affairs, including even reports of sermons. The usual concerns of a city chronicler were, however, predominant: the price of food, peculiar weather conditions, Mayor Thomas Lodge's beard (it was the first) and his bankruptcy, and so on. Partly, this parochialism must have been due to the fact that this sort of information was most readily available, that to many of these events Stow was an eyewitness. But this must not be overstated. The notes were certainly written well after the event—when Stow wrote of Lord Darnley's departure for Scotland, he added "who afftarward maried the Quene of Scotts, &ct." [36] and it must be assumed that when Stow wrote them (sometime during the 1560's, at the beginning of his career as a chronicler) he still shared the outlook of those city chroniclers whose manuscripts he was using. Since even the 1580 *Chronicles of England* was still in the form of the old Chronicle of London, it is clear that Stow's ideas changed slowly, and one may say that even after Camden's suggestions were incorporated into his text, Stow still thought of himself as continuing the old tradition.

The difference between Stow and his predecessors was substantial nevertheless. Stow was much more interested in accuracy, and his protestations of concern for truth were not the usual commonplaces. In 1565 he had written that truth was the essential ingre-

[35] *Three Fifteenth-Century Chronicles,* ed. James Gairdner, Camden Soc. (Westminster, 1880), pp. 94–147.
[36] Ibid., p. 132.

dient of history; forty years later he was still saying the same thing, still searching for records so that the history could be corrected further. Stow disliked making errors, but he disliked leaving them still more. So he went to great trouble to ascertain what had happened. He had always liked the Arthur story and was more prepared than Camden to believe it. Cooper's chronicle had been mildly skeptical; Stow at first borrowed that view and then, with time, seems to have moved closer to the traditional view and away from that of the modernists. But he backed his opinion with some independent investigation. Arthur's twelve battles against the invading Saxons might be looked into:

> The twelfth at the hil or town of *Bath,* then named *Bathen-hil,* where many more were slaine by the force of *Arthur,* for he alone (saith *W. Mal.*) having the Image of our Lady sowed upon his armor, set upon *900.* of his enemies & with an incredible slaughter put them to flight, but now concerning this *Bath* before mentioned, it is to be noted, that *Bath* in Somersetshire standeth low, compassed above with hils, wherby it is evident, that either it is removed from that place where it stood in *Nenius* time, or els that the place which he called *Badonicus Mons,* was not this town it selfe, as *Leiland* & other conjecture, but some other high place neere, which is not unlikely, for at this day within a mile of it, over a town called *Bannar downe,* which is so called, either corruptly for *Bathendowne,* or els in memory of the banners displaied there, *Bannerdowne,* & seemeth to me both upon the sight of the place, and report of such as have gathered caps full of mens teeth in following the plow there, to bee the same that *Nenius'* (corruptly called *Gildas*) or *Beade* meaneth, though *Polidor* mistakes it for *Blanchemore.*[37]

Stow, so we are told, could never afford a horse, and it was a long walk from London to Bath but worth it. Another trip took him to Kits Cotyhouse, the supposed site of the burial of Vortigern's brother.[38] But most of his investigations demanded common sense rather than shoe leather. Like Foxe, Stow told the story of the death of King John, and it was a full and circumstantial one. But

[37] Stow, *Annales* (1592), p. 59.
[38] Ibid., p. 55.

Foxe was inclined to believe another story, that John had been poisoned by a monk, and here Stow parted company with him:

> Thus have I set downe the life (though much abridged) and death of king John, after the writing of *Rog. Windover, Rad. Niger, Rad. Cogshall* Canon of Barnewel, and *Mathew Paris,* and other, who all lived when the king raigned, and wrote for that time what they sawe, or heard credibly reported. Notwithstanding, I think good (as heretofore) to set downe concerning his death, as is reported in the common English Chronicle, sometime penned by a namelesse Authour, and continuer of *Geffery Munmouth,* and since printed by William Caxton, and therefore called Caxtons Chronicle. . . . But to conclude, howsoever hee died, certaine it is, that hee raigned with trouble ynough, as by the premisses may appeare.[39]

The materials, the references to the chroniclers, all could be found in Foxe; and Stow, like Foxe, printed both the variants. The difference is that Stow recognized the importance of the proximity of a writer to the events he is recounting, whereas Foxe was content to take Caxton's word, but it was nonetheless true that Stow received lessons in source criticism from Foxe's *Acts and Monuments*.

Stow's infinite care was the result of a love of the past for its own sake, and by the end of his career he no longer apologized for it. History was still useful to instill morality and patriotism, but it was much closer to the center of life than it had been and was no longer the shamefaced activity of monks who should have been at their prayers nor of merchants taking a holiday from their accounts. Stow pursued accuracy because he loved the past enough to do it justice. The increasing nationalism of Elizabeth's reign also played its part in transforming Stow from a London chronicler into something more. London was as important as ever, perhaps more so, but the pressure of events had altered the focus so that the city was no longer a quasi-independent microcosmic organism but part of a larger whole. The expansion of interest was nothing new; it had been going on at least since Polydore, who as a foreigner in the employ of the monarchy was more likely to con-

[39] Ibid., p. 256.

centrate on the history of the realm than on that of the city. Stow reached the same point by way of patriotism but reached it just as surely, and by so doing he recapitulated the whole development and thus moved from being a chronicler of small pretensions to something very like a historian.

Whether Stow could ever have become a true historian it is unfortunately impossible to say. His great history could not find a publisher because the market had been spoiled by Holinshed, and the manuscript has vanished. The result is that we know Stow only as a chronicler and cannot judge how he would have handled causation, nor how he would have welded the history of England into some sort of whole. As it is, even the relatively simple causative scheme of Hall was abandoned, and Stow limited himself to taking from Hall what he needed and supplementing it with an ever-increasing array of new material; and something of the sort was the case whenever Stow borrowed.

Stow selected his materials by the principles of relevance (and those altered, for example, from local interest to national) and source criticism, by which a bad story was replaced (not supplemented) by a better. But Stow's principles were not applied very rigorously because he learned them only gradually, and some seemingly dispensable facts survived from edition to edition. So the first attempt to write a general history of England as a single uninterrupted narrative was that of John Clapham. What Clapham thought necessary was ". . . one continued History collected out of approved Writers, and digested in such maner, as the Reader might neither be tired with the length of fabulous, and extravagant discourses: nor left unsatisfied in any materiall pointes, or circumstances worth his knowledge." [40] Clapham accomplished just that, as far as he got, but never finished his task: his second edition, much larger than the first, only reached the reign of Egbert. Moreover, Clapham's remark about "approved writers" represented a possible danger, and the sources he listed for his own work, while high in quality, were very few indeed in number. This new method of "continuous history," which was to

---

[40] [John Clapham], *The Historie of England* (London, 1602), fol. A3ʳ. Clapham's second edition was entitled *The Historie of Great Britannie* (London, 1606).

become part of the technique of the politic historians, thus was easily amenable to a kind of cleverness where bright phrases replaced solid thought; on the other hand, the method it replaced, that of Polydore, which left decisions to the reader, had the disadvantage of tedium if used too often. The solution to the problem was a kind of footnoting, and this was in fact coming into use at just this time.

John Speed was substantially influenced by Clapham's book, as he was by Camden's *Britannia* and others of the newer histories. The result was a history different from any of the chronicles that had preceded it. The *History of Great Britaine* was in a sense the pendant of an atlas and may have grown out of a feeling on Speed's part that his *Theatre* (which had done for Britain what Ortelius had done on a global scale) did not present enough information. The material printed on the reverse of the maps was, most of it, derived from Camden; if Speed wished to do something different, a history of the island (which Camden insisted his *Britannia* was not) offered the best opportunity. How much interest Speed had in history for its own sake is arguable; his mind seems to have been oriented toward the visual rather than toward the analytical.[41] Thus, some of the best pieces in the *History* were the descriptions of the lives and mores of the various invaders of Britain, an idea again derived from Camden but rather more "anthropological" than in *Britannia*. Camden required his descriptions as background; for Speed, they were essential if the changing character of English history were to be clarified. Hence, the illustrations which were prepared for the *History* were not only decorative. However, Speed's visual sense frequently put him in the position of including material purely for its attractiveness. Little was made of the numerous coins which were used to illustrate each reign, and even the inscriptions Speed quoted were more decorative than necessary.

The methods of antiquarianism, though not fully integrated into Speed's text, nonetheless constituted one enormous break from the

---

[41] John Speed, *The Invasions of England and Ireland with All Their Civill Warrs since the Conquest* (London, 1600): a large historical map with battles indicated, and listed in the margin. This can be seen as an attempt to reduce the whole history of Britain to the visual level.

usual techniques of the traditional chroniclers. Adopting Clapham's method of choosing the best authority and then writing a straightforward account was another. It was indicative of the way Speed's mind was working that the histories of the individual kings were more or less proportional in length to the duration of the king's reign rather than to the quantity of information available. Speed, like Clapham, was not averse to compression and omission: "The multitude of memorable things which present themselves to us in the lives of our *English Monarches,* is such, that if wee did not use choise, and in their relation brevity, wee should not relieve our Readers of that molestation, with which the vaste volumes of former labours doe oppresse the memorie." Among the items to be omitted were the great descriptive pieces with which Hall had adorned his writing and the endless lists which the editors of Holinshed had foisted upon their readers: "The vulgar Annals can tell you the splendor and glorie thereof [referring to the wedding of Prince Arthur and Catherine of Aragon], in apparrell, jewels, Pageants, banquets, guests, and other princely complements, the onely weighty businesse of many weaker braines." [42]

If much of what had once been included in chronicles was now to be omitted, what was the proper content of a history? For the early history of the island, the antiquaries supplied the answer and Speed used Camden's *Britannia* and Sir Robert Cotton's immense collections as an armory. The fabulous had to be limited, and though there was something to be said on both sides of the dispute over Brutus, Speed plainly was opposed to the older stories, going so far as to point out that there was little enough honor to be found in a Trojan descent. The true history of Britain began with the Roman invasions, and there was no firm ground for a historian before Caesar. The only remnant of the British History that Speed tried to salvage was the story of the natives' opposition to the invaders, and by a little ingenuity he managed to derive that from the Roman accounts. For Speed, throughout, opposed invaders; his patriotism was such that the very men he had excoriated in one chapter became heroes later when they, in their turn, had to fight for their adopted country. Thus one finds a series of portraits of

[42] John Speed, *The History of Great Britaine* (London, 1611), pp. 600, 747.

those who led the defense against the Saxons, and King Arthur, to choose one example, figured more prominently as one of that gallery than he did in the main text.

The defense of Britain was one unifying theme in Speed's book; kingship was another. By Speed's day, the British kings no longer were appropriate as examples, and he reduced them to a series of petty rulers under the Romans. Indeed, pre-Julian Britain had been an aristocracy, not a monarchy, and the unification of the island (or at least of England) was one of the major accomplishments of the Romans. So, logically, the emperors of Rome were the true kings of Britain, and Speed told the history of Britannia accordingly. With the decay of Roman rule, the kingship passed to the Saxons, and once Egbert was firmly seated on the throne, Speed could continue his monarchical history. The intervening period was filled up by deserting politics for religion: when the progress of kingship became an impossible theme, the progress of Christianity made an admirable substitute. Moreover, Speed insisted on judging kings on the basis of their ability to rule rather than on their morality, despite his belief in God's intervention in the world. Henry VI's sanctity was undeniable, but

> We shall behold notwithstanding in the tragicall glasse of this *Henries* raigne, how farre the imbecillity of the kingly person may affect the body politicke with good or evill. If histories were ordayned to stirre affections, not to teach and instruct, never any Princes raigne since the Conquest did better deserve to bee described with a tragical style and words of horror & sorrow, although the beginning (like the faire morning of a most tempestuous day) promised nothing more then a continuance of passed felicities.[43]

Under normal circumstances, of course, kings should not be blamed, and active traitors or the passively disloyal were responsible for the difficulties which oftentimes threatened England. But if a king put other matters ahead of his primary duty of ruling—as Henry VI, and Edward the Confessor before him, had done—then the king was blameworthy.

For all the emphasis on politics, Speed cannot be called a

[43] Ibid., pp. 650–651.

"politic" historian. Even aside from the matter of style, in which he followed the model of Livy rather than that of Tacitus, Speed was in no way attempting to give political instruction to rulers or magistrates. His purpose was moral: the best way of differentiating his attitude from Holinshed's is to say that Speed considered incompetent kingship a moral failing. Speed's kings were liable to judgment on two quite different counts: leadership and morality. Of Henry IV's possible involvement in the murder of Richard II, he said, "O *Henry,* if thou wert Author, or but privie, (though for thine owne pretended safetie, and for that errors cause which is lewdly mis-called *reason of state*) of such a murther . . ."; [44] and this proved as well as anything that kingship must be defined as good rule, as able leadership, but must never be allowed to degenerate into what was already being called Machiavellianism. God's judgment remained operative in this world; it was not removed to some higher level, where it might be acknowledged only to be ignored. Speed believed in the notion of Fortune's wheel, and like many of those who did, he equated Fortune and Providence. But he did not follow Polydore and Hall in making sin and its punishment the mainspring of history, and the intervention of the Deity was likely to be masked by politics:

> Wofull experience [the loss of Normandy] had now taught *King John* a lesson fitte to be learned of all Princes, whom the fawning world enstyleth most *Mighty,* that this their *might* is not onely lyable to the checke and dispose of that Highest all-ruling power, who unthrones them at his will; but even depends of the waving humors, and wils of those inferiour vassals, of whom they thinke themselves unresistable Commaunders.[45]

Thus God continued to rule his universe, but the activities of men had their place in it as well. A king should rule, and a historian should praise him and perpetuate his name; and the two, magistrate and subject, should be linked by the love for their native land.

The chronicle had undergone a variety of changes during the Tudor century. While Speed still shared certain theological pre-

[44] Ibid., p. 614.
[45] Ibid., p. 493.

suppositions with his medieval predecessors, almost everything else had altered out of all recognition. The influence of humanism, first in its literary and critical form, through Polydore Vergil, then as antiquarianism, by way of Camden, had forced the chronicle into new shapes. Polydore had taught two lessons: doubt and order. The world history, beginning with the Creation, ceased to exist, and as Polydore's skepticism, together with the new theories and new sources of information of the antiquaries, began to take effect, the pre-Roman part of British history became more and more abbreviated. Geoffrey of Monmouth's history became the subject matter for poets, but good historians, even those with some lingering faith, placed less reliance in the old stories. Instead, they substituted a history based as much as possible on the classic writers and, where they used Geoffrey at all, used him merely to fill in the gaps. So the early chroniclers wrote the history of Roman Britain in terms of the British kings and made what they could of Caesar and Tacitus; Speed, going to the other extreme, organized his history of Britannia by dividing it up under the rubrics of the Roman emperors and ignoring the British kings almost entirely.

Much the most important lesson the Tudor chroniclers learned was that of limitation, and it became more and more important to learn it as the chroniclers absorbed the humanist habit of searching for the sources behind the great compilations and thus vastly increased their stock of facts and documents. In the course of the century they abandoned the view that sheer quantity of information was somehow equivalent to quality. The reason for this was the gradual introduction of political motives into history writing. Hall, for reasons having to do with his defense of the Tudors, wrote about a relatively brief period because that was all that was relevant to his theme. Stow changed from a London chronicler to a national chronicler under the impetus of a rising patriotism. Grafton gave a similar reason for writing purely English history. And much the same was true of the antiquaries, such as Lambarde and Camden, who were becoming increasingly influential during the last quarter of the sixteenth century. Indeed, the increasing insistence on the reign as a building block in the chronicles, replacing (at least in emphasis) the Four Monarchies or some other theological unit, was due to similar causes. Polydore, who did more than anyone else to popularize the idea, must have been influenced by the fact that he was hired to write in defense of the Tudors. Hall did not need even so much encouragement. In an age of danger internal and external, it is not surprising that kingship should be defended to the utmost. And this may help account for the fact that More's attack on Richard was not widely adopted as a pattern for history writing; Polydore's method better fitted the exigencies of the times. With the emphasis on politics, a standard of relevance was available to the historian; but since none of the Tudor chroniclers entirely gave up the idea of history as teacher of morality and even theology, the standard when applied was applied unevenly.

Finally, the concept of anachronism was more fully understood than it had been, and this again enabled the historians to apply a limitation on their work. That, of course, happened slowly, since a good deal of historical information was necessary before anyone could use the idea. It is necessary to know something about a past age before one can argue that some reported fact or event simply will not fit into one's mental picture of that age. Thus the earlier chroniclers, already hampered by their theological predilections, were extremely reluctant to abandon any views on grounds of anachronism and solved the problem by printing variant accounts of the same event. By Stow's time, the quantity of detail had multiplied enormously and that reluctance was overcome, so that Clapham and Speed had no hesitation in scrapping an old and false story in order to replace it with another obviously more accurate.

VI

The Popularization of History

The Elizabethan age was more historically minded than most, and by the time the great queen died, books with at least some historical content constituted a fairly substantial bloc of the total production. Moreover, these were books of all sorts, written for a variety of audiences.[1] This fact, in turn, creates confusion for the historian of ideas. He not only must consider the phenomenon of cultural lag but must worry about the class of audience. It is easy enough to recognize the extremes, a Samuel Daniel writing for the aristocracy, or a William Elderton penning broadsides for the teeming populace. But what about the rest? Lumping together the unruly city apprentice and the staid country gentleman and calling the resultant mixture the middle class does not really help. Moreover, this kind of classification is itself ill-conceived. There is no difficulty in imagining a merchant with a relatively refined taste in chronicles whose appreciation of the poetry of, say, Spenser was negligible; and the courtier who followed the latest taste in sophisticated love lyrics might well have been content to get his history from one of Stow's pocket manuals. This consideration tells us something about cultural lag as well: obviously it varied with the individual, and the notion that the entire culture, or some large segment of it, was far behind a small group of leaders makes no sense. Some people—the poverty-stricken husbandmen, for example—no doubt were cultural laggards, but their very poverty prevented their buying anything more expensive than a broadside,

---

[1] There are no very complete statistics on the subject matter of sixteenth-century books: the best available are in Edith L. Klotz, "A Subject Analysis of English Imprints for Every Tenth Year from 1480 to 1640," *Huntington Library Quarterly*, I (1938), 417–419. Much the best study of popularization is Louis B. Wright, *Middle-Class Culture in Elizabethan England* (Ithaca, 1958), to which I am heavily indebted.

and the occasional picture we are given of a crowd of countrymen listening to a ballad singer makes one wonder if they even bought many of those. These members of the population have to be ignored, and about the rest it is surely impossible to generalize. The only solution to the problem is to look not at the readers but at the books and try to determine, where it seems useful, the audience aimed at by a particular author writing a particular book at a given time, and to judge the book in terms of what else was readily available.

The great flowering of historical literature did not take place until Elizabeth was well settled on her throne. One obvious reason for the slowness of development was the general disquiet of the times. The previous thirty years had not encouraged long projects, and the problem of keeping alive had overridden all other considerations. Nor had the humanist impulse had time or opportunity to ripen. Poets and playwrights and popularizers needed a body of information to use, and none such existed. Even the achievements of foreigners, ancient and modern, had not been made available, and the great age of history writing had first to be preceded by an age of translation. The translation of classical histories especially made rapid progress in the first two decades of the reign. Prior to 1558, there had been published the part of Caesar relating to Britain, Alexander Barclay had turned Sallust's *Jugurtha* into English to assist gentlemen (or schoolmasters) having difficulties with their Latin, and Sir Anthony Cope had rewritten Livy on Hannibal and Scipio.[2] The notices attached to the latter two works both mentioned that readers would be encouraged in "marciall prowesse, feactes of chivalrie," which was not quite the point.[3] Thomas Nicolls' Thucydides, however, must have been part of the humanist revival: it was dedicated to Sir John Cheke, though one is inclined to wonder if that learned Grecian would have approved of Nicolls' method, a translation of Claude de Seyssel's French which

---

[2] Caesar, *Julius Cesars Commentaryes . . . as Much as Concernyth . . . England* ([London], 1530); Sallust, *Here Begynneth the Famous Cronycle of the Warre . . . agaynst Jugurth,* trans. Alexander Barclay, 2nd edn. (London, [1525?]); Livy, *The Historie of Two the Moste Noble Capitaines of the Worlde, Anniball and Scipio,* trans. Sir Anthony Cope (London, 1544).

[3] *Anniball and Scipio,* fol. [a1ᵛ].

was in turn taken from Lorenzo Valla's Latin.[4] Nonetheless, Seyssel's preface, which Nicolls duly rendered into English with everything else, struck the right tone: gentlemen should put away their tales of Lancelot and Tristram and take up instead those of Pericles and Nicias. True eloquence and true morality came from the classic past, not from the imaginings of the Middle Ages.

There was back of all the early translations, from Nicolls' Thucydides on, the humanist's faith that proper action could be based on reading the right books.[5] Preface after preface repeated the classical story of Lucius Lucullus, who, on being sent to the East while still ignorant of military matters, studied all the historians, checked his conclusions with the soldiers around him, and then went on to a successful career as a general. Thus the translators, by making histories available, were doing their country a service. But such teachings were not the only reasons for translating or reading histories. Eloquence could be learned from the great historians; so could an understanding of God's purpose, for history showed the rise and fall of nations and God's judgments upon the wicked. More could be learned than personal humility; with the proper effort, the state could be maintained and divine punishment averted. The growing unity of England and the developing monarchy called forth the efforts of the translators, and the fact that many of them were young gentlemen at the Inns of Court, that is, near the center of administration, and that their books were dedicated to the great men at court only serves to confirm the view that a new patriotism was responsible for much of the educative effort.

This view was best summed up in the prefatory matter to Sir Thomas North's translation of Bishop Amyot's Plutarch. North himself pointed out that there was no "prophane studye" better than history, because "All other learning is private, fitter for Universities then cities, fuller of contemplacion than experience, more commendable in the students them selves, than profitable unto others. Whereas stories are fit for every place, reache to all per-

---

[4] Thucydides, *The Hystory*, trans. Thomas Nicolls (London, 1550).

[5] C. H. Conley, *The First English Translators of the Classics* (New Haven, 1927); Henry Burrowes Lathrop, *Translations from the Classics into English from Caxton to Chapman 1477–1620* (Madison, 1933). I have used both works in this discussion, though Conley overstates his point and requires cautious handling.

sons, serve for all tymes, teache the living, revive the dead, so farre excelling all other bookes, as it is better to see learning in noble mens lives, than to reade it in Philosophers writings." [6] Amyot's introduction carried the argument further. History supplied the examples for moral philosophy, but it went further by showing, and teaching, the operation of states. Amyot admitted that reading was no substitute for natural ability, but he insisted that history developed that ability in the best and most expeditious manner. No man could live long enough to gain by experience the skill he could acquire by reading. This was most important for rulers, who otherwise might have had difficulty in evaluating their experience. A court was full of flatterers who applauded whatever the prince did, but a history showed them similar actions and their results, and a historian long dead was no sycophant.

Despite the high-flown rhetoric of the introductions, much translation was the result of the translator's desire to satisfy the curiosity of his readers, that is, simply to impart information. The sentiments which were appropriate in a translator of Plutarch were less so when the works involved were the summaries of Eutropius or Justin or the anecdotes of Aelianus. Moreover, with the exception of Meredith Hanmer's collection of church histories, the translations were not in any sense scholarly.[7] Almost all of the renditions of Greek works came through intermediaries, sometimes Latin, more often French. Finally, it must not be forgotten that some of the early translators had definite political purposes in mind. The preeminent example is Sir Thomas Wilson's version of Demosthenes' orations, intended in this case to strengthen the English spirit against another Philip; but one might name as well Thomas Norton's expansion of Justin, written probably in 1569 with the recent northern rebellion very much in mind.[8] Norton had had previous experience in turning history to political account in his play of *Gorboduc;* now he put together a book of selections,

---

[6] Plutarch, *Lives of the Noble Grecians and Romans,* trans. Sir Thomas North, ed. George Wyndham, Tudor Trans. (London, 1895–96), I, 7.

[7] Eusebius, *The Auncient Ecclesiasticall Histories,* trans. Meredith Hanmer (London, 1577); see above, p. 113–114.

[8] On Wilson, see Lathrop, *Translations from the Classics,* pp. 193–194; [Pompeius Trogus], *Orations, of Arsanes,* trans. [Thomas Norton?] (London, [1569?]).

some classical and some modern, to persuade men to defend the cause of England and the true religion.

It was not until near the end of the century that the great Roman historians began finally to be made available in good editions: Sir Henry Savile translated Tacitus; and the Translator General, Philemon Holland, followed, first with Livy, then with Suetonius and Ammianus Marcellinus.[9] Holland, who somehow found time for his immense volumes in the intervals of schoolteaching and doctoring, produced translations of real value. Not only did he dress the Latin in an English which was becoming to it, but he made the reader aware of the complexities involved in studying the classical historians. The Livy included a chronology, explaining the problems of dating, a topography of ancient Rome, and a translation of Florus' abridgment to fill in the gaps where Livy's original was lost. For those who believed that Livy taught oratory as well as history—and Holland as a schoolmaster was among them—classified lists of the speeches, arranged by rhetorical type, were provided. Much the same pattern was followed in the other books: marginal explanations of difficult points and annotations, based on the latest scholarship, were appended to explain what was doubtful. Holland and Savile established the classical translation as prestigious, and one result was that some of the professional literary men took it up: Thomas Lodge prepared a Josephus (from the French and Latin) and Thomas Heywood a Sallust (again, primarily from the French), with an introduction borrowed from Jean Bodin's *Methodus*.[10] By 1610, the great days were over, but at least some part of each of the most important classical historians was ready to hand.[11]

A somewhat parallel movement, providing translations of more

[9] For Tacitus, see below, pp. 250–251; on Holland, F. O. Matthiessen, *Translation, An Elizabethan Art* (Cambridge, Mass., 1931), pp. 169–227; Charles Whibley, "A Translator Generall," in *Literary Portraits* (London, 1904), pp. 147–178. Livy, *The Romane Historie*, trans. Philemon Holland (London, 1600); Suetonius, *The Historie of Twelve Caesars*, trans. Philemon Holland (London, 1606); Ammianus Marcellinus, *The Roman Historie*, trans. Philemon Holland (London, 1609).

[10] *The Famous and Memorable Workes of Josephus*, trans. Thomas Lodge (London, 1602); Sallust, *The Two Most Worthy and Notable Histories*, trans. Thomas Heywood (London, 1608).

[11] Caesar had been done by Arthur Golding (1565), part of Polybius by Christopher Watson (1568), Appian anonymously in 1578, some of Herodotus (again anonymously) in 1584. Lathrop prints a complete list.

recent histories, was going on simultaneously. Lord Berners' Froissart emphasized chivalry in the same way that Barclay and Cope
had. Thereafter, the translations usually had an obvious political
purpose. Rendering Lorenzo Valla's treatise attacking the Donation of Constantine was part of the propaganda of the Reformation; Thomas Paynell's translation of the humanist Constantius
Felicius' book on the conspiracy of Catiline was a tract on obedience to rulers whose appropriateness to the last years of Henry
VIII is clear.[12] Similarly, there was a great interest in the Turks,
who constituted an ever-present danger, and in George Castriot
(Scanderbeg), who had proved, however briefly, that resistance to
them was possible.[13] Besides, there was an attempt to assimilate the
Protestant historiography of the Continent: some of Carion had
been absorbed by Lanquet and Cooper, and two editions of Johann
Sleidan's chronicle within five years presumably were the result
of similar motives.[14] Again, the quantity of translation increased
rapidly after Queen Elizabeth's accession. By the 1570's, moreover, a spate of books explaining contemporary Europe was also
being published, a reflection of England's increasing involvement
in Continental politics.

It must be mentioned once more that the ostensible motives for
translation were not the only ones. Many men simply were cu-
rious, and to slake the thirst for knowledge was one reason for
translating:

> Furthermore, seinge that everye man even naturally, is desirous
> to know suche thinges, as he is ignorant in, & that now a dayes
> especially (I know not by what motion) we desyre of all thinges

[12] [Constantius Felicius], *The Conspiracie of Lucius Catiline*, trans. Thomas
Paynell (London, 1541).

[13] Paulus Jovius, *A Shorte Treatise upon the Turkes Chronicles*, trans. Peter
Ashton (London, 1546); Andrea Cambini, *Two Very Notable Commentaries*,
trans. John Shute (London, 1562); [Pompeius Trogus], *Orations, of Arsanes*,
trans. Norton, at end; C. A. Curio, *A Notable Historie of the Saracens*, trans.
Thomas Newton (London, 1575); Jaques de La Vardin, *The Historie of George
Castriot, surnamed Scanderbeg*, trans. Z. I. (London, 1596); *The Mahumetane or
Turkish Historie*, trans. from French and Italian by R[alph]. Carr (London,
1600). The anonymous *The Policy of the Turkish Empire* (London, 1597) was
seemingly not a translation but should perhaps be included here, as should
Richard Knolles, *The Generall Historie of the Turkes* (London, 1603).

[14] John Philippson [Johannes Sleidanus], *A Famouse Cronicle of Oure Time*,
trans. John Day (London, 1560), and *A Briefe Chronicle of the Foure Principall
Empyres*, trans. Stephan Wythers (London, 1563). There was a later translation
as well: *The Key of Historie*, trans. Abraham Darcie (London, 1627).

to heare newes and tydinges, and to know of strange ambassa-
dours what is done in farre landes, I marvayle verye moche, why
then we be so ydle and slacke, to aske and serche for the same.
For trulye there is no ambassadour that can more playnlye and
certainley declare unto us what hath bene done from tyme to tyme
in everye countreye, then the cronicles & histories of the same
countreye. . . . These tydinges in verye dede and suche other lyke
allthoughe they be rather owldes then newes, yet trulye to all those
as hereto fore have not hearde tell of theym, they may well be
called newes.

We wil not sticke to spend a quarte of wyne or two of a caryer
or servingman that commyth out of the northe partyes to heare tel
what skyrmisshes hath ben betwixt us and the Scottes, & to know
which of our warryours played the valyauntest parte and pretyest
feate. . . .[15]

Then why not spend the time in reading histories? Similarly, it was
a good thing for merchants to know about distant lands. This
would encourage trade by removing unjustified fears and by tout-
ing the great riches that might be available. The burden of José de
Acosta's history of the East and West Indies was to show that the
natives were reasonable men, not savages, and knowing that fact
should make it easier to rule them.[16] The territories involved were
not English when Edward Grimeston published his translation,
but the information was as relevant to North America as to South,
and there were those—especially Richard Hakluyt the younger,
who commissioned many of these translations—who saw the
Spanish as perennial enemies and had no difficulty in envisioning
the Spanish lands in the hands of English merchants.[17] Curiosity
about the far away could thus be assuaged without guilt at wasting
time.

Moreover, as the dangers represented by the political aspects of
the Counter-Reformation increased, books were written to meet
the challenge. Some were intended for the military. In 1578 John
Polemon made up an anthology of famous recent battles, derived

---

[15] Jovius, *A Shorte Treatise upon the Turkes Chronicles,* trans. Ashton, foll.
[*iii^v–*iv^r].
[16] *The Naturall and Morall Historie of the East and West Indies,* trans.
E. G[rimeston]. (London, 1604).
[17] George Bruner Parks, *Richard Hakluyt and the English Voyages* (New
York, 1928), pp. 161–166, 262–267.

from a variety of foreign historians—a book which included, among other things, the first translation of any of Guicciardini; the popularity of the book was sufficiently great to warrant a continuation.[18] At least one classical translation was produced for the same reason, for Clement Edmondes' *Observations* on Caesar were principally comments for military men.[19] The advantages of a strong monarchy had to be emphasized, and the numerous writers on the Turks never failed to point out that the great powers of the Sultan produced a unity which, when matched against the divisive self-interest of the Christians, produced success after success. In the troubled circumstances of a country in the midst of Reformation, facing the power of Spain, the lesson was taught in a myriad of ways ranging from the Homilies to translations ostensibly about something altogether different. The same argument was frequently propounded in the books concerning contemporary France. The dangers of disunity were clearly evident across the Channel, and when the histories of the religious wars were translated, even good Protestants, who saw the French civil war as the struggle between God and Satan, were inclined to take up a *politique* position emphasizing the dangers of discord. This had the additional advantage of enabling them to argue that the Catholic position was essentially political: the Guises were described as seeking personal power rather than Catholicism, and as willing to hand their country over to the hated Spanish in the process.[20] Applying the moral to England was not difficult.

For modern politics as for Roman history there was a "Translator Generall." Philemon Holland is well known; Edward Grimeston has received less than his due.[21] Where Holland had been a schoolmaster, Grimeston, appropriately, had been a minor public

[18] [John Polemon], *All the Famous Battels* (London, [1578]) and *The Second Part of the Booke of Battailes* (London, 1587).

[19] *Observations, upon the Five First Bookes of Caesars Commentaries* (London, 1600).

[20] See J. H. M. Salmon, *The French Religious Wars in English Political Thought* (Oxford, 1959), Appendix A; see, e.g., A. Colynet, *The True History of the Civill Warres of France* (London, 1591), which depicts the Guises as conspiring against the Crown; and Anon., *The Mutable and Wavering Estate of France* (London, 1597), which shows France as a looking glass for England.

[21] On Grimeston, see F. S. Boas, "Edward Grimeston, Translator and Sergeant-at-Arms," *Modern Philology*, III (1906), 395–409. Boas lists all the works translated by Grimeston.

servant of the English mission in France who, upon being relieved
of his post, turned to translation and kept at it even after becoming
Parliamentary-Serjeant. Grimeston provided detailed histories of
those countries with which the English had most dealings: the East
and West Indies (published at about the time that the treaty with
Spain was being negotiated), France (based on de Serres, much of
whose work was already available because of its emphasis on the
wars of religion), the Low Countries, Spain. In 1615 he translated Pierre d'Avity's *The Estates, Empires & Principalities of the
World*, a general history more brief for each country than his
earlier studies and in the current fashion of general guidebooks
then popular. Once the Thirty Years' War had broken out, an
Imperiall History naturally followed. In the meanwhile, as the idea
of history as politics gained ground, he translated Pierre Matthieu
on Louis XI. Unlike Holland, Grimeston was no scholar, but he
was willing to alter his methods as tastes changed. The first edition
of his translation of de Serres was a vast compendium of information, not all of it French: the book was an enormous chronicle.
But learned taste found this insufficient, so Grimeston added some
political causation to his second edition and also removed the
non-French material, thus improving the organization. A similar
pandering to current taste probably accounted for the alterations
in the history of the Netherlands, where the increased emphasis on
the heroic deeds of Englishmen in the Dutch struggle for independence may be traced to a cooling of the friendship between
Dutch and English in the years between 1609 and 1627. Thus
where Philemon Holland taught his readers, Grimeston was taught
by his; all the same, the array of his translations made it easy for
ordinary Englishmen to educate themselves on the subject of the
history of Europe.

There was, then, in the years after 1558, a substantial growth
in the knowledge of history. Some of it was due to the influence of
humanism; some, as England more and more appeared belea-
guered, to patriotism. At the same time there was a development in
native chronicling which marched step by step along with the
translations. All this was in a sense necessary. The increasing
pressure from Spain made isolation impossible, and men needed to
know about the theater of operations and wished to know, for the

sake of inspiration, about their own past. Moreover, as we have seen, English Protestantism itself encouraged a historical outlook, and if Calvinists were less interested in the development of religion than in its biblical roots, still the Puritan ethic encouraged education in any form. Arthur Golding made the point as early as 1564. Time, he tells us, is given us by God, and we should not waste it: if we cannot ourselves actively do good for others, at the least we can write about those who have done so.[22] Good deeds are essential, but so is the historian who records them and permits goodness to inspire posterity. A lover of England, be he Puritan or Anglican, had to read histories and, if he could, write them or translate them.

The translations and the great chronicles were written for the members of the upper and middle classes, that is, for those with sufficient education and money to buy them and understand them. These works in a sense were themselves already popularizations; it was their fate to be vulgarized by men who were content to rewrite them for those who were poorer either in money or training. This was due, in part, to the fact that it was easier to boil down a book in English than one in a foreign tongue, and some of the popularizers seem to have been only a notch above their audiences in learning; more important, though, was the fact that the translations and the chronicles made the market for popularizations. Shakespeare read Holinshed; his poorer customers, inspired by his chronicle histories, presumably read Stow's manuals or books of the sort of John Taylor's collection of woodcuts of English monarchs with attached verse descriptions. And here the notion of cultural lag is appropriate. Taylor and Anthony Munday, and others like them, writing for the least educated segment of the populace, continued to enshrine myths that more serious historians had treated skeptically a generation or more earlier.[23]

The pocket chronicles were a link between the tomes of the serious historians and the pastiches of the popularizers, simply because Stow's and Grafton's little books had a double derivation. On the one side, they descended from the London chronicles of

[22] Pompeius Trogus, *Thabridgment of the Histories . . . Collected . . . by . . . Justine,* trans. Arthur Golding (London, 1564), fol. [*v^r].
[23] John Taylor, *A Memorial of All the English Monarchs* (London, 1622); Anthony Munday, *A Briefe Chronicle, of the Successe of Times* (London, 1611).

the fifteenth century; on the other, their popularity was due to the increasing taste for historical literature which is so obvious during Elizabeth's reign. The features which made popularizations of their little books were grafted on as time progressed, so that one has the feeling that they become less sophisticated rather than the reverse. What began as an abbreviation gradually took on an individual character as the emphasis was shifted back toward the activities of Londoners and away from more general history and as the almanac material attached at both ends increased in scope and quantity. One can only suppose that the wealthier merchant bought the sumptuous folios of Holinshed or the less grand but still large *Annals* of Stow, while his poorer brother—or his apprentice—purchased the abridgments.

There would be a similar step down the ladder from the great classical historians and their modern successors to the handbooks such as that of John Bishop. Bishop's *Beautiful Blossomes* (1577) provided the moral substance of history without the pain of narrative by reducing the march of events to a series of little stories, carefully explained: here one could learn to beware of Fortune, and to trust in God, without having to extract the lessons for oneself. For those unwilling to put forth even so much effort, Richard Johnson and Thomas Deloney converted the more amusing episodes of English history into ballads; [24] but there is a question here whether those remarkably inept poetasters were attempting to cash in on the taste for history or the more recent craze for historical poetry in the manner of Daniel and Drayton. There is, however, little to be gained from elaborating a description of this sort of historical writing; it is enough to say that it existed, and that its existence indicates the widespread demand for history writing even on the lowest levels.

This is not to suggest that the poets need not be taken seriously. The best of them not only spread a knowledge of history but made positive contributions to its study. Beginning with the authors of the *Mirror for Magistrates* and continuing to Daniel, Drayton, and beyond, the poets helped to give a shape to historical narrative that was previously lacking. A poet had to do more than retell facts: he

[24] Johnson, *A Crowne-Garland of Golden Roses* (London, 1612); [Deloney], *Strange Histories* (London, 1602).

had to select certain parts of the chronicler's narrative as more important than others, and his principle of selection would inevitably give some sort of shape to the tale as he told it. If this was done unconsciously or clumsily, the result was likely to be a bad poem; if an appropriate pattern was used consciously, the resulting poem would have a unity and a force not in the chronicle from which it was drawn.

When William Baldwin collected together the men who were to write the *Mirror for Magistrates,* the only models for this kind of selection were the *de casibus* tragedies of Boccaccio and his follower John Lydgate and the *History of Richard III* of Sir Thomas More. The latter was still very new and the implications of achieving unity by psychology still unexplored. Thus it was entirely natural that the pattern to be followed should be Lydgate's *Fall of Princes,* and the original plan was to reissue that work with a series of added lives "chiefly of suche as Fortune had dalyed with here in this ylande." [25] The original plan collapsed when the lord chancellor applied the Marian prohibition of histories to the projected continuation; when Elizabeth's accession removed this constraint, the publisher decided to issue only the continuations. Thus the book that appeared was a collection of lives, mostly from relatively recent English history, each ostensibly told by the ghost of the hero or heroine to one of the authors of the anthology; and to hold the book together, prose links recorded the conversations of Baldwin and his collaborators as they set about their task.

The basic conception lying back of the book was that of history as a "glass," as "a myrrour for al men as well noble as others, to shewe the slyppery deceytes of the waveryng lady [Fortune], and the due rewarde of all kinde of vices." The advantages of reading history were thus twofold: in princes, it encouraged virtue; in ordinary men, a lack of faith in their own ambitions and a healthy distrust of the constancy of Fortune. By and large, it was better to be good than to be a success, and the man who performed well in the rank that God had assigned him was better off than he who

---

[25] *The Mirror for Magistrates,* ed. Lily B. Campbell (Cambridge, Eng., 1938), p. 68; the introduction is essential. See also the same author's *Tudor Conceptions of History and Tragedy in "A Mirror for Magistrates"* (Berkeley, 1936) and Willard Farnham, *The Medieval Heritage of Elizabethan Tragedy* (Oxford, 1956), pp. 271–303.

tried to alter to his own advantage the relationships established by the Deity. Inevitably, there was a notion that history is repetitive, for this could not be avoided in any history resting on a moral base. Like crimes had to have like punishments; to escape the latter, it was enough to avoid the former. Inevitably, too, there was a good deal of difficulty in the matter of assigning motives. How much can one blame a man who has been torn from the heights by the claws of Fortune? Moreover, if Fortune was overemphasized, what of God's providence? And if God's vengeance was to be demonstrated, then it was necessary to extend that vengeance over several generations: "Blood wyll have blood," though that might involve punishing men who had themselves done nothing to deserve the lightning of the Lord. Even purely human motives raised difficulties. Richard II's chief justice, Tresilian, was certainly greedy and deserved his fate, but part of his crime had been a too-eager obedience of his master: "To serve kings in al pointes men must sumwhile breke rules." [26] How was the lesson of obedience to rulers to be squared with that of responsibility to God?

It is easy to pose such questions and almost as easy to avoid answering them. More than one smooth-flowing poem mixed man's will, Fortune, and Providence with no concern for logic or the subtleties of interplay. Whatever we think of Baldwin and his friends as poets (and their stanzas often plod leadenly enough), they deserve admiration for facing the questions they posed. The individual lives might teach virtue in a simple sense—do good or you will be punished—but the book as a whole was concerned with the related but great problem of free will. The structure of *de casibus* tragedy inevitably led to an emphasis on Fortune simply because the pyramidal pattern of rise and fall suggested it. Fortune's wheel first raised, then lowered; indeed Fortune commonly raised a man in order to lower him:

> For whyles that Fortune lulde me in her lap,
> And gave me gyftes mo than I dyd requyre,
> The subtyll quean behynde me set a trap,
> whereby to dashe and laye all in the myre:

[26] *The Mirror*, ed. Campbell, pp. 68, 99, 77.

But this was too capricious. Instead, a compromise was proposed:

> I blame not Fortune though she dyd her parte,
> And true it is she can doo lytell harme,
> She gydeth goods, she hampreth not the harte,
> A vertuous mynde is safe from every charme:
> Vyce, onely vyce, with her stoute strengthles arme,
> Doth cause the harte to evyll to enclyne,
> Whiche I alas, doo fynde to true by myne,

The emphasis was now on man, but Fortune had retained some place, however insignificant; and since that place was unspecified, the confusion remained. The author of Jack Cade went further. Cade himself asked

> Shal I cal it Fortune or my froward folly
> That lifted me, and layed me downe below?

and then answered his question by stating that in every man lust (will) and reason warred, and that in most there was such weakness that lust won out.

> Now if this happe wherby we yelde our mynde
> To lust and wyll, be fortune, as we name her,
> Than is she justly called false and blynde,
> And no reproche can be to much to blame her:
> Yet is the shame our owne when so we shame her,
> For sure this hap if it be rightly knowen,
> Cummeth of our selves, and so the blame our owne.[27]

The logical ending to this line of reasoning was a recommendation to quiet and otherworldliness.

In Jack Cade's tragedy, man was made responsible for his own misdeeds with no excuses. Yet when the authors met in conclave, they found such doctrine too strong, for they saw in Cade's rebellion an example of how "God dysposeth all thynges," and in Cade himself "one of Fortunes whelpes." Providentialism had at all costs to be saved, and though Cade was personally guilty and justly destroyed, still "this I note . . . concernyng rebelles and rebellions. Although the devyll rayse theim, yet God alwayes useth them to his glory, as a parte of his Justice. For whan Kynges and

---

[27] Ibid., pp. 87, 102, 171, 172.

chiefe rulers, suffer theyr under officers to mysuse theyr subjectes, and wil not heare nor remedye theyr peoples wronges whan they complayne, than suffreth GOD the Rebell to rage, and to execute that parte of his Justice, whiche the parcyall prince woulde not." [28] With that the circle was once more complete, the tragedy could serve as a glass to kings and subjects alike, and the issue of free will was once more disposed of as satisfactorily as it was likely to be.

If any emphasis were to be placed on man's will, then a moral judgment could not be made on the basis of an action's result.

> I say the cause and not the casual spede,
> Is to be wayed in every kinde of dede.

This, in turn, led to criticism of the chronicles, and rightly so:

> Unfruytfull Fabyan folowed the face
> Of time and dedes, but let the causes slip:
> Whych Hall hath added, but with double grace,
> For feare I thinke least trouble might him trip:
> For this or that (sayeth he) he felt the whip.
> Thus story writers leave the causes out,
> Or so rehears them, as they wer in dout.

> But seing causes are the chiefest thinges
> That should be noted of the story wryters,
> That men may learne what endes al causes bringes
> They be unwurthy the name of Croniclers,
> That leave them cleane out of their registers.
> Or doubtfully report them: for the fruite
> Of reading stories, standeth in the suite.[29]

But here other difficulties supervened. The sources which the authors of the *Mirror* had used did not supply much causation, yet the causes had somewhere to be found. Moreover, the authors sometimes disagreed among themselves. Two suggestions were made. One was that the nobility should see to it that the sources lying back of the chroniclers should be published, and this was admirable. The other was considerably more dangerous. It was decided, sensibly enough, to follow Hall in most cases, but "where

[28] Ibid., pp. 170, 178.
[29] Ibid., pp. 144, 198.

we seme to swarve from hys reasons and causes of dyvers doynges, there we gather upon conjecture such thinges as seeme most probable, or at the least most convenient for the furderaunce of our purpose." [30] Once the purpose of a history was allowed to control the sources, there could be no end to the confusion that resulted.

The achievement of the *Mirror* was thus great, and the lackluster poetry and carelessness with sources should not be allowed to overshadow an honest and quite successful attempt to solve the basic problems facing a historian who wished to preserve man's free will and God's providence together. The *Fall of Princes,* to which the *Mirror* was to have been appended, had already begun the process of selecting some aspects of a man's career as more worth recording than others: the wheel of Fortune had to be exemplified. The *Mirror,* with its insistence on causes and on the responsibility of the hero, carried this further, and so the personages represented were less like types than they would have been in Lydgate. This is not to suggest that a full-fledged drama of character appeared miraculously and at one stroke, but a first step—and a long one—had been taken.

To an age which considered light reading sinful, the *Mirror* was a blessing: it had all the advantages of history and was easy to read. However lightly we treat it, in its time the *Mirror* was thought of as a profoundly serious book, and its readers were right to think so. This explains why the book was so often added to, so often imitated, why the line of the progeny of the *Mirror* extended well into the seventeenth century, and why men should still wish to read it when much better poets were at work. The additions of 1563 closely resembled the originals, and it seems probable that most of these had been ready in Queen Mary's time: they included Sackville's Buckingham and his Induction, and Thomas Churchyard's Jane Shore, the best poetry and the most famous of the lives respectively. These additions and those of 1578 and 1587 continued the original pattern in that the personages came from recent history. Others saw an opportunity to turn Baldwin's success to their own account, and they did so by writing of men whose lives were found earlier in the chronicles. In his *The First Parte of the*

[30] Ibid., p. 267.

Mirour (1574), John Higgins still thought of his work as a "glass" for princes, and his introduction spoke of the virtues of Prudence and Temperance, but the order within the individual lives escaped him. Higgins was too much given to narrative, to presenting Geoffrey of Monmouth in verse, with the result that the pattern of rise and fall was submerged beneath a mass of trivial and frequently irrelevant detail. As for Thomas Blenerhasset's *Second Part* (1578), the less said the better. There was hardly anything historical in his imaginative portraits, and it is clear that he, like Higgins, never quite understood what Baldwin's intentions had been. Their additions were blemishes on the original, and it is their work which has given the *Mirror* a bad name.[31]

The popularity of the *Mirror* continued unabated. As the century neared its close, better poets than Baldwin (let alone his continuators) took up the idea. Samuel Daniel's *Complaint of Rosamund* demonstrated that character could be put at the center of an episode and extraneous historical matter severely pruned away. With that as inspiration, others leapt into the arena. The elder Giles Fletcher brought the mysterious Richard III to life once more; so, twenty years later, did Christopher Brooke.[32] By that time, the political atmosphere had changed; so perhaps had the moral. Richard was still a hardened villain, but a villain of a different sort. Fletcher saw him as trapped by his own ambition, unable to leave off his villainy; and, for all the talk of evil, Fletcher had Richard unrepentant—a radical departure from the *Mirror* tradition—and certain that a crown was worth securing at whatever danger to one's soul. Brooke carried the emphasis on psychology further than anyone before, but added to it the newer fashionable emphasis on "policy." His Richard had planned everything from the beginning and had killed Prince Edward, Henry VI, his own brother the Duke of Clarence, and his nephews with no other intent than to seize the throne when opportunity offered. Richard had become a Machiavellian villain, and the talk of For-

[31] Higgins and Blenerhasset were edited by Lily B. Campbell in *Parts Added to The Mirror for Magistrates* (Cambridge, Eng., 1946).

[32] "The Rising to the Crowne of Richard the Third," in *The English Works of Giles Fletcher, the Elder*, ed. Lloyd E. Berry (Madison, 1964), pp. 123–132; Brooke, *The Ghost of Richard the Third* (London, 1614).

tune being overmastered and in turn overmastering stemmed from the Italy of Machiavelli, not from that of Boccaccio. Compared to this, Thomas Storer's Wolsey was conventional and Christopher Middleton's Humphrey, Duke of Gloucester, negligible.[33]

One point that has emerged already from this discussion of the *Mirror* tradition is that in the course of fifty years the proportion of history to moralizing altered in favor of the former. In the years that had elapsed since the first two editions of Baldwin's work a vast number of chronicles had been printed, and these, far from slaking the thirst for historical information, had only whetted it. Patriotism, connected to the war with Spain, must have been one reason. For a time, indeed, the Privy Council even ordered Christopher Ocland's *Anglorum praelia* to be used in schools as a Latin exercise, and that book was no more than a paean in praise of the English ability to win battles.[34] Moreover, during the queen's reign, Englishmen seem to have learned to be a little less serious. Writers like Robert Greene might pretend that their books had some educative value, but no one could have been fooled. More and more purely entertaining literature appeared, and so the amusing aspects of studying the past, whose existence had always been acknowledged, came to have a place of their own on the literary scene. Serious historians still thought of their endeavors as useful, and Puritans frowned on mere entertainment as godless self-indulgence—witness Golding. Other Englishmen, however, were prepared to enjoy their history in the form of drama or poetry, and there were plenty of writers to see to it that they could.

The very popular *Albion's England* (1586 ff.) of William Warner is one example of the sort of book that this new taste produced. Around a framework of history, much of it Galfridean, Warner wove a series of tales. Some were from classical mythology, some from the mythological history of England. There was enough information about events to keep up some sort of chronological progression (though even this collapsed toward the end), but the history was nearly irrelevant. The dialogue between Vul-

[33] Storer, *The Life and Death of Thomas Wolsey Cardinal* (London, 1599); Middleton, *The Legend of Humphrey Duke of Glocester* (London, 1600).
[34] Foster Watson, *The Beginnings of the Teaching of Modern Subjects in England* (London, 1909), pp. 79–88.

can and Mars, in Book VI, took much more space than all the events of the reigns of Henry IV and Henry V. If anyone doubts Warner's quest for popularity, it is only necessary to compare his passing over Rosamund in Book V, where she belonged, with her obtrusion into Book VIII (added 1592), where she appeared in the unlikely company of Mary Tudor—but then Daniel had just published his *Complaint*. Warner's book goes far to document the insatiability of the late Elizabethan craving for history in any form: a dull book, written in plodding fourteeners, it went through seven editions in twenty years and remained popular even when more talented poets had turned their attention to similar subjects.

In Michael Drayton almost every form of historical poetry can be found. Over a long career, he tried all sorts of narrative poetry; and, because he was a pathological reviser, each poem exists in several versions. In the 1590's he adopted the fashionable mode of historical romance, and the heroine of his *Matilda* (1594), who preferred death to the advances of King John, is the converse of Daniel's more pliable *Rosamund*. A few years later he invented a new mode, adapted from Ovid, in *Englands Heroicall Epistles,* a series of pairs of letters exchanged by famous lovers of the past, and in these romance has all but submerged history. The *Mortimeriados* was a somewhat similar production, a mixture of romance and comment about kingship, full of sententious dogma but not at all analytical. At the same time Drayton was also writing in the vein of the *Mirror*. *Piers Gaveston* was drawn from the chronicles—Drayton had Stow's help and used his manuscripts—but the old emphasis on mutability, on Fortune, remained, though overlaid with a cloying eroticism. Indeed, of the early poems the most interesting, if least successful, was the *Tragicall Legend of Robert, Duke of Normandy,* which, instead of following the pattern of the *Mirror,* began with a long discussion between Fame and Fortune and then divided up Robert's far from spectacular career between the two as each of the ladies laid claim to him. The resultant confusion leaves the reader with two pictures of Robert and makes it almost impossible to follow his career; moreover, Fame had to triumph over Fortune (which means, really, that virtue had to defeat vice), and since Robert's real career was a heedless and unsuccessful race toward self-aggrandizement, Drayton had to falsify it in order to achieve the result he wanted. Nonetheless, if the historian's task was to judge the past, this poetic balance sheet marked a step toward a system of evaluation.

The popularity of the historical romances did not long survive the turn of the century, and when the newer analytic vein became fashionable, Drayton rewrote his poems accordingly. Much of the eroticism vanished from *Piers Gaveston,* and the caprices of Fortune gave way to the steadier if still baleful influence of Fate. The *Mortimeriados* was transformed into *The Barons Warres,* in imitation of Daniel's *Civil Wars.* The "sentences" remained, but politics became much more obtrusive; realism replaced the romantic, but the causes of events were still very general, and the attempt to become philosophical, in the manner of Daniel, failed. Only in the new *Legend of Great Cromwell* (1607) did Drayton finally achieve a coherent picture. Cromwell became more than Foxe's Reformation figure: he was seen as the pattern of the "new man" rising to the top by his own merits. Fortune still turned her wheel—*Cromwell* was the only one of Drayton's poems to be included in the final rescension of the *Mirror*—but it was a new man's Fortune, specially adapted to peculiar circumstances. Moreover, in this poem Drayton achieved his aim to be analytical. He saw Cromwell as the first modern politician, carrying the methods of Wolsey to their logical extreme, but doing so by introducing Italian statecraft:

> And my experience happily me taught
> Into the secrets of those Times to see,
> From whence to *England* afterward I brought
> Those slights of State deliv'red there to mee,
> In t'which there then were very few that sought,
> Nor did with th'humour of that age agree,
> Which after did most fearefull things effect,
> Whose secret working few did then suspect.[35]

Not until *Poly-Olbion* was finished did Drayton return to the older forms of historical poetry. *The Miseries of Queene Marga-*

[35] Michael Drayton, *The Legend of Great Cromwell,* in *The Works of Michael Drayton,* ed. J. William Hebel (Oxford, 1931–41), II, 458. Much of my commentary is drawn from the notes in the fifth volume of this edition, prepared by Kathleen Tillotson and B. H. Newdigate.

rite and *The Battaile of Agincourt* were both attempts at classical epic poetry, and both were, in a way, successful. In *Queen Margarite,* Drayton dropped the categories of Hall: there was no talk of blood calling forth blood. Instead, Drayton saw the mid-fifteenth century as a cockpit for the ambitious, and he created a unity for the period (perhaps following Shakespeare) by putting Margaret rather than Henry VI at the center. The Queen and Suffolk had been confederates from the beginning, seeking their own advantage; and it was this very ambition that brought such troubles on their own heads:

> For they betwixt them turn'd the Wheele of *Chance,*
> Tis they cry up, tis they that doe debase. . . .[36]

Thus Fortune became a metaphor for human frailty, and her reappearance throughout the poem was intended to suggest the unexpected turns that can occur when too many selfish men seek their own way. For all that, the poem was too diffuse, too close to history in verse, saved only by its emphasis on Margaret as a person, a mixture of good and evil, not a type.

Of Drayton's historical poems, the epic *Battaile of Agincourt* is the most successful, simply because of its limited subject. The causes of events were not given in any detail, nor did they need to be. There was no problem of internal conflict, of psychology. The usual comparison to Drayton's superb ballad on the same theme is unfair: obviously a short poem, having no narrative freight to carry, moves more easily. But in the longer poem Drayton's self-conscious epic borrowings work: the list of the ships sent, the county pennants, provided the right sort of color and allowed everyone to identify with the heroes. The account of the battle was perhaps too long and too gruesome, but the need to create a few personalities made that inevitable. The mixture of poetry and history, of invention and fact, was perfect. The Homeric catalog of ships was pure invention but was inspired detail all the same. In small compass Drayton managed beautifully; the grand manner, Daniel's manner, was beyond him.

Not that Drayton lacked ambition. Few men would have made the decision to versify Camden's *Britannia;* fewer still would have

[36] Ibid., III, 78.

persisted in the effort regardless of discouragement. Drayton probably conceived the idea of writing an epic around 1594 and was busy on it a few years later. But he had his living to earn and little time to spare for his great project. So the first part was not printed until 1612, and the complete *Poly-Olbion* had to wait another decade. By 1612, however, epics (and especially historical epics) were no longer in fashion, and Drayton's preface was a lament for an opportunity lost:

> In publishing this Essay of my Poeme, there is this great disadvantage against me; that it commeth out at this time, when Verses are wholly deduc't to Chambers, and nothing esteem'd in this lunatique Age, but what is kept in Cabinets, and must only passe by Transcription; In such a season, when the Idle Humerous world must heare of nothing, that either savors of Antiquity, or may awake it to seeke after more, then dull and slothfull ignorance may easily reach unto: These, I say make much against me. . . .[37]

Indeed, one wonders whether the poem would have been very popular at any time. Not only was it very long—this would have been counted in its favor—but the verse form, Alexandrines, lacked variety. Moreover, the allegory leaves the impression of having been superimposed. Camden had organized *Britannia* around the river systems of the various shires; Drayton borrowed the idea and converted the rivers to nymphs. There was a gain in that much of the poem could be put in direct discourse but a loss in that some confusion resulted. Drayton, too, felt that the various legends, beginning with Brute, had to be included; then he asked his friend John Selden to append historical notes, and Selden was more than a little skeptical of the British History. The result was a kind of warfare between poetical text and prosaic notes, from which only one conclusion could be drawn: hereafter the British History might serve the poets but not the historians. By removing Geoffrey to the land of fancy, Drayton performed an important service, but whether he served the cause of poetry, or even that of topography, remains an open question.

Daniel shared Drayton's ambition but was in a better position to indulge it. The advantages of patronage were surely somewhat

[37] Ibid., IV, fol. v*.

dubious, but they were preferable to the strenuous exertions needed to earn a living in London's literary underworld. Daniel had the blessing of time, not only time to write long works but time to think about their construction. That even this was not an unalloyed blessing is true, for one result was that he did not finish any of his major works, but even the truncated carcasses were substantial. In any case, it took some daring to embark on a poem whose scope was to be the same as that of Hall's history, for this meant that Daniel was setting himself up to compete not only with Hall but with Baldwin's *Mirror*. These circumstances and Daniel's own cast of mind insured that he would write a philosophical poem: characterizations would be general, because men were at all times in essence the same. Thus the civil wars were treated not as actions interesting in themselves but as paradigms demonstrating the deformities of dissension and rebellion. And Daniel glorified once more the attitude expressed by Hardyng and Hall, that ambition was bad but was excused, at least somewhat, by weak kingship. Unlike Hall or Hardyng, however, Daniel saw ambition in political terms rather than as a mortal sin; and where Baldwin and his friends had used the *de casibus* method to demonstrate that whoever tried to rise must inevitably fall, and that the best way to save oneself not only in the next world but even in this one was to remain quietly in the station that God had assigned, Daniel argued the same conclusion on political as well as personal grounds:

> And how much better for him, had it beene,
> T'indure a wrong with peace, then with such toyle
> "T'obtaine a bloody Right? since Right is sinne,
> "That is ill sought, and purchased with spoyle.
> But, this so wretched state are Kingdomes in,
> Where one mans Cause, shall all the rest imbroyle:
> And oft, t'advance a Tyran to a Crowne,
> Men run t'undoo the State, that is their owne.[38]

Daniel, as we shall see again, is a historian of great interest, but a reader has qualms whether this makes for good poetry. A reading of Drayton and Daniel, who do more with historical poetry

[38] Samuel Daniel, *The Civil Wars*, ed. Laurence Michel (New Haven, 1958), p. 189; Daniel's philosophy is considered in terms of politic history below, Ch. vii.

than any of their contemporaries, makes one feel the justice of
C. S. Lewis' remark that "the historical epic is . . . a *genre* dis-
eased at the heart." [39] At their best, the historical poems were chal-
lenges to thought: this was true of the *Mirror,* of some of Drayton,
of much of Daniel. But while no one wishes to argue that poetry
should be bereft of thought, it is fair to say that a play of ideas is
not by itself enough to make a good poem. And historical poetry
degenerated too easily into romance or verse-chronicling, into the
unredeemable epic of Warner or the still worse attempt of William
Slatyer to revive all the old legends in his imitation of Drayton,
The History of Great Britanie (Palae-Albion), or the sheer bom-
bast of Thomas May's *Edward the Third.*[40] At their best, the
poet-historians taught that history should be seen through character or through some controlling idea; at their worst, they made of
history a plaything for idle minds.

Much the same may be said of the dramatists. The problem to
be solved was similar: how could a series of tenuously related
events be portrayed in such a way as to give the action unity? The
solution to some extent depended on the past history of English
drama. The morality play had tended toward concentrating on a
single characterized abstraction—Mankind or Everyman—and
using him as a focal point. The very earliest history plays, Bale's
King Johan and Sackville and Norton's *Gorboduc,* were rather
more diffuse but succeeded in achieving a minimal cohesion by the
use of politics. Bale had written against the pope and in favor of
the monarchy; Sackville and Norton were suggesting marriage to
the young Queen Elizabeth and made their case by showing the
dire effects of a disputed succession. Thus when Marlowe and
Shakespeare came upon the scene, two roads lay open. Marlowe
chose the former and concentrated on personality, though his hero
no longer demonstrated the effects of vice and virtue but instead
exhibited the Italianate trait of *virtù.* If the hero were prepossessing enough—if he were a Tamburlaine—the result could be exciting. Even a bad king, an Edward II, could be placed at the center,

[39] *English Literature in the Sixteenth Century excluding Drama* (Oxford,
1954), p. 532.
[40] Slatyer, *The History of Great Britanie* (London, 1621); May, *The Victorious Reigne of King Edward the Third* (London, 1635).

provided that the defect of character thus revealed was actually the wellspring of the action. After a point, however, Marlowe's answer to the question of unity ceased to be valid. It was no help when the king was a minor or otherwise incapacitated; nor did it assist the playwright whose conception of history extended beyond the events of a single reign. Unity by force of personality thus gave way to something new or at least was relegated to particular situations. To create order out of the confusion of the episodic chronicle play was the achievement of Shakespeare, and he did it by rejecting the idea of "plot" (an orderly progression of events toward a climax) and substituting for it the method of "construction." [41]

As Shakespeare practiced it, construction meant the organization of a seemingly episodic play around some central idea.[42] The first part of *King Henry VI* had no plot in the traditional sense of the word. The play had a beginning but no real end; it was to be continued in the second and third parts. The action moved between France and England, between court and battlefield. Yet clearly the play was about something and was not merely an attempt to stage the variegated happenings of the first part of a long reign. In this case, it may be argued, the hero was *Respublica,* the commonweal of England, and the action centered around the effects on England of the personal ambition of overweening noblemen. The movement back and forth across the Channel was symbolic, offering the spectators a contrast between the disunity at home and the concentration of the French; similarly, the selfishness of the courtiers was contrasted to the singlemindedness of Talbot. The result of jealousy and ambition was the loss of France, of the heritage of Henry V. Much the same may be said of the rest

---

[41] The idea of construction is stated most clearly by Hereward T. Price, "Construction in Shakespeare," *University of Michigan Contributions in Modern Philology,* No. 17 (May 1951). My discussion of the dramatists is indebted also to Lily B. Campbell, *Shakespeare's "Histories": Mirrors of Elizabethan Policy* (San Marino, 1947); E. M. W. Tillyard, *Shakespeare's History Plays* (London, 1944); M. M. Reese, *The Cease of Majesty* (London, 1961); Irving Ribner, *The English History Play in the Age of Shakespeare* (Princeton, 1957); and to the various editors of the Arden Shakespeare (new series).

[42] It is possible that Shakespeare adapted the idea from the *Gorboduc* of Thomas Norton and Thomas Sackville, where some elements of construction are conspicuously present.

of the trilogy, but as Henry VI grew up and himself took more and more a part in events, it became clear that a parallel line was being developed. The discord was inevitable, a result of the usurpation of Richard II's throne by Henry IV, and once this was granted, it was obvious that only a very strong king, a Henry V, could conceivably ride the storm. Henry VI was nothing of the sort. Pious and amiable, his character was such that his wife and son preferred him away from the field of battle for fear that his lack of enthusiasm would demoralize the troops. Thus the trilogy was a study in kingship and its failure as well as a study of discord; and when discord itself rose to occupy the throne—as it did in the fourth play of the series, *Richard III*—the whole order of heaven and earth snapped asunder. Only with the end of the curse of usurpation, with the advent of concord—that is, of a strong king—could harmony be restored, and that function was performed by Henry VII. Thus Shakespeare managed to hold together not only each individual play of the series but the whole tetralogy.

In his first three histories Shakespeare had demonstrated his mastery of the art of construction, and this carried over into *Richard III*. But in writing *Richard III* Shakespeare had prepared himself by reading "Hall," and in this case that meant the near-dramatic chronicle of Sir Thomas More. More's Richard differed from a typical Marlowe hero in being rather more subtly drawn: where Tamburlaine was characterized by *virtù* (or mere overinflated ego), Richard had besides some remnants of the purely human—moments of self-doubt, of conscience. More, as we have seen, introduced psychological unity into English history writing, but the weapon had been too dangerous, and no one had had sufficient courage to seize it and wield it as it could be wielded. Nor did Shakespeare entirely succeed in his maiden endeavor. Too much of his play had to be given over to narrating the events of Edward IV's reign, and with relatively little time remaining, it was simpler to draw Richard with broad strokes. There was a good deal of Tamburlaine in Richard III as Shakespeare presented him, though there was something of More's Richard as well.

In *Richard II,* the lesson had been learned. Instead of Marlovian temperament, Shakespeare's young king exhibited a clearly defined, if malformed, character. The shadings were now of the appropriate subtlety; and to More's paradigm Shakespeare added his own technique of construction. The political theme in drama could in any event be broken down into two general components, *Respublica* and *Rex,* and, as Shakespeare's first tetralogy demonstrated, it was possible to use them together in a kind of counterpoint. But character, properly conceived, could be made part of *Rex,* and kingship could be looked at both generally and as the problem faced by an individual ruler, thus producing a play like *Richard II.* So in this case there is little point in arguing whether the play is political or personal, when it plainly is both: Richard's character would matter little if he were not king. In Shakespeare it is difficult to find a case where the private character of a ruler is the center of attention. The interest lies in the conflict between personality and duty, between the private and the public, not in either one taken in isolation. Richard II could not bridge the gap; the following two plays of the second tetralogy show how Prince Hal learned to adjust his private interests to his public responsibilities, and in *Henry V* Shakespeare demonstrated how much could be accomplished by a monarch who had learned the lesson well. One suspects that the criticism lavished on *Henry V* is due to the lack of conflict: King Henry no longer had choices to make, at least not of the sort he had faced as Prince Hal. But the play was necessary to complete the series, not only to fill the space between 1413 and 1422—that is, to complete the dramatization of Hall—but also to round off the series of variations on a theme which had begun with *Richard II.*

Most of the history plays, where they made use of any organizing scheme at all, followed either the pattern of Marlowe or that of Shakespeare. Peele's *Edward I,* though still episodic, was held together by the personality of the king; much the same can be said of the plays of Cromwell and Sir Thomas More. Inevitably, the Shakespearean plays were more complicated. *The Life and Death of Jack Straw,* by being rather more a tract than a drama, was concerned with discord and its effects; Thomas Middleton's *Hengist, King of Kent* was a study of the character of tyranny. Kingship and discord were two themes around which to construct a play, the two used by Shakespeare and most of his successors.

There were, however, other possibilities. The operation of Fortune was one. The authors of the *Mirror* had made much of this, and few of the dramatists were able to avoid Fortune altogether. The historical Cromwell, certainly, had owed much to the turning of her wheel, and the author of the play could hardly help mentioning Cromwell's excessive ambition and the retribution which followed. Nonetheless, that play was one of character, and it was the personality of Cromwell which joined together its variegated episodes. Only in the *True Tragedy of Richard III* did Fortune play a major role, and its author more than most made use of the *Mirror*. Even here, Fortune had to share the stage with character, but because of the traditional welding of rise and fall with ambition, this was possible. The danger of making much of Fortune's operations was too great impersonality, and so dramatists, sensibly enough, put people on the stage, considering no theme at all to be better than one which made their characters puppets.[43] Later, with the coming of "policy," that idea was dramatized. Ben Jonson did it in *Sejanus* and emphasized his point by drawing heavily on Tacitus, one of the patron saints of the "politic" historians. The anonymous author of *The Tragedie of Claudius Tiberius Nero* tried the same thing but overdid it: everyone in that play harbored treasonable thoughts, even the "good" Germanicus, with the result that the "evil" Tiberius seems justified in his villainy. Had the object been to exemplify the discord caused by too much subtlety, the author might have succeeded; as it was, all that resulted was confusion. Oddly enough, little was made of policy in the history plays with an English setting. There was something of this in Shakespeare's *Richard III*, but the theme was not dominant nor even, I think, very important. One purely "politic" character appeared in *Edmond Ironside*, but the author did not know what to do with him, and the politician, though he has the largest part in the play, ended by being tangential to the main action.[44]

Although the ways of unifying historical drama were relatively limited in number, there was no such inhibition in the choice of

---

[43] On this, see Farnham, *Medieval Heritage*, esp. Ch. x.

[44] This play is so inconclusive that it has been suggested that a sequel must have existed: Ribner, *The English History Play*, p. 243; *Edmond Ironside*, ed. Eleanore Boswell, Malone Society Reprints (London, 1927), p. xii.

subject. Almost any period could be made to produce some rea-
sonably exciting events, and then it was only necessary to bind
them together according to one of the recognized patterns. The
Elizabethan stage was remarkably hungry for new plays, and like
most highly competitive enterprises, it spawned imitations of the
successful. Once a Roman play appealed to the audience, a dozen
would follow; once the English historical play was established,
virtually every reign was set on the stage. Only a few of the
classical plays have survived, and it is difficult to judge the genre,
especially since the plays left to us were by the better dramatists
(Shakespeare and Jonson supplying the majority). The construction here closely resembled that already discussed. Of "British"
plays, much the same may be said. Once the craze for chronicle
histories was fully developed, the dramatists felt no hesitation in
borrowing from Geoffrey of Monmouth. Again, judgment is difficult. Most of the plays have vanished, and the survivors have in
common the fact that their authors did not take the "chronicle"
very seriously. *King Lear* was, in this sense, a chronicle history; so
was *Macbeth*. No one now thinks of either play in this
connection; [45] interestingly, the Elizabethans also refused to accept
these plays as history. Thus the increasing historical sophistication
of the late sixteenth-century antiquaries affected the drama sufficiently to prevent the survival of "British" histories qua histories,
and only if some extraneous interest were generated did the plays
continue on the boards, let alone see print.

So the majority of the plays putting history on the stage chose
the English past and, the political motif being strong, either the
relatively recent past or certain special reigns such as those in
which rebellion or deposition figured. Along with these there was a
line of contemporary history. If the subject were native English—as in Thomas Heywood's *If You Know Not Me You Know
Nobody*, which was about Queen Elizabeth—then a political approach was dangerous, and Heywood began by dramatizing Foxe's
encomium on the marvelous preservation of Elizabeth and ended,
in his second part, by putting on a series of London scenes.
Heywood in any case was given to seeking the domestic in history.

[45] Actually Ribner discusses them, *The English History Play*, pp. 247–259, but
as plays on a political theme.

It is an indication of the gulf which separated him from Shake-speare that the principal character in Heywood's *Edward IV* was Jane Shore, and that what we remember most clearly is the effect of her submission to Edward IV, not on the king but on Matthew Shore, while Shakespeare, in *Richard III,* omitted her altogether and instead emphasized the role of the Cassandra-like Dowager Queen Margaret (who had in fact died in 1482 and had to be resurrected especially for the occasion).[46] Once in a while happenings abroad were staged, but the tendency to propaganda always came to dominate the play. Marlowe's *Massacre at Paris* was largely antipapal, and the characters resemble cardboard cutouts in an advertising display. The play of the *Battle of Alcazar,* probably by George Peele, contained passages attacking Philip of Spain, presumably because the opportunity was too good to miss. The main difficulty with these plays, however, was their didacticism: their primary purpose seems to have been historical exposition, and so the method of construction, of order around a theme, was never attempted.

The dramatists managed to set a vast amount of history on the stage, and had they accomplished nothing else, they would at least have made the Elizabethans familiar with the more obvious episodes of their own past. In fact, the better playwrights did much more. Shakespeare popularized not only Hall's history, that is, the events covered in Hall, but also his interpretation of them. The problem of providentialism, faced by the authors of the *Mirror,* reappeared in Shakespeare as well. Warwick, in *2 Henry IV,* was able to explain King Richard's view of the future in purely personal terms, even though Richard's vision was essentially Hall's:

> There is a history in all men's lives,
> Figuring the natures or the times deceased:
> The which observed, a man may prophesy,
> With a near aim, of the main chance of things
> As yet not come to life, who in their seeds
> And weak beginnings lie intreasuréd:

[46] In spite of this, Heywood believed that "playes have made the ignorant more apprehensive, taught the unlearned the knowledge of many famous histories, [and] instructed such as cannot read in the discovery of all our *English* Chronicles." Quoted by Arthur Melville Clark, *Thomas Heywood* (Oxford, 1931), p. 78.

> Such things become the hatch and brood of time;
> And by the necessary form of this
> King Richard might create a perfect guess
> That great Northumberland, then false to him,
> Would of that seed grow to a greater falseness,
> Which should not find a ground to root upon,
> Unless on you. (III.i.80–92) [47]

But even the purely human may become necessitous, may generate its own reply, and King Henry chose to emphasize that interpretation in his answer:

> Are these things then necessities?
> Then let us meet them like necessities—
> And that same word even now cries out on us: (III.i.92–94)

So matters eventually turned out. Lord Clifford, who earlier had killed Richard, Duke of York, and had ordered his head impaled above the Duke's own town, now suffered the same fate:

> From off the gates of York fetch down the head,
> Your father's head, which Clifford placed there;
> Instead whereof let this supply the room;
> Measure for measure must be answered. (II.vi.52–55) [48]

Shakespeare thus repeated Hall's theme of an implacable destiny at work but kept the motivating force human. Fortune and Providence were not suppressed, nor did Shakespeare argue the case outright, but his selection of historical materials and his shaping of them made his attitude clear.

It was precisely in this realm that the playwrights were able to teach the historians a lesson. Whatever his factual inaccuracies—and they were both numerous and deliberate—Shakespeare was an improvement on Holinshed, his principal source. The editors of the second edition of Holinshed had worked on a principle of agglomeration; Shakespeare used selection instead. Holinshed's method was precisely comparable to that of the playwrights who presented history in episodes, and Holinshed in

---

[47] *The Second Part of the History of Henry IV*, ed. J. Dover Wilson (Cambridge, Eng., 1953).
[48] *The Third Part of King Henry VI*, ed. Andrew S. Cairncross (London, 1964).

one way marked a step back from Polydore Vergil, who saw history in terms of reigns and whose analogue was Marlowe. The majority of the playwrights, whatever their source and method, did emphasize the political nature of history and the lessons that might be learned from the past, so that even Thomas Heywood (who was more interested in the personal life of Jane Shore than in the public life of Edward IV) made a point of showing the iniquities of rebellion. But Shakespeare, of whom this is true as well, innovated. His method of construction saw history in terms of the operation of ideas. There is a resemblance to Hall in this, but Shakespeare was much less mechanical. And because he was a dramatist, with only a brief space at his disposal, his selection had to be more rigorous. The unity in Hall is considerably more apparent in his table of contents than in his text: vast blocs of information which were never fitted into the overall scheme had to be included for the sake of completeness. No one expected that of a playwright. Organized history, which became much more common with the "politic" historians, appeared first in the theater, and Sir John Hayward and Lord Bacon, two of its principal exponents, were well aware of the fact.[49]

The enthusiasm for history plays was short-lived. It began somewhere in the 1580's—exact dates are hard to come by—and reached a peak around 1598. Not long after the accession of James I, the genre ceased to have any life, and only one play of any importance, Ford's *Chronicle Historie of Perkin Warbeck*, came out of the years after the middle of James's reign.[50] The precise reasons for the decline have been a matter of argument, and no wholly satisfactory theory has so far been evolved. Certain points are clear enough. The material itself was becoming overworked: most reigns had already been staged, some of them several times. Ingenuity would certainly have located new "plots," but for the plays to be effective as didactic history, a certain familiarity with the basic story on the part of the audience seems to have been

[49] On Hayward's debt to Shakespeare, *King Richard II*, ed. Peter Ure, 5th Arden edn. (London, 1961), pp. lvii–lxii; for Bacon's awareness of the play of *Richard II*, see the quotation below, p. 257.

[50] The rise and fall of the history play can be seen most readily in Alfred Harbage, *Annals of English Drama*, 2nd edn., rev. S. Schoenbaum (Philadelphia, 1964).

considered necessary, and obscure incidents long ago and far away presented difficulties. The increasing incidence of romance in history must also have helped the decline along. Dekker's *Shoemaker's Holiday* was a London play with a historical setting, but the history in it was negligible, and it was not long before the playwrights realized that a contemporary background offered advantages lacking in an artificial past. The result was plays of the order of Jonson's *Bartholomew Fair* or *The Alchemist*. Besides this, the rise of "politic" history as a prose genre may have been involved. The improvements in historical thought which were the result of the activities of Shakespeare and his fellow dramatists were absorbed by the historians themselves, and having a larger canvas on which to work, they were able to do the job better. Shakespearean history did not vanish altogether but was altered so as to reappear in the form of Sir Robert Cotton's *Henry III*. Finally, the shift in politics may have had an influence. The pressure of Spain, which included attempts to murder the queen, made men conscious of political stability, a theme which haunted many of the history plays; in addition, there was the matter of the Earl of Essex's revolt. But James came to the throne quietly and brought two sons with him, thus ending the problem of the succession; and the peace with Spain, signed in 1604, terminated the immediate threat from that direction. Nor was there any replacement for Essex as a center for discontent and possible rebellion. Instead, men turned from an examination of the state to an examination of themselves, and that then became the dominant theme of Jacobean drama.

From about the middle of the 1580's a typical Englishman must have found it more and more difficult to avoid having any knowledge of the past. Regardless of his purse, his background, or his tastes, sooner or later he was bound to be exposed to history. A scholar would have his Camden, a courtier his Daniel or Drayton; a merchant had his choice among historians, including Stow and Holinshed, while his apprentice could enjoy the ditties of Deloney. Any or all of them might have gone to the theater; or, if they lived in the country, not uncommonly the theater came to them. If they were preparing for the grand tour of Europe, handbooks for travel and descriptions of the major countries across the Channel were coming into being; the same books would be of use to a merchant planning investments abroad or to his factor isolated in a strange land. After 1585 the English ceased merely to react to events abroad and began to help shape them; after 1588 it was clear that English intervention was a potent force. English history had been full of such excursions across the Channel. Agincourt had not been forgotten. It is not too surprising, then, that a taste for English history developed, nor that there should be a lively market for books about the world which the English were again entering. To this should be added the effects of humanist education. Introduced first in Henry VIII's day, the humanist view required time to reach its full impact, that is, to affect not only a small group of scholars but the community at large. More and more, the nobility and the gentry were sending their sons to the new grammar schools, to the universities, to the Inns of Court. However deficient the curriculum might have been in the teaching of history, the humanist emphasis on service to the state was bound to produce an interest in politics which was most easily and most effectively assuaged by reading histories.

For a variety of reasons there was an urgent demand for histories, and, as we have seen, to match the demand came a vast supply. Of most of these books, and especially of most of the popularizations, it may fairly be said that they are of no historiographical importance, and that they serve only as evidence that this was a most historically-minded age. The literary men, however, the poets and playwrights, had other problems to solve than meeting the demand for new histories in any and all forms. Limited as they were in the amount of space they had available, forced by the nature of their craft to find some sort of unity in the jumbled incidents of the past, they broke away from the tendency toward all-inclusiveness represented by the revised Holinshed and saw in the events of long-gone days a variety of patterns still applicable to the present. They understood the validity of Sir Philip Sidney's argument that the poet was better able to tell the "truth" about the past than the historian, because he was not as bound to the details. They had to see the past as a kind of drama, filled not only with incidents but with characters, and thus they had, perforce, to learn the lesson of selection. When the lesson was applied by the historians themselves, as happened with the rise of "politic" history, some strange hybrids were bound to result, but in the end the writing of history was never to be the same again.

VII

Politic History

Toward the end of the sixteenth century there grew up a new form of history writing whose usual characteristics were a laconic and epigrammatic style, a radical condensation of subject matter, and, most important, an insistence that the purpose of writing history was to teach men political wisdom. The poets and the playwrights had prepared the way for this new method of looking at the past, at least in terms of style and terseness; and when the historians took this up, their enthusiasm for politics meant that they would search for the causes of events. Like their predecessors, they accepted Providence as the ultimate cause of all happenings, but they looked beyond (or below) Providence for the secondary causes. It was no longer enough to say that some ruler had behaved in a particular way, and that such behavior was morally right or wrong. The new historians assumed that monarchs knew enough to make their own decisions regarding the morality of an action, but that the same monarchs might be grateful for advice concerning its expediency. Logically the most obvious way to analyze past actions would be through the use of some form of psychology; but although this was done, if carried too far it would lead away from the principal purpose of the new history simply because the emphasis would be on the particular actor rather than on the universal situation. If the question to be answered was, "How did Scipio or Alexander or Caesar come to succeed?" then psychology was of some use; if, instead, it was a more general question such as how to pacify a newly conquered territory, then such disciplines as political science, geography, and the like were more relevant. From these considerations the characteristics of the new history stemmed: a brief period, such as the reign of one monarch, or the story of one event, simplified and made more cogent the process of exhibiting political virtuosity; and the discursive style of Livy, admirably suited to narrative, had to be replaced by the more compact style of Tacitus.

The new history began in Italy three quarters of a century before it reached England, and the names usually associated with its origins are those of Machiavelli and Guicciardini. Both men were in the grip of the same tragedy, the Italians' loss of Italy, and this affected everything they wrote.[1] Italy during the *quattrocento* had not been a place where a moral prince survived easily; after the French invasions and the Spanish and Hapsburg domination, it was hard for any Italian prince, even an amoral one, to survive. The Italians had lost their liberty, and with it their historians lost their innocence. Domination bred suspicion and cynicism. There is no need to justify the "Machiavellianism" of Machiavelli, nor did Machiavelli ever push matters to the extremes which his later legend suggested. Machiavelli was not an atheist, but God played no great role in *The Prince:* God had not saved the Italians from their own folly, and the purpose of *The Prince,* and of Guicciardini's *History of Italy,* was to turn the dominant role back to man, with some instructions for acting it. Machiavelli's *Prince* posed a choice: if a ruler wished to act morally, he might so choose, but his chances of survival on this earth were small; if a ruler wished to survive here, and preferred to risk his soul, Machiavelli was prepared to offer him advice which led to success in the temporal sphere.

The Prince is usually taken to be a work of political theory and has been not infrequently compared to other works superficially similar because they also dealt with the problems of rulers. The similarities are there, but they mask a crucial difference: while Machiavelli's predecessors (and many of his successors as well) began with an a priori moral system and deduced their politics from it, Machiavelli began with political reality, as he found it in history both recent and ancient, and derived his maxims from that. The procedure is obvious in the *Discourses;* but while most of the "working notes" have been trimmed from *The Prince,* there is no

---

[1] Felix Gilbert, *Machiavelli and Guicciardini: Politics and History in Sixteenth-Century Florence* (Princeton, 1965), analyzes the whole matter of the effects of 1494 in great detail; he adds to this a discussion of the effects of local Florentine politics.

question that Machiavelli's methodology in writing that book was virtually the same as that which went into the *Discourses*. Machiavelli's reputation as an atheist (or worse) hindered the acceptance of his method, and it was not until a few others adopted it, sometimes while in the act of reviling its originator, that his influence was properly felt.

One result was that Machiavelli's younger contemporary Francesco Guicciardini soon became better known as a historian. Whereas even so innocent a work as Machiavelli's *Florentine History* was not translated into English until 1595, Guicciardini's *History of Italy* appeared in 1579 and was reissued in 1599 and 1618. *The Prince* had no published translation until 1640, though much could be learned about the book from attacks on it, especially from the fulsome work of Innocent Gentillet, published in Simon Patricke's translation in 1602.[2] But while those interested in Machiavelli had to turn to foreign languages or to his traducers, mastering Guicciardini was much simpler. Besides Fenton's translation—a rather bulky volume—readers had available Remigio Nannini's *Civill Considerations* (1601), a handbook of political advice drawn almost entirely from the *History of Italy*, in which all the causes were carefully set out and the morals drawn, without the benefit of Guicciardini's lengthy narrative; and there was also an abridgment of the narrative, enabling one to follow the action without being deterred by the numerous speeches.[3] Even the passages omitted from the third and fourth books of the *History* were published separately in 1595, the second passage being reprinted in 1613 by Robert Dallington as an appendix to his *Aphorismes Civill and Militarie*, a work which was itself a commentary on Guicciardini's *History*.[4] Nor was it possible for anyone to mistake the import of the work: the Table, even of the first

---

[2] The details of the transmission of Machiavelli can be studied in Felix Raab, *The English Face of Machiavelli* (London, 1964), pp. 30–101; the editions and variations of Guicciardini's writings are detailed in Vincent Luciani, *Francesco Guicciardini and His European Reputation* (New York, 1936).

[3] [Nannini], *Civill Considerations upon Many and Sundry Histories . . . and Principallie upon Those of Guicciardin* (London, 1601), from a French translation of 1584; *A Briefe Collection of All the Notable Things in the Hystorie of Guicciardini* (London, 1591).

[4] *Two Discourses of Master Frances Guicciardin* (London, 1595); Robert Dallington, "A Briefe Inference upon Guicciardines Digression," appended to *Aphorismes Civill and Militarie* (London, 1613).

edition of Fenton's translation, was full of headings of the sort
"New Princes have new councells, and of new councells commonly resorte new effects," or "Dissimulacions very daungerous in
the persons of great men." Fenton was not exaggerating when he
wrote:

> And for the generall matter of his worke, it doth not onely
> conteine the warres and diverse accidentes hapned in Italy and
> other partes for almost fortie yeres, but also he doth so distinctly
> set downe the causes, the counsells, and the fortunes of every
> principall partie introduced into those actions, that by his studie
> and judgement, is traced & made easie to the reader, the way to all
> those swete and plentifull frutes which with paynfulnes are sought
> for in Histories of this nature.[5]

To make certainty still more certain, Fenton heightened his original by lengthening the speeches and pointing morals not obvious
enough to suit Englishmen still slightly naïve in historical matters.[6]

Machiavellian history writing thus made its first great impression through the work of Guicciardini, with Machiavelli's own
reputation acting as a brake. That much of the distaste was irrelevant to Machiavelli's own thought hardly mattered. Some of it
pertained to that distrust of contemporary Italy which all good
Englishmen felt: "An Englishman Italianate is a devil incarnate."
The distrust was not lessened by Italy's position as the headquar-
ters of Catholicism. At the same time, men accused Machiavelli of
atheism, principally because he considered religion from a political point of view. But other layers were added to the legend:
Gentillet, who wished to characterize Catherine de' Medici, pinned
the tag of greed to the Machiavellian prince, a view which was
fairly accurate regarding Catherine but diametrically opposed to
Machiavelli's own teaching. Worse than this, the entire vocabulary
of Machiavellian political theory developed connotations which
made it suspect. Such words as "policy" and "practice," "aphorism" and "maxim" implied something sinister and best kept in
darkness, which made it difficult to discuss political realities with-

---

[5] *The Historie of Guicciardin*, trans. Geoffrey Fenton (London, 1579), Dedication to Queen Elizabeth, fol. *iiij^v.
[6] Rudolf B. Gottfried, "Geoffrey Fenton's *Historie of Guicciardin*," *Indiana
University Publications*, Humanity Series, No. 3 (Bloomington, 1940), pp. 15 ff.

out implying that any such discussion was, and had to be, im-moral.[7] This and the inevitably moralistic outlook of the typical Elizabethan made it virtually impossible to take a reasonable atti-tude toward Machiavelli. The Elizabethan mind in any event tended to be divided between a pious underpinning and a realistic shell: and Machiavelli's translators (and critics) attacked him on the incompatible grounds that his morality was abysmal and his advice false. Moreover, Machiavelli's assumption that ruler and ruled were usually at odds and his patent enthusiasm for democ-racy made him a serious danger to those of royalist sympathy. Both Thomas Bedingfield (in 1595) and Edward Dacres (1636, 1640) defended monarchy from the strictures of the Italian, and the latter went so far as to devalue *The Prince* by treating it as a variety of cony-catching pamphlet.[8] The moral problem, and the reality, were expressed clearly by an anonymous annotator of one of the unpublished manuscripts of *The Prince:*

> This booke not only discovers the knowledge of much evill, but also the shortest and most effectuall waies to perpetrate the same. Here is shewed that we should not with a rude heate or naturall instinct or by other example but artificially as it were only for a further end follow ether vertue or vice, making noe difference but by the profit we may receive when we have occasion to use them. the Author teacheth what men doe and not what they ought to doe.[9]

---

[7] Napoleone Orsini, " 'Policy' or the Language of Elizabethan Machiavellian-ism," *Journal of the Warburg and Courtauld Institutes,* IX (1946), 122–134. Orsini demonstrates that these words sometimes had a sinister meaning long before the coming of Machiavelli's thought, but by the late sixteenth century the connection was frequently made. See also Mario Praz, "The Politic Brain: Machiavelli and the Elizabethans," in *The Flaming Heart,* Anchor Books (New York, 1958), pp. 103 ff.

[8] Niccolo Machiavelli, *The Florentine Historie,* trans. T[homas]. B[edingfield]. (London, 1595), foll. [A4ʳ–A5ʳ]; *Machiavels Discourses,* trans. E[dward]. D[acres]. (London, 1636), pp. 261–262; Machiavelli, *Prince,* trans. E. D. (Lon-don, 1640), The Epistle to the Reader: "if thou consider well the actions of the world, thou shalt find him much practisd by those that condemne him; who willingly would walk as theeves doe with close lanternes in the night, that they being undescried, and yet seeing all, might surprise the unwary in the dark. . . . And he that means well, shall be here warnd, where the deceitfull man learnes to set his snares."

[9] *Machiavelli's The Prince: An Elizabethan Translation,* ed. Hardin Craig (Chapel Hill, 1944), p. 177.

The connection between a new politic history and the popular
conception of Machiavellianism made it difficult to write in the
new vein. Certain other tendencies, seemingly unconnected to this
problem, worked the opposite way. For one thing, the position of
history among the arts and sciences was gradually shifting. During
the course of the sixteenth century, literary theory became more
and more important as a subject for debate, and, under the double
impetus of an attempt to absorb Aristotle's treatise on poetry and
to fit into classical theory the newer types of literature evolved
during the Renaissance, Italian critics found it necessary to revise
entirely the scheme which governed the relationships among the
various forms of discourse. Originally history had been classed
with poetry (as well as with rhetoric and grammar) as one of the
verbal disciplines, and the relationship between history and poetry
had been especially close because both dealt with ancient deeds
and with the description of people and places, and because both
condemned vice and praised virtue. After the middle of the century
it was not unusual to class both history and poetry with moral philosophy, which meant that the principle of classification had been
altered from a grouping by the fact of discourse to one by the purpose of discourse. This had the effect of making the differences between history and poetry clearer than they had been. It was agreed
that both, in some way, were "true," but poetry was more universal, history more particular, simply because poetry was more consistent in its portrayals. Moreover, poetry represented a single action by one man, history a single action by many men. Poetry thus
had the advantage of being able to isolate whatever factors were
relevant and to ignore the others, while history, unless it were to
falsify what really happened, had to include them all. In terms of the
purpose of discourse, history ran a poor second to poetry, and this
was so because of the very virtues which were usually acclaimed as
being the unique graces of the historian. The poet could be imaginative, and his example followed his precept closely; the historian,
bound to tell the truth in all its complexity, not uncommonly
found himself disproving the efficacy of the ethics he ought to have
been demonstrating. Admittedly, all of this was not quite as logical
as it might have been: omitted, for one thing, was the matter of
selection in history; and since much of the theory was written by

poets, there was a natural tendency to inflate the value of poetry vis-à-vis what might be looked on as a competing discipline. The literary critics thus came close to expelling history from their domain altogether, thereby giving it a certain autonomy; the next step, that of classing history with politics, was not explicitly taken by anyone, though it was implied in the work of the Italian historians and later in the writings of Jean Bodin.

The first appearance in England of this new attitude toward poetry and history came in a treatise on literature, Sir Philip Sidney's *Defense of Poesy*.[10] That work is interesting to us because Sidney took up a comparatively large segment of his essay discussing history, and because Sidney, as a courtier and as the heir to a political tradition, had read widely and carefully in the best historians. Moreover, in the course of a career much taken up with literary patronage, he had made the acquaintance of a number of practicing historians, among them William Camden. In the case of Sidney's treatise, it is possible to be sure that, whatever the author's feelings about the superiority of poetry to history, at least the criticisms of contemporary history writing would not be based on poetic prejudice alone. Many of Sidney's comments on the interrelation between history and poetry almost certainly derived from his reading of the Italian theorists, but some of his remarks on history, and among them the most cogent, were original and were probably the result of his study of Machiavelli and similar writers. Sidney adopted the connection between history and poetry and moral philosophy and repeated the argument that poetry was to be preferred because both forms of writing were intended to be didactic and poetry succeeded better.

> Now to that which commonly is attributed to the praise of history, in respect of the notable learning is got by marking the success, as though therein a man should see virtue exalted and vice punished—truly that commendation is peculiar to poetry, and far off from history. For indeed poetry ever sets virtue so out in her best colors, making Fortune her well-waiting handmaid, that one must needs be enamored of her. . . . But history, being captived to the

[10] I have discussed this in detail in "Sir Philip Sidney and the Idea of History," *Bibliothèque d'Humanisme et Renaissance*, XXVI (1964), 608–617.

truth of a foolish world, is many times a terror from well doing, and an encouragement to unbridled wickedness.[11]

The result of this analysis was that history did not, in fact, supply the example for which philosophy gave the precept. It must not be inferred from this that there were no precepts for which history might supply examples; they might be political rather than moral, and elsewhere Sidney said as much.[12]

Sidney, however, advanced still another step. Not only did he show that the usual professions concerning the utility of history were false, but he also demonstrated that historians had, on occasion, to borrow their methodology from the poets. The usual claim that the historian was superior to the poet because he dealt in truth was itself suspect. "Many times" the historian "must tell events whereof he can yield no cause; and, if he do, it must be poetically." [13] The poet had the advantage because he could invent the story and its wellsprings; the historian could only search old records in the hope of finding enough. The poet had to worry about verisimilitude, not truth, and the historian, for all his searching, frequently came to the same point. The historical poets— especially Drayton and Daniel, who were much under Sidney's influence—proved the point. They demonstrated that a good historian had to adopt some of the methods of the poet if he were to do more than elaborate a narrative. The severe difficulties involved in combining two subjects which were becoming more and more disparate ensured that the genre of historical poetry would eventually fail, and it was not long before the poets gave up history. But the two could be combined in the opposite proportions. The English politic historians, Sir John Hayward, Sir Francis Bacon, and Samuel Daniel, made a virtue of the necessity that Sidney had stressed. They deliberately made history writing more poetical, and they did it through ruthless selectivity, by the use of imagination in the writing of fictitious explanatory speeches, and by the construction of human causes for otherwise inexplicable events.

Not all of the hunt for causes was conducted by mere imagina-

[11] *The Defense of Poesie*, in *Literary Criticism, Plato to Dryden*, ed. Allan H. Gilbert (Detroit, 1962), pp. 425–426.
[12] In a letter to his brother, *The Complete Works of Sir Philip Sidney*, ed. Albert Feuillerat (Cambridge, Eng., 1922–26), III, 130–133.
[13] Sidney, *Defense*, p. 424.

tion. Along with the new enthusiasm for history as an illustration of politics came a devaluation of the purely biographical approach to historical thinking. When the Tudor history grew out of the medieval chronicle, the principle upon which the raw material of the former was organized was usually biographical: that is, the center point was the deeds of some monarch or great man. What causation there was had to do with Providence and Fortune and with personality. Extra-human causes were rare. The whole point of politic history, however, was to establish maxims which, applied to given situations, produced predictable results. Personality was still an issue: if anything, more power was given to the individual ruler—one reason Machiavelli was called an atheist was because he took decisions from God and gave them to men—but it was a power of choice between politics and morals, and if politics was chosen, then one had to obey the relevant rules, just as one did if the choice were morality. A politic historian had to take into account the same factors as a politic prince, or the councilors of a politic prince; and so if one wished to learn something of the way in which men grasped the principles of action, the best place to begin the search would be in the books of advice written for councilors.

Among the more useful classes of books for this purpose were those giving advice to travelers. By the end of the sixteenth century the idea that gentlemen needed to know no more than courtly matters and country sports was all but dead. The scions of gentle families found their way to the universities and to the Inns of Court, and from there numbers of them paraded around Europe on the Grand Tour. Sir Philip Sidney had been one of the earliest of such students, as well as the most successful. He had been sent to learn languages—French, Italian, a little German—and to make the acquaintance of men of his own social position in other lands. It was hoped that he would learn something of the way in which Continental nations were governed, not only in theory but in reality: who were the men who really made decisions and how they did it. As such tours became more common, handbooks appeared which categorized what one should see and do and how one should make notes of a unique experience. Jerome Turler's *The Traveiler* (1575) was written for budding humanists, and his

notes on Naples, supplied as an example of the method he proposed, were primarily of architectural and classical interest, while
the government of the city was given very short shrift. This was no
help to aspiring politicians, who already sought for other information. These might turn to Albrecht Meier's *Certaine Briefe, and
Speciall Instructions for Gentlemen, Merchants, Students, Soul-
diers, Marriners, &c.*, which emphasized the necessity for a study
of "the state, manners, lawes, governement and natures of the
people." [14] Meier, unfortunately, was overambitious, and his final
schema would have served better for the author of an encyclope-
dia. Nonetheless, the questions to be asked about the political state
were comprehensive and included the form of government of the
whole country as well as of the cities, the laws, the spirit of the
inhabitants, and the relation of the ruler with his neighbors. The
traveler should ask about the prince and his council, and especially should discover the "perpetuall care of the Prince to with-
stand all the pollicies, inventions, invasions, violences, hostilities
and indignities of other Princes, his or her enimies, and to preserve
the realme, and people in peace, tranquillitie, securitie, and pros-
peritie." [15] Here were the materials for a politic councilor, but
mixed among all manner of things irrelevant for his purpose.

It was not long before such handbooks became more specific.
Sir Robert Dallington, whom we have already met as a student of
Guicciardini, wrote as well *A Method for Travell* (1605?), which
used as its example a view of France taken in the year 1598.
Dallington had himself been a traveler and, rather than limit
himself entirely to theory, included highly practical matter such as
the details of arranging financing or the best cities in which to
learn languages (Orleans, Florence, Leipzig). The description of
France that followed was extremely detailed and included the
geographical features (and their relevance to military matters),
the government, the laws, and so on. But Dallington went much
farther than Meier: he asked questions about the officers of the
court, the military, the revenue of the nation, administration, the
various social classes, and the character of the people. The history

[14] *Certaine Briefe, and Speciall Instructions,* trans. Philip Jones (London,
1589), fol. A3ʳ.
[15] Ibid., p. 21.

of France, especially such recent history as the religious wars, was applied where relevant, and the vast array of extraneous matter so prominent in Meier was quietly dropped. Moreover, Dallington's organization, while quite as rigid as Meier's, was more suitable to his subject. Having finished France, Dallington next turned to the Grand Duchy of Tuscany and performed the same task.[16] Within a few years even larger compilations began to appear: Edward Grimeston translated and supplemented Pierre d'Avity's *The Estates, Empires, & Principallities of the World* (1615), a book which did in brief for all the nations of the world what Dallington had done for two; and Gabriel Richardson's *Of the State of Europe* (1627), which handled a somewhat more limited subject matter in a highly illuminating fashion. Indeed even before Richardson's excellent book appeared, the situation had reached a point of full circle: Bishop Joseph Hall could, for religious and moral reasons, insist that English youth should remain home because travel was unnecessary as all that was really essential could be learned from books.[17] A traveler could add to this only a knowledge of "Machiavellianism" and of assassination.

From this sort of travel writing, the step to political theory was short. Of contemporary writers the best known was certainly the Frenchman Jean Bodin, whose *Methodus* (1566) and *Republic* (1576) both had a considerable vogue in England. Precisely what the English derived from his work is not easy to determine: the *Methodus* especially became a kind of mine from which men dug what they needed to the exclusion of all else.[18] Since Bodin visited England in 1579–1581, a number of courtiers found opportunity to see him, and among them was Sir Philip Sidney. From this it is no surprise to learn that Gabriel Harvey and Edmund Spenser rapidly became aware of Bodin's work, though it is more difficult to explain why William Harrison and Thomas Nashe found him attractive. The best that may be said is that Bodin became fashionable so that even before Thomas Heywood translated the fourth chapter of Bodin's *Methodus* as an introduc-

---

[16] *A Survey of the Great Dukes State of Tuscany* (London, 1605).

[17] *Quo vadis? A Just Censure of Travell* (London, 1617).

[18] Leonard F. Dean, "Bodin's *Methodus* in England before 1625," *Studies in Philology*, XXXIX (1942), 160–166.

tion to his rendition of Sallust (1609), a minor writer such as
Charles Merbury made use of him, and the obscure Edward Forset defended his conception of sovereignty.[19] Bodin's idea of history fitted into a vast scheme of universal knowledge, with natural
and divine history constituting segments as large as human history
and certainly as important. Human history was obviously the eas-
iest to grasp and hence constituted the beginning of knowledge;
but Bodin knew that divine and natural history followed immutable laws, and thus felt certain that the history of man, too, had its
regulations. So wisdom could be thought of as the ability to separate the mundane from the eternal, the changeable from the
immutable. It was for this reason that Bodin was so interested in
the effects of climate on men's spirits and in numerology as a way
of finding law in human history. But reduced to a more prosaic
level, history was of utility for teaching generals the art of war or
councilors the art of advice. In all of this men had to seek the
eternal; and so Bodin, like others we have mentioned, concentrated on laws, maxims, and causes, not on the vagaries of the
individual. Of all the aspects of human history, governance was
the one that most needed to be explained, and Bodin offered his
answer in the *Six Books of the Republic*. But that treatise, though
it was longer than the whole of the *Methodus*, had already been
adumbrated in the sixth chapter of the earlier work, and the whole
of the *Republic* was but a segment of the work that needed to be
done. For our purposes the *Methodus* is the more important work
simply because it was the more influential, at least at this stage, and
because Bodin's view of historical causation appeared most clearly
in it.

The argument of those who, like Bodin, wrote of the theory of
history and politics, and of the others, like Richardson or d'Avity,
can be summed up in a statement made by Giovanni Botero, who
himself wrote books of both a theoretical and a descriptive sort. In
his work on the greatness of cities, Botero wished to find why some
cities flourished (that is, in his terms, grew large in population)
while others stagnated. His reasons for the growth of cities began

---

[19] Merbury, *A Briefe Discourse of Royall Monarchie* (London, 1581), esp. p.
51 (from Bodin's *Methodus,* Ch. vi); Forset, *A Comparative Discourse of the
Bodies Natural and Politique* (London, 1606).

with obvious considerations such as the site, the soil, and the accessibility of transportation and then continued with schools, justice, industry, and the residence of the prince and of the nobility. The reasons why a great city should suddenly stagnate were much more difficult to find. Plagues, wars, and the like constituted part of the answer, but enough cities survived those calamities to make it desirable to seek still further for causes: "Some others say, it is, bycause God the governor of all things, doth so dispose, no man doth doubt of that. But, forasmuch as the infinit wisedome of God, in the administration and the government of nature, worketh secondary causes: My question is, with what meanes that eternall providence maketh little, to multiply; and much, to stand at a stay, and go no further." [20] That in the end Botero was reduced to speaking of the "virtue generative" of man and the "virtue nutritive" of cities does not mean that the statement could not stand as his motto and as that of a host of others.

A new era required a new way of looking at the past, and that in its turn called for new gods to worship. Whereas the favorite Roman historian of the early humanists had been Livy, now men sought out the more difficult and more politically conscious Tacitus. Partly this was a question of snob appeal: men loved Tacitus just because he was difficult, and his circle of admirers had necessarily to be small.[21] Partly, too, changes of stylistic appreciation were coming over all of literature, not over history alone, and these may have been related to the alteration of the categories into which literature was divided. The fulsome turn of the old gave way to a laconic, epigrammatic brevity, the explicitness of Sidney to the riddles of the Metaphysicals. In history writing, narrative was replaced by maxim, completeness by selectivity. How much all this had to do with the changing political scene is difficult to say. The men who had characterized the early part of Elizabeth's reign—the scholar Burghley, the courtier Leicester, the Puritan Walsingham—all were dead before the queen herself. In 1601

---

[20] *A Treatise, concerning the Causes of the Magnificencie and Greatnes of Cities,* trans. Robert Peterson (London, 1606), p. 91.

[21] George Williamson, "Strong Lines," in *Seventeenth Century Contexts* (London, 1960), p. 121. See also the same author's *The Senecan Amble* (Chicago, 1951) and F. P. Wilson, *Elizabethan and Jacobean* (Oxford, 1945), for further discussion of the change in language.

the old queen, perhaps a little disillusioned with the shadows who had replaced the former substance, told an admirer: "Now the wit of the fox is everywhere on foot, so as hardly a faithful or virtuous man may be found." [22] The new place hunters, still more prevalent under James, had need of moral advice but no inclination to take it; instead they preferred the works of the politic historians.

The European political situation had much to do with the change. The fifteenth century was by no means an age of democracy, but on the other hand it was not as radically monarchical as the sixteenth century, let alone the seventeenth. The republic of Florence gave way to the Grand Duchy of Tuscany, the old humanist historians to the disillusioned Machiavelli and Guicciardini. In the same way, Livy, the historian of republican Rome, was replaced by Tacitus, the historian of imperial Rome. For men who had to live in monarchies, Tacitus was the more relevant: it was from him that one learned the techniques of survival.[23] Tacitus was a weapon that could cut both ways, a guide to profitable servility or a way of showing a carefully hidden antagonism to ruthless princes. Traiano Boccalini defended Tacitus, who was most commonly read as a Machiavellian before Machiavelli, by claiming that *raison d'état* could be found only in the Florentine, and that Tacitus instead enabled men to see through the dishonesties of princes.[24] In that, Boccalini erred: Machiavelli could have been read the same way; *The Prince* could be taken as an exposure of "practices" rather than as a recommendation of them. Tacitus and Machiavelli shared the attribute of ambiguity because the political situations in which they lived necessitated it. England, certainly from the 1590's, was no different.

That all this began as an academic exercise explains the origins of the interest in Tacitus and his descendants but not their popularity. It is hardly cause for surprise that the academics of Oxford

[22] Quoted in Sir John Neale, *Essays in Elizabethan History* (London, 1958), p. 79.

[23] Morris W. Croll, "Muret and the History of 'Attic' Prose," *Publications of the Modern Language Association*, XXXIX (1924), 298–299, quoting a lecture given by Muret at Rome in 1580–81.

[24] *The New-found Politicke*, trans. John Florio et al. (London, 1626), pp. 29–32.

and Cambridge discovered the works of their Continental contemporaries before the mass of Englishmen. Even before 1580, Gabriel Harvey wrote of his fellow Cantabrigians that they were all engrossed in Italian books of manners, in Aristotle's *Politics,* in Comines and Guicciardini and Machiavelli. "You can not stepp into a schollars studye but (ten to on) you shall litely finde open ether Bodin de Republica or Le Royes Exposition uppon Aristotles Politiques or sum other like Frenche or Italian Politique Discourses." [25] A few years later a group at Oxford including Jean Hotman, Henry Cuffe, and Thomas Savile, with William Camden joining them by correspondence from London, were reading Tacitus.[26] It was from such groups that the message spread: Hotman and Camden knew Sidney, Cuffe became adviser and *éminence grise* to the Earl of Essex (who adopted his political credo), and Savile's brother, Sir Henry, became the first translator of Tacitus into English. In the 1580's Tacitus and politic history were idle, if exciting, adventures. When Essex became ascendant, so did the Taciteans. The earl himself encouraged politic history—there is some evidence that he wrote the preface to Savile's translation of Tacitus—and his followers, Francis Bacon, Sir Henry Savile, John Hayward, and Henry Cuffe, all wrote in the same genre.[27] Cuffe went further, urged Essex forward, and was executed with his master; Savile and Hayward were both imprisoned. Tacitus had become practical politics, and the historians had left their posts as observers and had stepped into the arena. The danger was such that when, later, Isaac Dorislaus, the first history lecturer on Fulke Greville's foundation at Cambridge, began by analyzing Tacitus, the king sent word "to prohibit the history-reader to read." [28]

[25] *Letter-Book of Gabriel Harvey, A.D. 1573–1580,* ed. E. J. L. Scott, Camden Soc. (London, 1884), p. 79.

[26] F. J. Levy, "The Making of Camden's *Britannia,"* in *Bibliothèque d'Humanisme et Renaissance,* XXVI (1964), 84–85.

[27] Tacitus, *The Ende of Nero and Beginning of Galba,* trans. H. Savile (Oxford, 1591), "A. B. To the Reader." A. B. may be Anthony Bacon, but Edmund Bolton and Ben Jonson thought it was the Earl of Essex: Edmund Bolton, *Hypercritica,* in *Critical Essays of the Seventeenth Century,* ed. Joel Spingarn (Oxford, 1908–09), I, 115, and *Ben Jonson,* ed. C. H. Herford and Percy Simpson (Oxford, 1925–52), I, 142.

[28] *The Whole Works of the Most Rev. James Ussher, D.D.,* ed. C. R. Elrington and J. H. Todd (Dublin, 1847–64), XV, 403.

The particular phase of historiography which is called "politic" history was of brief duration. Sir John Hayward's *Henrie IIII*, of 1599, was the first such book in English; before 1640 decline had set in badly, and for our purposes, at least, the vogue may be said to have ended there. Between lay the historical sketches of Sir Robert Cotton and Sir Francis Bacon and the longer narratives of William Martyn and Samuel Daniel. Between lay, too, what was to be the most enduring monument of the school, William Camden's history of Queen Elizabeth.

Because Bacon not only wrote history but theorized about it, the obvious order of chronology ought here to be abandoned. If the question of literary influence be raised, it must be admitted that Bacon knew of Hayward's work immediately after its publication—Bacon seems, indeed, to have defended Hayward when the *Henrie IIII* landed him in the Tower. Even so, specific indebtedness is difficult to prove, and there is evidence that Bacon had been in any case thinking along similar lines. If, as Spedding argued, the letter of advice to the Earl of Rutland which is sometimes attributed to the Earl of Essex was in fact written by Bacon, then as early as 1594 Bacon was already saying, as he was to continue to do, that "Histories . . . will best instruct you in matter moral, military, and politic," and he went on to analyze the way in which history might be instructive:

> The use of observation is in noting the coherence of causes and effects, counsels and successes, and the proportion and likeness between nature and nature, force and force, action and action, state and state, time past and time present. . . . The observation of proportion or likeness between one person or one thing and another, makes nothing without an example, nor nothing new: and although *exempla illustrant non probant*, examples may make things plain that are proved, but prove not themselves; yet when circumstances agree, and proportion is kept, that which is probable in one case is probable in a thousand, and that which is reason once is reason ever.[29]

The careful differentiation between the two possible uses of *exempla* would itself be good reason to say that the letter was Bacon's.

[29] *The Letters and Life of Francis Bacon,* in *The Works of Francis Bacon,* ed. James E. Spedding et al. (London, 1857–74), IX, 12, 14.

Moreover, in another letter, this time to Sir Fulke Greville and, one must admit, of more dubious authenticity, Bacon praised Demosthenes above Cicero, Tacitus above Livy, Thucydides above all the other Greeks.[30] These are the new preferences, the favorites of a Senecan stylist and—obviously—of a Tacitean historian. That Bacon was part of the "court" of the Earl of Essex, at least for so long as the earl remained a moderate, means that he came into contact with the Taciteans who circled around Essex. Thus, even if Bacon's views of his own university, Cambridge, were not very complimentary, he must have met the remnants of the group of Oxonian Taciteans—such as Cuffe and Sir Henry Savile—who were in close association with Essex, and he knew Camden as well. There is, in brief, no real doubt that Bacon was a Tacitean long before he wrote his *Henry VII* and even before Hayward published the notorious *Henrie IIII*.

Bacon differed from his contemporaries by insisting on putting anything he did into a theoretical framework, and this habit is the more impressive in that the theory preceded the practice.[31] In *The Advancement of Learning* history was firmly dissociated from poetry, the former being considered as part of the faculty of memory, the latter as part of imagination. Thus the work of the Italian literary critics and of Sir Philip Sidney was brought to completion by, henceforth, making the comparison of history and poetry irrelevant. On the other hand, politics was a subdivision of reason, and the only connection between history and politics was the fact that the analyst of politics used history as his raw material. Bacon thus did not go so far as to see the writing of history as a rational act: for him the historian was still essentially a recorder of the acts of the past. In this the theory was somewhat at variance with Bacon's own practice, for he insisted that for a politic historian political experience was of greater importance than any "academic" historical training. Bacon's statement of the point was so strenuous that a reader might be pardoned for suspecting an ulterior motive:

[30] Ibid., IX, 25.
[31] I am much indebted for this discussion to the excellent article of Leonard F. Dean, "Sir Francis Bacon's Theory of Civil History-Writing," *English Literary History,* VIII (1941), 161–183. Except for quotations, I have not given references to *The Advancement of Learning*.

But it is not to monks or closet penmen that we are to look for guidance in such a case [as that of Queen Elizabeth]; for men of that order, being keen in style, poor in judgment, and partial in feeling, are no faithful witnesses as to the real passages of business. It is for ministers and great officers to judge of these things, and those who have handled the helm of government, and been acquainted with the difficulties and mysteries of state business.[32]

As an advertisement for Bacon's history this could hardly be bettered. But there was here a divergence between theory and practice caused perhaps by the fact that normally Bacon's comments on history were separated from the actual writing of it.

However, human history was only one part of human knowledge, with natural history and supernatural history constituting the two others. Simply because we know more about human history, the application of Baconian inductive method was easier there; and there was the additional point that it was a simpler matter to bring the human faculties to bear on human history than it was to analyze the principles of nature, let alone the providence of God. There was in this something of the grand theory of Bodin, though it is perhaps doubtful that Bacon would have gone quite so far as to say that an understanding of human history would lead to an understanding of the history of nature and the supernatural. In any case, the "scientific method" could be applied to human history: induction would allow the historian to draw general principles from the raw mass of deeds done, even if in so doing he turned philosopher. Oddly enough, Bacon never himself made much use of the critical tools that he invented. With a little adjustment the four groups of idols, those subtle delineations of how thought can be distorted, would have made admirable testing devices for judging historical sources; instead Bacon used them to expunge time-honored but erroneous concepts of natural history. He applied only the much more dubious theory that the stream of time washes down the lighter objects leaving the weightier behind to be excavated by the historian, and then only by adding statutes to the usual sources; most of the time Bacon was content to exercise his reason

[32] "On the Fortunate Memory of Elizabeth Queen of England," in *The Works of Francis Bacon*, VI, 305.

on facts left him by just those antiquated historians whom he
professed to despise.

One result of this disparity between practice and theory was that
Bacon's definition of history became unduly complicated. He differentiated the chronicler, the mere collector of material, from the
true historian, who did not present that material but instead used
it. Here would lie the distinction between Hall's or Speed's account
of Henry VII's reign and Bacon's. But it was possible to go a stage
beyond this: "And therefore the form of writing which of all
others is fittest for this variable argument of negotiation and occasions is that which Machiavel chose wisely and aptly for government; namely, *discourse upon histories or examples.*"[33] For this
there are no Baconian parallels. Instead, Bacon altered the form of
Machiavellian discourse and moved still another step from the raw
historical data. The sort of material that Machiavelli might have
included in his *Discourses* was mixed either with psychological
generalizations, as in the *Essays,* or with general epistemology, as
in *The Advancement of Learning.* Bacon, instead of commenting
on a specific history, subsumed his historical examples under subject headings: his model, in short, was Machiavelli's *Prince* rather
than his *Discourses.* If one wishes to find what political wisdom
Bacon drew from his reading (and writing) of history, there is
little use in seeking it in his *Henry VII.* If further illustration of
this be needed, it may be found in the use that Bacon made of the
Henry VII in his *Essays:* two references only are of importance,
one referring to the king's misuse of his noblemen, the other to his
use of councilors. Both come from the same paragraph of the
history, one of those in the concluding summary; and it was only
in this summary that Bacon generalized outward from Henry to
other kings.[34] Elsewhere, certainly, Bacon showed that particular
acts of the king might have a more general application, but that
application did not refer the reader outside the book or beyond the
character of Henry. Except for the last few paragraphs, in which

[33] Bacon, *The Advancement of Learning,* in *Works,* III, 453.
[34] Bacon, *Works,* VI, 422 ("Of Empire"); VI, 425 ("Of Counsel"). The
famous reference in the essay "Of the True Greatness of Kingdoms and Estates,"
which sends the reader to the *History* in order to learn about Henry's method of
ensuring a proper army, seems to refer to his acts in Parliament. The passage
does not occur in the summary, but neither is it of genuinely universal import.

Bacon the chronicler momentarily stood aside, the division between the recorder and the analyst of history remained unbridged.

The dichotomy between record and analysis, between memory and reason, must not be pushed too far. The chronicler, if he was reasonable, presumably tailored his record to fit its eventual end as the mine of the analyst. Thus Bacon was anxious to write the history of Tudor times because he felt that a "union of the two most noble and illustre houses of England and Scotland" would complement Hall's similar account of the union of York and Lancaster. More than that, the period had a peculiar attractiveness of its own, meeting as it did certain standards and criteria of inherent interest: "For they be not the great wars and conquests (which many times are the works of fortune and fall out in barbarous times) the rehearsal whereof maketh the profitable and instructing history; but rather times refined in policies and industries, new and rare variety of accidents and alterations, equal and just encounters of state and state in forces and of prince and prince in sufficiency, that bring upon the stage the best parts for observation." [35] A more detailed examination indicated that the Tudor period saw alterations in religion, a series of reigns of great variety —a new king, a minor, a queen married to a foreigner and, stranger still, a queen who refused to marry at all—as well as a series of corresponding rebellions and conspiracies and, finally, a varied foreign policy mixed with new discoveries and adventures overseas. Thus "there will be no doubt but the times which I have chosen are of all former times of this nation [the fittest] to be registered." [36] Peaceful times, of small but well-chosen scope, were the most instructive.

It is against this background that Bacon's own *Historie of the Raign of King Henry the Seventh* should be examined. His general theory epitomized the various forces operating to change the sixteenth-century concept of history: the development in critical theory which finally separated history from poetry, the interest in Tacitus and in the Senecan-Tacitean style, the connection to educative travel literature, the overtones of contemporary applicabil-

---

[35] Ibid., VI, 19 ("The History of the reign of K. Henry the Eighth, K. Edward, Q. Mary, and part of the reign of Q. Elizabeth").
[36] Ibid., VI, 20.

ity not only in terms of political maxims (which in Bacon, if not in his contemporaries, are shunted off from history writing proper) but also in terms of implied references to the situation of the day. When in 1621 the disgraced lord chancellor sat down to write history, he had to show a mastery of the discipline; perhaps more important, at least to the author, he had to demonstrate that his political advice was still worth seeking. That Bacon had planned such a history long before, that he had indeed done much of the research earlier, is inconsequential; when Bacon finally wrote, these were the purposes he had in mind. Thus, the references to a union with Scotland—the outcome of Henry's policy—were apropos; thus there was point to outlining at considerable length how Henry had handled pretenders to the throne, an issue which in the hands of Catholic apologists was not yet buried. That the parallel between James and Henry was far from perfect is not surprising; nor does the lack of perfection mean that no parallel was intended. Whatever Bacon's criticisms of Henry, Henry remained one of the good kings. "And for your comparison with Richard II. [so he told Oliver St. John], I see you follow the example of them that brought him upon the stage and into print in Queen Elizabeth's time; . . . But let me intreat you, that when you will speak of Queen Elizabeth or King James, you would compare them to King Henry VII. or King Edward I. or some other parallels to which they are like." [37] This did not and was not intended to mean that Henry VII was perfect, for the simple reason that James was not perfect either. A perfect king had no need of Bacons; but Henry had used and controlled Fox and Morton, and James could do the same with his councilors. If Henry VII had been greedy and amassed treasure, James might find that example useful—he was given more to spending. The very fact that the story of Henry's penny-pinching was largely a Baconian invention lends point to this: the lesson had to be taught somehow.

Bacon invented the past as well as reporting it, and this argues again the fundamental inconsistency of his position. That the *Historie of . . . Henry the Seventh* may not be treated as a source for that reign has been evident since it was demonstrated that

[37] Ibid., XII, 145.

Bacon used very little besides readily available chroniclers such as Polydore Vergil (through Hall), Bernard André, and Speed.[38] Again, what additional material he found was by no means recondite: the Statutes, some manuscript Parliament Rolls, and Hakluyt. The list is probably not exhaustive, but those few works comprise the greater part of Bacon's sources. The speeches of which the *Historie* is full were invented, even if occasionally there was evidence that some speech had indeed been given—but there was classical precedent for that, though Bodin did not approve. The errors were, many of them, due to Bacon's working from memory: the terms of his exile precluded further checks in Cotton's library, let alone the records. But then the details of chronology did not seem too important to a politic historian. That causes frequently had to be invented was inevitable: Sidney had seen that, and Bacon understood it as well. But the invention of causes meant that both the imaginative and the reasoning faculties had to be used in writing history; and this cast doubt upon the use of the ensuing history as raw material for politics. It was not the past that taught lessons, but the interpreters of the past. Bacon, when he sat down to write a history, found that his own theoretical distinction between the recorder of facts and the analyst of chronicles simply did not work, and his vain attempt to follow his own precept did little more than make his history less interesting than it might have been had analysis been more overtly included. Because of the emphasis on causes, there had to be some analysis in any case, and Bacon's attempt to hide the fact (or, less likely, his lack of awareness of it) only confounded what was already a serious problem in his philosophy. Bacon's separation of the historian from the philosopher had to lead, inevitably, to confusion; his own attempts to allay the confusion did little but compound it, and the other historians sensibly ignored the distinction.

Sir John Hayward, whose account of Henry IV's accession has already been mentioned, adopted no theoretical framework at all; nonetheless, if Bacon supplied some sort of epistemology, Hayward supplied the best example of "politic" history writ-

[38] Wilhelm Busch, *England under the Tudors, Vol. I: King Henry VII,* trans. Alice M. Todd (London, 1895), pp. 416–423.

ing.[39] Because of Hayward's early difficulties with the law, we have some information about his own views of historical method, and because he wrote a number of histories, scattered over nearly thirty years, he enables us to see what development, if any, was possible in the genre. *The First Part of the Life and Raigne of King Henrie the IIII* appeared in 1599; the eventual clamor made such a *cause célèbre* of the book that three other editions, all fraudulently dated 1599, also exist.[40] In retrospect it is somewhat difficult to see why there was so much excitement: granted that the *First Part*—there were no others—was concerned primarily with the deposition of Richard II, since that act conditioned most of the events of Henry IV's reign, it was hardly surprising that a historian would emphasize it. It was, of course, true that Queen Elizabeth had often been identified with Richard II; that the queen was accused of having favorites (Robert Cecil), that Ireland appeared as a crux in both stories, and that an earl played a prominent part in each. Had Hayward not dedicated his book to Essex, all might still have gone well. But Essex was the natural patron for such a book, not because his difficulties with Queen Elizabeth resembled those of Bolingbroke with Richard II, but because he was a powerful and wealthy nobleman with court connections who, moreover, had already shown some interest in just such subjects as Hayward's. This is not enough to exculpate Hayward: he may have known that he was treading close to treason, but, at the same time, his denials of any such intent cannot be dismissed. It is true that in the dedication Essex was covertly compared to Henry Bolingbroke; since a comparison of the patron to one of the characters of a history was natural and normal, and since Richard was patently inappropriate, there was still no necessity to cry treason. The remaining prefatory material was innocent enough: there was some expatiation on the value of histories to men of action, with a very standard reference to Lucius

[39] Hayward also has had the benefit of a good study: S. L. Goldberg, "Sir John Hayward, 'Politic' Historian," *Review of English Studies,* N.S., VI (1955), 233–244.

[40] W. A. Jackson, "Counterfeit Printing in Jacobean Times," *The Library,* 4th Ser., XV (1934), 372–376.

Lucullus, who, so the story went, learned to be a fine general
purely by reading such works. Hayward was aware of the meth-
odological problems—"what thinges are to bee suppressed, what
lightly touched, and what to be treated at large: how creadit
may be won, and suspition avoyded: what is to bee observed
in the order of times, and description of places and other such
circumstances of weight; what liberty a writer may use in fram-
ing speeches, and in declaring the causes, counsailes and eventes
of thinges done . . ." [41]—but having mentioned the difficulties, he
refused to discuss them further. It is undeniable that he made things
as difficult for himself as possible.

The evident ambiguities extended into the text. On the one
hand Hayward blamed and castigated the fitful changeability of
the mob; on the other he could hardly approve of Henry's pandering to that mob. That Richard behaved badly was soon evident but did not mean that Henry behaved well. The very mob
that had pitied Henry because of Richard's actions soon showed
its instability by pitying the imprisoned Richard. Richard,
dying, pointed out the justice of his own deposition by considering it as divine vengeance for Edward III's deposition of Edward II, and Hayward ended by showing that the same pattern
would repeat itself in the next century: which is simply a restate-
ment of Hall's thesis, with an extension back into the
fourteenth century. The crux of the volume, however, could be
found in a pair of speeches, attributed to Archbishop Arundel
(a "solemne oration in these words, or to this sence following")
and to the Bishop of Carlyle, which debated the right of revolution.[42] Afterward Hayward thought the second speech a sufficient answer to the first; the prosecutor, Sir Edward Coke,
disagreed. Since the archbishop's oration did lead to a successful
revolution, Hayward made it as impressive as he could and attributed to Arundel statements which seemed appropriate but for

---

[41] *The First Part of the Life and Raigne of King Henrie the IIII* (London,
1599), fol. A4^v. At least one reader was unable to see what the fuss was about:
John Chamberlain to Sir Dudley Carleton (March 1, 1599), *The Letters of John
Chamberlain*, ed. Norman E. McClure, in *Memoirs of the American Philosophical Society*, XII (Philadelphia, 1939), Pt. I, p. 70. The whole affair has been
treated by Margaret Dowling, "Sir John Hayward's Troubles over His *Life of
Henry IV*," *The Library*, 4th Ser., XI (1930), 212–224.

[42] Hayward, *Henrie the IIII*, pp. 61 ff.

which there was no sort of evidence: "he [Hayward] confessed
that the stories mencioned in the Archb. oration tendinge to
prove that deposers of kings and princes have had good successe,
were not taken out of any other cronicle, but inserted by him-
selfe. . . ." [43] Hayward was a trifle too successful, but any follower of the ancients would have done the same.

The heightening of the material was not, however, confined
to the speeches, where traditionally some license was permitted.
Hayward admitted that while the first benevolence he knew of
had been collected in the reign of Richard III, he had no objec-
tion to transferring the event to Richard II, thus blackening that
monarch further and adding to the justification for Henry's revolt. Shifting material from a later period into an earlier was patently inexcusable; the reverse could be justified, for "he taketh
that to be lawfull for any historiographer to insert any hystorie
of former tyme into that hystorie he wright albeit no other hystorian of that matter have meved the same." [44] But by this Hayward seems to have referred to speeches, and it was a defense
once again of Arundel's oration: the assumption was merely that
a man in Arundel's position would know the precedents as well
as, say, Hayward, and would cite them, and that the historian,
even without specific evidence, could assume that he had done
so. Here was a poor precept and, in the case of the benevolence,
a worse example.

Yet, for all of this, Hayward's *Henrie IIII* was more than propaganda in favor of Essex. The debt to Tacitus, to Guicciardini,
and to Machiavelli is fairly evident. In the case of the first, Bacon's comment that the author was guilty of larceny rather than
treason is true enough.[45] Hayward owed Tacitus more than his
language: the whole *mise en scène* was, in a sense, Tacitean
even if the opponents of the Roman emperors never managed to
mount a full-scale revolt. Hayward's approach to the problem of
portents resembled that of Guicciardini: an ostensible disbelief
hid a remnant of credulity which could be excused by saying that

[43] Dowling, "Hayward's Troubles," p. 214.
[44] Ibid., p. 216.
[45] Edwin B. Benjamin, "Sir John Hayward and Tacitus," *Review of English Studies*, N.S., VIII (1957), 275–276.

the men of Richard's time believed such things even if the historian did not. Thus, though such matters were patently trivial, they could (indeed, should) be included.[46] Even after admitting Hayward's debt to Tacitus and Guicciardini, one still feels the aura of Machiavelli surrounding the piece. If Hayward posed a question, it was that of how a prince should act who wished to lose his kingdom, with its converse, the actions necessary to gain it. It was the problem of the transfer of power that concerned him here, just as the problem of the consolidation of power was the subject of his *Lives of the III. Normans*. To Hayward the issue was as much political as historical, and it was this fact that justified transferring details from one reign to another: here was to be the textbook example of a deposition, and any and all causes for such an event might be adduced. The events of the last few years of Richard's reign, and of the first of Henry's, provided the factual base; the orations of Arundel and the Bishop of Carlyle provided the theoretical groundwork. Thus there was no reason to complain that a history of Henry IV's reign should not be taken up with an account of Richard; a history of how a new prince established himself could not logically avoid doing this. Moreover, viewing the work as a Machiavellian treatise helps to explain how Hayward could think of it as a defense of monarchy, even after his personal danger was long past. It has been pointed out that Machiavelli and Tacitus were essentially ambiguous, that they could be read as manuals for tyrants or as explications of the ways of tyrants for those wishing to go into opposition. Hayward later claimed that his book backed the authority of princes and the legitimacy of royal blood, and he was right.[47] He made as clear as he could (in the relatively few pages his essential structure allowed him) that Henry's lack of legitimacy had to lead to infinite trouble. There was no way to exculpate Richard II, and if a warning to tyrants could be read into that section, one suspects that Hayward would not have minded; but that is far from saying that he enjoined revolution, by Henry IV or by the Earl of Essex.

[46] Hayward, *Henrie the IIII*, pp. 51–52.
[47] *An Answer to the First Part of a Certaine Conference, concerning Succession* (London, 1603), fol. [A3ʳ].

· The penalty for ambiguity was serious: Hayward managed to
escape execution but most probably spent the years until the
queen's death in prison. Upon James's succession, most of Essex's
followers were restored to honor, and Hayward now had an opportunity to ingratiate himself with a new monarch. For a well-
trained civil lawyer this was not too difficult. In 1603 Hayward
defended James's claim to the throne against the attacks of the
Catholic Dolman (R. Parsons), at the same time affirming his
own loyalty to the principles of royalism. As far as Hayward was
concerned, laws, Parliament, and councils all took their origin
and authority from the king: that view was, even in 1603, already a little extreme; under the sledgehammer blows of Coke
and his fellows, it was to become downright unpopular. Nonetheless, such views were appropriate to civil lawyers, if not to
their common law brethren—a point which, by the way, suggests
that Hayward's claim that his first book had been misinterpreted
was not completely unjustified. Having defended the king's title,
Hayward went on by offering support for James's project of a
union between Scotland and England, mainly by showing that
the legal systems of the two countries were not incompatible.[48] Finally, in *A Reporte . . . concerning Supreme Power in Affaires of
Religion* (1606), Hayward demonstrated that religion should be a
part of the sovereignty of a state, by arguing from a definition of
sovereignty resembling Bodin's and by citing numerous historical examples, biblical and secular, that this had indeed been the
case and that the practice of the English monarch was in no
way an innovation. Thus, by a series of learned pamphlets, Hayward demonstrated his loyalty to kingship and to James. This
gives point to the suggestion that the 1609 forgery of the *Henrie
IIII* may have been printed at Hayward's request in order to
supply him with copies for presentation purposes: if this is so,
then Hayward received his reward quickly, for in 1610 he was
appointed one of the historiographers of His Majesty's new college at Chelsea.[49] Since the college never became operative, other

---

[48] *A Treatise of Union of the Two Realmes of England and Scotland* (London,
1604).

[49] Jackson, "Counterfeit Printing," p. 374; Anon., "Sir John Hayward," *Notes
& Queries,* CCII (1957), 288–290.

preferment followed: the lucrative post of commissary to the
dean and chapter of St. Paul's and, in 1616, a mastership in
Chancery, followed by work on the Court of High Commission.
In the struggles between king and Commons, Hayward (not surprisingly) was consistently on the side of the former, to the point
of bearing an attack by his fellow members of Commons for in-
fringing on the privileges of the House. Having once erred,
Hayward never again set a foot wrong, and his royalism remained
unsullied.

Only after his future was assured did Hayward return to practicing history. *The Lives of the III. Normans* (1613) may be
considered a pendant to the earlier biography of Henry IV: the
one book analyzed the means by which power was acquired, the
other the ways by which newly gained authority might be con-
solidated. The new book was intended to teach "rules of Policie," [50] and for an English ruler (it was dedicated first to Prince
Henry and then, after Henry's untimely death, to Prince Charles)
the history of England was the most appropriate vehicle. The
mechanics of William's conquest were not worth much study:

> Hee that winneth a State surmounteth onely outward difficulties;
> but he that assureth the same, travaileth as well against internall
> weaknes, as external strength. To attaine a Kingdome is many
> times a gift of Fortune; but to provide that it may long time
> continue firme, is not onely to oppose against humane forces, but
> against the very malice of Fortune, or rather the power and wrath
> of time, whereby all things are naturally inclineable to change.[51]

Hayward eventually arrived at the not entirely surprising conclusion that William used much the same technique for getting
as for holding, that is, the rigorous application of superior force.
Still, once victory and peace had been achieved, force could be
channeled from arms into law, and the rigor of the Conqueror's
laws—which lasted in Hayward's opinion until Magna Carta—
was worthy of commendation. William, indeed, appears more as
a Renaissance prince than as an eleventh-century Norman: his
difficulties with Bishop Odo, for instance, were interpreted not

---

[50] *The Lives of the III. Normans, Kings of England* (London, 1613), fol.
[A4ʳ].
[51] Ibid., pp. 45–46.

as feudal insubordination but as William's allowing a subordinate to collect both money and odium, thus permitting the king at one stroke to please the populace by despatching a hated oppressor while at the same time keeping the money for himself. One recollects something similar in Machiavelli—not that the Italian invented the idea.

William's achievement could be measured by his success in forcing the English to accept his younger son as their king; once William Rufus was seated safely on the throne of his father, Hayward could turn his attention to other matters. In the *Lives of the III. Normans* there is an advance in historical method. The matter of establishing power was only one of Hayward's themes, that most appropriate to the Conqueror. Two subordinate themes were introduced: the question of legality, relevant to William's title, came up again in greater detail when Rufus' right to the succession had to be discussed, and the same point arose again, less strongly, in an investigation of Henry I's right; and church-state relations were mentioned as relevant to the activities of both of the first two Normans, but this point did not become of major importance till Hayward came to Henry. Thus, although Hayward kept the division of history by reigns, he added to it a division by problems. Each of his themes was fully explored in one of his lives, but each was adumbrated in the other two. This is not to say that all other matters were suppressed: there is an attempt to fill out the portraits of the three monarchs. For all that, the organization of the book is extremely subtle, and Hayward solved in it the very difficult problem of giving unity to the history of more than one reign.

Hayward's last works are less exciting. The posthumously published history of Edward VI's reign was at once a return to old themes and an attempt to extend the organizing principles developed in the book on the Normans. The annalistic approach had been dropped in the earlier work simply because the lives of the two Williams and of Henry were mere sketches: the problem had been how to bridge reigns. But annals still were considered a necessity for a full-scale regnal history. In the case of Edward the reign was short and the problem of transition from year to year relatively simple. Hayward thus simply stated that he would go by "coherence or propinquity of matter" rather than by "just order of time," and that he would include only facts "such as I esteeme most fit for history, both as being publique, and as contained matter of some regard." [52] Certain points were taken together: rebellions, religion, Scotland; but the primary division was into the acts of a tragedy, these following chronology rather than strict regnal years. Warwick's doing away with Somerset began Act Three, for instance, while Warwick's own troubles constituted Act Four. While such a division was overtly stated,[53] and while Hayward undoubtedly realized that he could learn something about dramatic unity from the playwrights, one nevertheless feels that the play structure is superficial. Hayward, for all his faults, was too honest a historian to select his materials as drastically as Shakespeare, and the essential point, problems rather than (or at least together with) years, had already been adopted anyway. When one comes to ask what the unifying themes were, there is a sudden return to some of the problems raised in Hayward's earlier books. The instability of the mob once again was the subject of attack, and joined to this, a hatred of Somerset for seeking "popularity." Perhaps the people, seen from Charles I's reign, seemed more dangerous than they had in 1599; and in any case Hayward strongly disagreed with Somerset on the effects of enclosure. If so much sounded an echo of the *Henrie IIII*, then the theme of the Scottish war no less echoed *A Treatise of Union*. In retrospect the attempts to solve the Scottish problem by invasion and marriage seemed a waste of energy and blood, and Somerset was blamed for continuing a policy which was not his in the first place, and for being unable to predict the peaceful accession of the Stuarts. After the *Lives of the III. Normans*, Hayward's *Edward VI* was disappointing, and its only advance upon its predecessors came in the author's use of sources— such as the young king's journal—rather than other men's chronicles.

Judging Hayward's *Annals of . . . the Reign of Queen Elizabeth* is still more difficult. It is impossible to tell when the book was begun, nor can one guess whether it remained unfinished be-

---

[52] *The Life and Raigne of King Edward the Sixt* (London, 1630), p. 143.
[53] Ibid., p. 129: "And now to begin the third act of his tragedie. . . ."

cause of the author's death or because the inevitable failure of his attempt became obvious. Structurally the *Annals* was an attempt to extend the earlier technique to a long reign. Camden had already published his biography of the queen, but because his bridging of the annalistic scheme was rudimentary, Hayward must have thought the work could be improved upon.[54] That task turned out to be more difficult than it appeared. Hayward completed only four of Elizabeth's forty-four years of rule, and in those he merely organized each year around some specific theme. In the first the emphasis was on the queen's personality and on the alteration in religion; in the second and third the focal point was Scotland, with the fire at St. Paul's coming in as a minor leitmotiv in the latter; the fourth year centered on France. Again, briefer accounts of other happenings were included, as they had to be. There is, however, no doubt that the *Annals* was a failure: Hayward had only exaggerated the sort of thing that Camden had done earlier and, in the face of that example, had been unable to nerve himself sufficiently to give up the annalistic structure altogether. For Hayward, detailed history centered only on problems was impossible, and his technique of compromise with older forms had gone as far as it could.

What Hayward and Bacon accomplished was to join the methods of the ordinary chronicler to those of the politic historian. In his first book Hayward tended to emphasize the new technique at the expense of the old; later the balance became more even. To a large extent we have discussed that point in terms of organization, simply because the most important change took place in the way in which the raw materials of history were arranged. The topical approach sprang directly from the practice of using history to teach political lessons, that is, from the basic premise of politic history; it was only a short step from that to arranging the materials of history so that the lessons would emerge more easily. Hayward took that step in his first book and then, as we have seen, went beyond it. A serious question arises, however. Hayward himself stated that the three essential qualities of good

[54] The suggestion that Hayward attempted to rival Camden is Goldberg's: "Sir John Hayward," p. 240; Hayward's *Annals* were not published until the nineteenth century (ed. John Bruce for the Camden Soc. [London, 1840]).

history writing were "Order, Poyse and Truth." [55] Order has been discussed at length and so has "poyse," for that is what makes a history politic; both, in Hayward's hands, came off well. Truth, alas, frequently had to follow at a sorry distance. Hayward's freedom with chronology when he wrote his first book has been mentioned before. Because motive and causation were so important to a politic historian, he ended by taking some liberties with the facts. Most classical historians solved that problem by confining their imaginative reconstructions to the speeches; since tradition hallowed this, and since readers were quite as aware of the tradition as writers, no harm resulted. By the time Hayward wrote, the old tradition had come under attack, the oration was no longer a safe haven for the imagination, and an author had either to give up working his causes into his narrative at all or to exercise his inventiveness elsewhere in the story. Hayward had learned his lesson in the hardest possible school. So one finds speeches in the life of Edward VI that were not invented but which came ultimately from Foxe, with Speed as a possible medium; on the other hand, Hayward on one occasion moved a fact backward in time (which even he thought improper) and many times invented his character sketches. This last was, one supposes, as good a compromise as increasing standards of historical accuracy allowed. And if Hayward did sometimes invent, he also researched. *The Lives of the III. Normans* may have been based on the Elizabethan chroniclers, but its author also read in the newly published anthologies of Camden and Savile and in Matthew Paris and William of Newburgh as well; in the same way, the Cotton manuscript of Edward VI's diary augmented the account in Speed. Nor, in all this, did the politic aphorism go forgotten. In Hayward's first book many such came, appropriately enough, from Tacitus. Later they came from his own experience and, since Hayward never mastered the art of the epigram, became correspondingly fewer. But in his work were all the accouterments of the politic historian, tempered increasingly by responsibility.

A number of small works proved, however, that it was possible to adopt the surface polishing of Hayward and Bacon with-

---

[55] See Goldberg, "Sir John Hayward," p. 237.

out at the same time adopting their solid core of fact. A discussion of such a writer as William Martyn, whose sweep was wide, had best be postponed; but Thomas Gainsford, an intelligent hack with an ability for capitalizing on current fashion, fits superficially into the category of Hayward and Bacon. Of all of Gainsford's substantial production, *The True and Wonderfull History of Perkin Warbeck* (1618) is the only properly "historical" work, though Gainsford did, on occasion, comment on the immediate past elsewhere. The introduction contained all the proper clichés: the advantages of precept and example, the usefulness of caution, and the fact that history taught the divine attributes of majesty, the secrets of religion, the policies of government, and the workings of fortune, with the additional comment—typical of Gainsford—that history was pleasurable. Unfortunately, the text did not live up to the advance billing, and the body of the book was not concerned with the highly interesting matters adumbrated in its introduction but was merely a tract against rebellion set in a slight theological framework. Of "policy" there was very little, and the introduction, it is clear, was tacked onto the book in order to make it appeal to a new taste.[56]

Gainsford's book tells us no more than that by 1618 there was enough popular interest in "politic" history writing to make it worthwhile engaging in a species of fraud. Two works of a decade later indicate what might happen to the new style when the author's interest in contemporary affairs completely overshadowed any attempt at historical verisimilitude. Sir Robert Cotton, as the possessor of the largest collection of documents in private hands, ought to have been in a position to write accurate and well-authenticated history, perhaps along the lines of Hayward. Instead, his *Short View of the Long Life and Raigne of Henry the Third, King of England* was little more than a tract for the times. Written, so the title page informs us, for King James, it applied equally well to his son and successor. Contemporaries, at least, were in no doubt as to Cotton's intentions: "There is a

---

[56] One earlier example is amusing. Henry Crosse, in 1603, wrote an uninspired moral treatise entitled *Vertues Common-wealth, or The Highway to Honour;* two years later, the unsold sheets were bound up with a new title page as *The Schoole of Pollicie.*

litle booke published comprising severall passages of state historically related, as they were carried in the long raigne of King
Henry the 3d. with some observations or application to our state
at this present which by reason of Favourites & discontented
peeres resembles in many thing that ancient government." [57] Cotton's biography of Henry III was essentially a *Bildungsroman,*
written as a not very oblique warning to the Stuarts. The style
was "Baconian," though the text was even more studded with
epigrams:

> Denials from Princes must bee supplyed with gracious usage, that
> though they cure not the sore, yet they may abate the sence of it;
> but best it is, that all favours come directly from themselves;
> denialls and things of bitternesse from their Ministers. . . .
>
> Thus Parliaments that before were ever a medicine to heale up
> any rupture in Princes fortunes, are now growne worse then the
> mallady, sith from thence more mallignant humors beganne to
> raigne in them, then well composed tempers. . . .
>
> Thus doe the wrongs of our Enemies more then our owne
> discretions, make us sometimes both wise and fortunate.[58]

There was in all of this no attempt to write a proper history of
the reign, though the trappings of scholarship (such as the
sources cited in the margin) were in evidence: on one occasion,
thirty years were dismissed in a sentence. Nonetheless, the aphorisms and the choice of materials all conspired to prove that
Crosfield's judgment of the case was accurate. Cotton's work was
the product of a loyal if somewhat disillusioned supporter of the
monarchy who hoped desperately to demonstrate what effects its
errors were likely to have, and who dared not write more openly.

The History of the Life, Reign, and Death of Edward II,
while more fully developed, was both exactly contemporaneous
to and exactly parallel to Cotton's work. Edward Cary, Lord
Falkland, had also become disillusioned with the rule of favorites, and he too had chosen a reign appropriate to teaching lessons about the dire results of misplaced faith in unworthy men.

---

[57] *The Diary of Thomas Crosfield,* ed. F. S. Boas (London, 1935), p. 12
(March 3, 1627).

[58] *A Short View of the Long Life and Raigne of Henry the Third* (London,
1627), pp. 12–13, 25, 49.

Henry III, however, had had to face only disturbances; Edward II was deposed. Thus, while Cotton's book was at least published, though anonymously, Falkland's had to remain in manuscript until 1680. Whether Falkland's book was "disloyal" is open to question, but there is no doubt that the reader must often have asked himself whether the true setting was 1307–1327 or 1627. So the epigrams are more frequent and more pointed, the orations are exaggerated, the style screwed to the highest pitch. That Edward II was guilty not only of homosexuality but also of bad judgment was made clear at the outset. Falkland clearly believed that the barons had a good case, since there was no doubt that Edward's "favoritism" led to unsuccessful French and Scottish wars and, more importantly, to the vicious fighting within England itself. Having said so much, Falkland drew back: Edward was wrong, but so was revolution. The problem, presumably, was not capable of solution: it would be best for the king to reform, or the nobility would be forced into illegal action. All that could safely be said was that favorites, and the illegal taxes they forced the king to levy, were wrong. The year 1627 was not yet a year for revolution: but it was not too soon to warn of it, and for that politic history made an ideal vehicle.

How far the methods of politic history could be stretched was a question that had not been satisfactorily answered. Certain reigns were obviously more amenable to such treatment than others, and if a writer was willing to use the surgeon's knife and was deft in its handling, still more could be forced into the pattern. Bacon had stated that the period of the Tudors was ideal material: he had then written of Henry VII, and Camden of Elizabeth, with Bishop Francis Godwin filling in the intervening reigns, of which Edward VI's was done again by Hayward and Henry VIII's was to be done by Lord Herbert of Cherbury. Other reigns with special problems—revolutions, conquests, and the like—also were attractive, especially if the problems represented current concerns. But what of an ordinary reign? William Habington tried to rewrite the history of Edward IV and, partly because of the nature of the subject but more especially because of his own incapacity, failed. Edward's reign did offer some advantages: the European situation was such that England was isolated and needed to fear

no intervention from abroad. Edward, however, was not a very
"politic" king: his marriage to Elizabeth Woodville proved that.
As if that were not enough, Habington was still so much in the
toils of the "kings and battles" school that he ended by concentrating on wars and conspiracies, the former of which were, by
his own showing, tedious. Had the book been conceived as the
struggle between a king and his overmighty subject, between
Edward and Warwick, something might have been made of it.
But Edward fitted into the mold neither of a Henry VII nor yet of
a Henry V, and nothing that Habington could do was able to alter
the fact. That Habington, moreover, was obsessed by the ordinary
rules of morality helped not at all: Edward was simply not very
virtuous. And Habington's custom of making historical equations
—Edward got rid of Clarence by a false accusation and so
Edward's own children were disposed of the same way—was opposed in its essence to the principles upon which politic historians
worked. All that was visible of the politic method were the *sententiae,* probably inserted after the narrative was written, and they
were not very impressive. Habington failed because he was too
honest to cut his cloth to fit the pattern, but also because his grasp
of the pattern was, at best, weak.

Politic history began, as we have seen, with a problem—the
reasons for the deposition of Richard II—and then was extended
to reigns. Even here, frequently, a reign was seen in terms of one
problem—say, favorites—with other events either omitted altogether or sharply compressed. There were, however, some
attempts to write a politic history of a broad stretch of time, and
two of these are worth further examination. *The Historie, and
Lives, of Twentie Kings of England* (1615) was written by William Martyn, a lawyer who served as Recorder of Exeter. As with
other works we have examined, there was more here of form than
of substance. Martyn wrote to educate the young gentlemen of
England, who ought to learn something of their own history
before they went abroad to learn that of others, but who did not
do so because the English chronicles were blemished by being excessively long, burdened "by too too many intervening Occurrences, and by a multitude of extravagant Observations." [59] Such

---

[59] Epistle Dedicatorie, [¶3ʳ].

confusion, he thought, was too much for the capacities of his readers, who turned instead to the digests of foreign history. Whereas Hayward abbreviated because one point struck him as more important than another, Martyn did so to make things simpler for his readers. This attitude extended still further, for Martyn did believe that causes and policy were the reasons men should read histories, but instead of detailed analysis he was inclined to give his readers lists. William's policies for holding England were reduced to sixteen, the principle uniting them being that of naked power. Similar lists could be found in the lives of other kings, though most of the items were a little vague: the precise value of the statement that it was a good policy of Henry I's to exile base flatterers from his court does not strike one as very great. Nor, in the context of policy, was it very helpful to analyze the defeats of Edward II by the Scots as caused by divine justice, by God "before whom Princes must fall as well as the common subjects, except their true and heartie repentance . . . procure his mercie and his favour." [60] It is not that Hayward or Bacon or Cotton would have disagreed, merely that they would have wondered what use such a statement would be to a prince in difficulties. As it is, the statement indicates a falling-off even from Martyn's never high standards, something which is true of most of the second half of his book. By the time Martyn reached the reign of Henry VII, the story had been reduced to mere chronology, and the closest he came even to the unsophisticated analysis of the beginning was in his description of Henry's sending agents to Burgundy to learn about Perkin Warbeck's rebellious plans as "a wittie policie." [61] Bacon must have found it difficult to repress a smile.

Martyn's was an amateur's attempt, and it proved little more than that the tricks of Tacitean history were easily learned—plus, presumably, that there was a market for such things. With Samuel Daniel, we are in a different world.[62] Daniel had been

[60] Ibid., p. 94.
[61] Ibid., p. 339, margin.
[62] Daniel has been the subject of much writing: May McKisack, "Samuel Daniel as Historian," *Review of English Studies*, XXIII (1947), 226–243; Rudolf B. Gottfried, "Samuel Daniel's Method of Writing History," *Studies in the Renaissance*, III (1956), 157–174; William Blissett, "Samuel Daniel's Sense of the Past," *English Studies*, XXXVIII (1957), 49–63; Cecil C. Seronsy, "The

reading history—and writing historical verse—long before *The First Part of the Historie of England* appeared in 1612. Even before Hayward published, Daniel had begun to think of history in terms of the transfer and consolidation of power, in terms of the state and the loyalties and disloyalties it engendered. Of the two verse dramas, *Cleopatra* (which took place in the period between Mark Antony's defeat and the queen's suicide) analyzed the methods of a conqueror and the delays of the conquered and described the aura of power which forced weak men into petty treasons even when they had no hope of gain. Cleopatra had not had the good fortune of Harold the Saxon: she survived her defeat, and the inexorable laws of power and conquest left her with the choice only between captivity (a progress, in chains, through the streets of Rome) or suicide. *Philotas* paralleled the career of the Earl of Essex—accidentally, so Daniel claimed—by demonstrating how easily treason came to those whose thoughts were already in any way disloyal. The power of Alexander the Great attracted envy—Philotas and his father had helped win Alexander's battles: were they not then as great as he?—as it also attracted sycophancy; and when Philotas showed himself guilty of misprision of treason, the sycophants, the mere administrators jealous of a man of action, saw to his ruin. Both *Philotas* and *Cleopatra* were dramas of character, but in both the theme was that of the relation of men to the manifestations of political power.

Much the same may be said of Daniel's *Civil Wars*. Ben Jonson thought it was an insult when he commented that "Daniel wrott civill warres & yett hath not one batle in all his Book"; [63] in fact, Daniel would probably have considered the remark a compliment, since in his view battles were only one way, and one of the least important, of settling political disputes. Bacon had thought that relatively peaceful periods were best for analysis; Daniel, a pacifist who was inclined to think that wars settled little, reduced the reports of the fighting to a minimum. Instead, the poet-

Doctrine of Cyclical Recurrence and Some Related Ideas in the Works of Samuel Daniel," *Studies in Philology*, LIV (1957), 387–407; William Leigh Godshalk, "Daniel's *History*," *Journal of English and Germanic Philology*, LXIII (1964), 45–57.

[63] *Ben Jonson*, ed. Herford and Simpson, I, 138.

historian should concentrate his attention on character, even if that meant inventing speeches:

> And although many of these Images are drawne with the pencil of mine owne conceiving: yet I knowe, they are according to the portraiture of Nature; and carrie a resemblance to the life of Action, and their complexions whom they represent. For I see, Ambition, Faction, and Affections, speake ever one Language, weare like colours (though in severall fashions) feed, and are fed with the same nutriments; and only vary but in time.
>
> Man is a creature of the same dimension he was: and how great and eminent soever hee bee, his measure and height is easie to be taken. And all these great actions are openly presented on the Stage of the World: where, there are ever *Spectators,* who will judge and censure how men personate those parts, which they are set to perform; and so enter them in the Records of Memorie.[64]

The problem to be faced was not one of war but of guilt or innocence, of what sort and how much justification was required to remove a tyrant and the inevitable effects of such a removal, for tyranny created chaos not only in its being but even in its ending. If Daniel's *Civil Wars* were bloodless, the cause was not in the paucity of battles but in the lack of delineation of the principal characters: one has the impression that the protagonists were ethereal ideas, not men, and that the motive forces were not human passions but gods far removed from the fray.

Daniel was too good a historian to be a good historical poet, and he realized that writing philosophical history was itself difficult enough without trying to force narrative and analysis into verse, while those things that made verse interesting—romance, for instance—might not be appropriate to philosophical history. Those lessons that writing historical poetry taught—condensation and characterization—he had learned; and long before the *Meisterwerk* of his apprentice years—the *Civil Wars*—was completed, Daniel had determined to write a prose history, with the result that the poem never did progress beyond the middle of Edward IV's reign. It did not at first trouble its author that the new work had an even grander sweep than the old, from William I through

---

[64] *The Civil Wars,* ed. Laurence Michel (New Haven, 1958), p. 68.

the Tudors. The results, unfortunately, were the same: the *Historie of England* arrived finally at the point where the *Civil Wars* began, and the final volume, intended to finish the narrative, was never written, nor was a supplementary volume of sources. Even as it stood, however, the work was highly original. Daniel, like Martyn, refused to go back beyond William the Conqueror, but where Martyn gave no reason for his refusal (and one suspects that laziness was one cause) Daniel stated firmly that the earlier period was too much subject to conjecture and that the possibilities of learning from that guesswork were slight. The whole of English history to 1066 was thus reduced to two dozen pages, and these were clearly in the nature of an introduction. Once William came to the throne, it was possible to be sensible. Daniel began his history with a survey of the events of the reign and then turned to an analysis of selected problems: the laws of England, tenures and taxation, and counselors, concluding with a brief portrayal of William himself. The problems clearly were those of a conqueror and of his relations to the conquered; but for Daniel there was interest also in the way in which a nation might absorb a conqueror. This pattern was continued throughout the book: always there were the events, necessary for completeness, then the problems, necessary for the didactic purpose of history to be fulfilled.

The *Historie of England* was intended to teach, and the subject taught was political behavior. Daniel claimed no originality in his matter, only in "the observation of those necessary circumstances, and inferences which the History naturally ministers." [65] The history of any nation could be made to teach, but a man learned best from the history of his own land; thus it was a pity that no analytical history of England existed, and it was Daniel's patriotism that prompted him to write one. Accuracy was worth striving for, but it was not essential. If the printer or the author made errors, that was not too important, for "these things being but of the By, the understanding Reader will not much care to set at them, and therefore I referre him to the Maine, of more important consideration." [66] Complete accu-

---

[65] *The Collection of the History of England* (London, 1634), fol. A3ᵛ.
[66] Ibid., fol. [A4ʳ].

racy was, in any event, impossible because "God in his providence, to checke our presumption, wraps up all things in uncertaintie," nor was it even necessarily desirable. "For had we the perticular occurrents of all ages, and all nations, it might more stuffe, but not better our understanding." [67] Men were always men, virtues and vices remained the same, though their combination in any one man was unique. A well-digested slice of recent history was enough.

So much was not, in fact, very unusual. What set Daniel apart from his contemporaries was not his intention but his practice. Daniel had the gift of not taking things at face value, and no source was sacrosanct. Even in the first section, which, being pre-Norman, was of little interest to him, he could not forbear to comment that the validity of Gildas was limited by his attitude, "as if he laboured to inveigh, not to enforme." Moreover, Daniel, for all his supposed didacticism (which involved a continual linking of past and present), had the sort of historical imagination which could try to see the past in its own terms and could realize that the present would never fully understand the past. Having censured Richard I for his crusading, in which Daniel could see little that was useful, he nonetheless was able to go on: "Pardon us Antiquity, if we mis-censure your actions, which are ever (as those of men) according to the vogue, and sway of times, and have onely their upholding by the opinion of the present: We deale with you but as posterity will with us (which ever thinkes it selfe the wiser) that will judge likewise of our errors according to the cast of their imaginations." For all his protestations to the contrary, Daniel was never altogether able to eschew commenting on events as he recorded and analyzed them. Just because he felt strongly and was unable to repress those feelings, Daniel's work is interesting; one thinks of his comment on Edward III's order that law pleadings be in English: "A blessed Act and worthy so great a King . . . ; but such is the Fate of Law, that in what language soever it speakes, it never speakes plaine, but . . . gives more affliction to the people than it doth remedy." [68] Assuredly, this is not one of the lessons of history

[67] *The First Part of the Historie of England* (London, 1612), p. 3.
[68] *Collection*, pp. 7, 119, 251.

advertised in the preface; just as surely, it is a lesson that any wise man, not himself a lawyer, might easily draw.

In one way, however, Daniel was closer to his Tudor predecessors than he was to the other politic historians. In spite of causes, circumstances, and other appurtenances of the new mode, Daniel retained a strong belief in the actions of the divine Providence, a belief so strong as to set up a serious conflict between free will and predestination. Early in his book, he had expressed the view that the death of Henry I's son in the White Ship was but the first example of a plague that was to trouble the kings of England for generations: that no dynasty seemed able to sit quietly on the throne for more than three inheritors. When Edward II was murdered, Daniel exclaimed that "the judgement of God fell heavily, not onely upon the great contrivers, but even upon the whole kingdome," as the nobility could testify, whose ancestors had died on "the many imbrued scaffolds" and "the divers bloudy fields." [69] And Edward III, though himself innocent, suffered too. But if this were so, and the taint were inherited, what purpose did the political lessons serve?

As if this were not bad enough, Daniel even doubted the effects of education. Had not Henry III's son, Prince Edward, been of an innate goodness, he might have proven a bad prince regardless of how he was taught, for bad princes "shall gaine litle by their education, wherein they are rather shewed what they are, than what they should be; . . . being ever soothed in all whatsoever they doe." [70] For a prince to be good was still necessary, or the curse would be continued for further generations; but Daniel left in doubt the problem of whether goodness could assist anyone in raising the shadow of the past. All that was left to a prince was to act in such a way as to earn the approbation of posterity: Daniel arranged matters so that the traditional boast of the poet—that he alone was able to lead his patron to immortality—had now to be applied to the relation between prince and historian as well. Since a similar view could be found in Caxton, and since the three-generations concept which Daniel elaborated derived from Hall and Polydore, the philosophical

[69] Ibid., pp. 65, 220.
[70] Ibid., p. 173.

substructure of the *Historie of England* may be said to be traditional, with Daniel adding to it only a fine intelligence which operated on the specific details rather than on the grander picture. How fine that intelligence was may be seen best in Daniel's brief analysis of the changes that took place during the Tudor century—an analysis that he never found time to work up into a history:

> A time not of that virilitie as the former, but more subtile, and let out into wider notions, and bolder discoveries of what lay hidden before. A time wherein began a greater improvement of the Soveraigntie, and more came to be effected by wit then the sword: Equall and just incounters, of State, and State in forces, and of Prince, and Prince in sufficiencie. The opening of a new world, which strangely altered the manner of this, inhancing both the rate of all things, by the induction of infinite Treasure, & opened a wider way to corruption, whereby Princes got much without their swords: Protections, & Confederations to counterpoyse, & prevent over-growing powers, came to bee maintained with larger pensions. Leidger Ambassadors first imployed abroad for intelligences. Common Banks erected, to returne and furnish moneys for these businesses. Besides strange alterations in the State Ecclesiasticall: Religion brought forth to bee an Actor in the greatest Designes of Ambition and Faction. To conclude, a time stored with all varietie of accidents fit for example, and instruction.[71]

Sir Francis Bacon, who also saw the possibilities, never saw them half so clearly.

The greatest accomplishment of the school of politic historians was the *Rerum Anglicarum . . . annales, regnante Elisabetha.* William Camden was able to combine the amplitude of the traditional chronicle with the incisiveness of the newer methods and was able, moreover, to bring about some changes in the way in which annals might be organized. The principal difference between Camden and the other politic historians was, however, the fact that when Camden began his *Annales,* he had already made a reputation with his *Britannia;* that is, he had very substantial

---

[71] *The First Part of the Historie,* fol. A3ʳ–A3ᵛ.

experience in the delicate tasks of collecting and weighing evidence and in the use of conjecture.

So far as one can tell, Camden had determined to be a historian from the beginning. Evidence remains which indicates that even before he began work on *Britannia,* he intended to write a history of England beginning with the Norman Conquest if not earlier.[72] That scheme was abandoned when Ortelius convinced him that a chorography of Britain was a more pressing task than another history, and its revival had to wait until 1596, when Lord Burghley persuaded him to undertake a history of the queen's reign. Even so, Camden waited until 1608 before he began to sort out the papers left him by the lord treasurer. In the interim he added to those papers whatever he could find in Cotton's library and in his own notes. Camden had always been interested in the history of his own times, and he had made a point of being present on such great occasions as the trials of Norfolk and Essex, the first of which occurred when Camden was only twenty-one and newly down from Oxford.[73] Whether, in the end, the *Annales* would have been written without official encouragement is doubtful, since Camden was all too aware of the dangers of contemporary history.

As a classical scholar Camden was bound to be influenced by past examples, but rather than choose as his models Livy or Plutarch, he instead based himself on Polybius and Tacitus. "That of *Polybius* I like well: *Take away from History Why, How and To what end, things have been done, and Whether the thing done hath succeeded according to Reason; and all that remains will rather be an idle Sport and Foolery, then a profitable Instruction."* From Tacitus, Camden learned to write annals as being the best way of digesting "Weighty and remarkable Occurrences." A curt style, coarse and undecorated, was appropriate to annals, although Camden went further than his master by eschewing the aphorisms and *sententiae* which normally graced the Tacitean style. From both his teachers Camden learned some-

---

[72] *Britannia,* ed. Richard Gough (London, 1789), I, cxxii.
[73] Camden, *The Historie of the . . . Princesse Elizabeth,* trans. Richard Norton (London, 1675), fol. a3ʳ; *V. Cl. Gulielmi Camdeni . . . Epistolae,* ed. Thomas Smith (London, 1691), Appendix, p. 85; *Historie,* pp. 176, 620.

thing of decorum, a solution to the problem of what was appropriate for a historian to include and what should be omitted. War and policy were proper subjects for a historian; in ordinary circumstances, ecclesiastical matters were the province of specialists, but no analysis of Elizabethan history could omit them "For Religion and the Commonwealth cannot be parted asunder." [74] Disturbances in nature and the minor peccadilloes of unimportant men—these required apology if they were to be included.

The solution of two interlocking problems gave the book what excellence it possessed, while at the same time those problems were the source of some of the more obvious objections. In his *Britannia,* Camden had had to face the problem of conjecture, and although he expressed his willingness to push his information as far as it could be made to go and a little beyond, he had always been apologetic about it. When a historian was trying to solve the mysteries of long-vanished place names, there might be justification for such a procedure; when the history was of yesterday and the day before, there could be no such excuse. Thus, when Camden said that "Circumstances I have in no wise omitted, that not onely the Events of Affairs, but also the Reasons and Causes thereof, might be understood," he meant that his access to records in his own hands, in Cotton's library, and in the Burghley archives made enough material available so that causes could be worked out without imagination. For the use of imagination was dangerous not only to truth but also to the health of the historian. "Things manifest and evident I have not concealed; Things doubtfull I have interpreted favourably; Things secret and abstruse I have not pried into." There was the second of his problems: it was dangerous for a historian to seek the answers to certain questions, let alone to publish them. With conjecture thus doubly barred from use, it taxed the powers even of a good historian to indicate the motives from which decisions sprang. Camden's solution was ingenious: he adopted, in essence, the method that Lord Burghley himself had used in making up his mind on key problems. Anyone acquainted with Burghley's papers is familiar with the long lists of arguments, pro and con,

---

[74] Ibid., "The Authour to the Reader," foll. b2ʳ, b2ᵛ, b1ᵛ.

that the old treasurer was wont to draft. Camden printed similar
lists, sometimes straight out, at other times absorbed into the
general argument.[75]

Thus in Camden it is not always easy to detect to what causes
an event is attributed; all one has are the reasons for and against
an action which passed, or might have passed, through the mind
of one of the principal actors. This slightly obscure method of
indicating causation must, however, be considered in conjunction
with the structure of the *Annales*. Although Camden proceeded
year by year, he grouped events within a given year and, where
it was feasible and expedient, put an action at the end of an annal
so that the story could be picked up immediately at the beginning
of the next. Camden's annals rarely had the scope or the vigor of
Tacitus', but they were far from being mere chronicle entries.
The result of all this was that a reader interested in politics would
find an action beginning in one annal where it might not seem
important; in the next annal, the event would be shown in sharper
focus (or, of course, if nothing happened, there would be no
mention of it); eventually, a decision regarding the matter would
have to be made, and the reasons for the alternatives were presented, though the notice of what the decision was might have to
wait for the ensuing annal; at last, the effects of the decision
could be evaluated. Thus, the *Annales* was a handbook for politicians, not in the usual sense of a list of "do's" and "don't's" but in
the sense of allowing the reader at each moment to make his own
prediction of what would happen next and enabling him to
check his prediction against the decisions that were actually
made and the results that followed. Thus Camden never pried
into the secrets of princes, nor did he engage in conjecture, but
causation was still indicated, and that in a most instructive manner. It was true, however, that the author's analysis frequently
appeared perfunctory and that, because of the annalistic
method, it was sometimes hard to follow what was going on.

This is not to suggest that the *Annales,* overall, was an aimless compilation, differing from chronicles only in the care with
which causes were introduced. For all the author's emphasis on

---

[75] Ibid., foll. b1ᵛ–b2ʳ, b1ᵛ; see, e.g., pp. 233–234, 319–320.

truth, his book was nonetheless a deliberate defense of the Elizabethan settlement in both politics and religion: "By means of
this Alteration of Religion, *England* (as the Politicians have
observed) became of all the Kingdoms of Christendome the
most free, the Scepter as it were manumitted from the forrein
Servitude of the Bishop of *Rome;* and more wealthy then in
former Ages, an infinite mass of Money being stayed at home,
which was wont to be exported daily to *Rome. . . .*" [76] The
mature Camden who wrote the *Annales* was far removed from
the young man who had lost a fellowship at All Souls because of
his Anglicanism, but the incident was never forgotten. Anglicanism in all its manifestations was always in the right, whether
in regard to the war against Spain, the persecution of Catholics
(and Camden emphasized the political nature of their crimes,
following the lead of the Elizabethan courts), or the difficulties
placed in the way of Puritans and sectaries. Camden remained
an Anglican and a royalist in James's reign, regardless of the
opinions of friends such as Cotton and Selden, and his book was
an *apologia* for the old-fashioned view which its author shared
with Lord Burghley. Burghley had chosen well.

If Camden gave way at all to the changing times, it was only to
please the king. Logically, had everything in the book been made
to fit into the Elizabethan pattern, Mary of Scotland would have
been one of the villains. With her son on the throne, that was impossible. James dictated to Camden, and to anyone else who
would listen, his own account of the events which had led up to
Mary's loss of her throne, and the Protestant Earl of Moray had
to be indicted for ambition before the Catholic Mary could be ac-
quitted of sheer foolishness. That account was the more satisfying
in that Moray's ablest defender had been the king's hated tutor,
George Buchanan, and now James could avenge himself on Buchanan and clear his mother simultaneously. Camden was virtually forced to include this story in his *Annales,* despite the fact
that he had earlier admired Buchanan as a man and as a writer.
Pages of the *Annales* had to be devoted to exposing Buchanan's
pretensions, and when Mary came to England, the author was

[76] Ibid., p. 31.

still left in the awkward position of being anti-Catholic and having Catholic plots against Elizabeth to explain without being able to present Mary as the logical center, indeed the originator, of those plots. The queen executed for treason had perforce to become a heroine, and her transformation left a gaping tear in the fabric of the book. Such were the penalties of writing contemporary history.[77]

The corresponding reward was the plethora of available information. Burghley's papers, Cotton's library, and Camden's own collections and observations could all be drawn on. He spoke to men of affairs "who have been present at the transacting of Matters, and such as have been addicted to the Parties on both Sides in this contrariety of Religion," and these included Sir John Fortescue, an officer of the royal household and an intimate of the queen, Henry Cuffe, who had been professor of Greek at Oxford before becoming adviser of Essex and his companion on the scaffold, and Sir Henry Docwra, whose exploits in Ireland were clarified between one draft of the *Annales* and another because their author set Camden right.[78] The manufactured speeches found in Bacon and Cotton thus became unnecessary because the full text was available and could be printed instead. Camden disliked invention:

> What matters *Parpalia* propounded I find not, for I do not think his Instructions were put in writing; and to roave at them, with the common sort of Historians, I list not. That Queen *Elizabeth* still persisted like Herself, *Semper Eadem, Always the Same,* and that the matter succeeded not to the Pope's desire, all men know. The report goeth, that the Pope gave his faith, "that he would disannull the Sentence against her Mother's Marriage as unjust, confirm the English Liturgy by his Authority, and grant the Use of the

---

[77] A section attacking Buchanan appears ibid., pp. 88–92, and an examination of Camden's manuscripts indicates that the blackening of Buchanan's reputation was progressive: British Museum, Cotton MSS, Faustina F.iv, foll. 112–113, Faustina F.i, fol. 132ʳ. Moreover, in this section Camden identified every document that he quoted, which was not his usual habit. James's view was explained by Camden to J. A. de Thou in a letter dated 1612, printed by John Collinson, *The Life of Thuanus* (London, 1807), pp. 142–145.

[78] Camden, *Historie*, fol. a4ʳ, p. 438; on Cuffe, ibid., p. 624; on Docwra, see the additions in British Museum, Cotton MSS, Faustina F.iii, foll. 133ʳ, 210ʳ–210ᵛ, Faustina F.vii, foll. 64ᵛ and 65ᵛ.

Sacraments to the *English* under Both kinds, so as she would joyn herself to the Romish Church, and acknowledge the Primacy of the Chair of *Rome"; yea, and that certain thousand Crowns were promised to those that should procure the same.[79]

The apology was, of course, due to the fact that on this occasion Camden did guess: his authority was no better than "the report goeth." But that case was highly unusual. Normally he obeyed his own dictum that "Speeches and Orations, unless they be the very same *verbatim,* or else abbreviated, I have not meddled withall, much less coined them of mine own Head." [80] Unlike his contemporaries, Camden was in a position to make good his boast.

The end result was a book that is still invaluable, partly because of the author's proximity to the subject, but partly also because Camden, of all the politic historians, was the most level-headed and the least likely to substitute the superficial tricks of Tacitean history for the reality of solid thought. The purely human causation, the emphasis on causes, the political nature of the analysis—all these were there. If the style was sometimes very plain, that only served to make the work appear more trustworthy. If compromises had to be made because past events were still too closely tied to present happenings, these were no different than the compromises that were necessary to make the reign of Richard II or Henry VII appear appropriate to the early seventeenth century. Of all the politic historians, Camden alone took amplitude seriously, and of them all, it was only he whose protestations concerning truth were worthy of serious credence.

[79] *Historie,* p. 47.
[80] Ibid., fol. b2ʳ.

Conclusion

In the century and a half which separated Camden from Caxton, how much change had occurred in the idea of history? In one sense, the comparison is almost impossible to make. The microcosm of the court of James I could hardly have been more different from that of Edward IV, nor did the learned Stuart much resemble the amorous Plantagenet. The anomalously erudite Earl Rivers might be paralleled by the Earl of Northumberland, but the former owed his reputation to encouraging Caxton (and translating for him), while the interests of the latter were very nearly exotic: mere literacy was no longer cause for wonder. And where could be found an earlier Bacon, let alone a Ben Jonson? Not that the matter of courts and courtiers is vital. Other things mattered more. When Edward annoyed his nobility, the king found himself on an unanticipated voyage to the Low Countries; James, whose subjects had good reason to be disillusioned, still died in uninterrupted possession of his throne. It required more than fifteen years of Charles before anyone again wished to remove a king from the seat God had allotted him. Stability made a difference. It meant that the minds of men could turn from threats of faction to a dream of England. It meant that England could survive the shock of the Reformation and, more, that the Reformation could make Englishmen stand together in a great protective wall, prepared to fight the foreigner who challenged them, reluctant to return to the bestiality of fighting one another. Stability meant, too, that the economic changes of the sixteenth century—changes the Reformation accelerated—could be absorbed profitably and could produce, among other things, a new and larger reading public, properly educated in the latest and best mode. As a result, while it is almost possible to speak of "the" idea of history prevalent in Caxton's time, it is questionable whether one could do so sensibly of a time which saw the writings of Bacon and John Taylor the Water Poet, of John Stow and Anthony Munday, of John Selden and William Slatyer. A single audience had become many; the taste for history that was common to both ages had spread far down the social ladder.

The changes that resulted from the growth of a national state, from the rapid expansion of the economy, and from the growth, in quantity and in quality, of literacy together are sufficient to be described as revolutionary—however much that overworked word may frighten us. Yet in history writing (as in much else), while the changes were enormous and far-reaching, much remained the same. Men were as strongly convinced in 1625 as in 1480 that they lived in a basically orderly universe. Even the kind of order remained the same, for the Copernican theory was only beginning to be assimilated. Everyone knew that God ruled the world in accordance with a plan known in its entirety only to Him, if partially discoverable by men, though they were gradually coming to the conclusion that God's plan was rational and that He would not alter it capriciously. That meant that an emphasis on second causes could be defended as not detracting too much from His glory. The sublunary world was still divided among the powers of Reason and Fortune and Providence, but the realm of Reason was gradually being extended at the expense of the others. And the same could be said about the purpose of history writing itself. Writing—and reading—about the past was justifiable only because men learned from it. Moral behavior was one lesson. The workings of God's providence might be another. But as Reason came to be more important, history writing began to emphasize lessons more useful in this world. Instead of seeking a more detailed knowledge of the ways of God, historians began to search for laws explaining the ways of men. The interest shifted from first causes to second. No one denied the preeminence of the first causes; instead, it was simply assumed that in a rational universe God acted rationally, and so the operations of the first cause might be taken as a precondition but otherwise ignored.

What changes there were in fundamental conceptions occurred slowly and gradually, and they took place beneath a seemingly tranquil surface of uniformity. In terms of structure, histories altered much more rapidly and obviously. A medieval chronicle such as the *Polychronicon* began as a universal history and only gradually shifted its center to the English scene. The organization was loose in the extreme, annalistic, with no obvious methods of selecting materials or of imposing order on them. Encouraging personal morality and demonstrating God's providence made admirable reasons for an author's desire to write but did not help much in the actual composition. One result was the operation of the principle of inclusiveness. With no very clear-cut criteria for selection, the author was inclined to put into his chronicle as much as he could for fear that otherwise some significant bit of information might be omitted. Part of the trouble was the result of the lack of the notion of anachronism. Without that, an author could not even ask how an action was significant to its participants; at most, he could ask how it was useful for his own generation. And this same emphasis on usefulness here and now meant that the analysis and criticism of sources was irrelevant. What really happened was less important than the meaning of what might (or might not) have happened; a "story" might be as useful as a "history," and indeed the latter term could be used to cover both. Instead of analysis there was documentation; quantity outweighed quality; the record was preserved not for its own sake but for whatever moral use posterity could find for it.

How then did a book such as Sir Walter Raleigh's *History* differ from the *Polychronicon*? Raleigh embodied many of the changes worked out during the sixteenth century, and we are so inclined to see him as a man quintessentially of his time, that it is easy to answer that he had nothing whatever in common with the great medieval chronicle.[1] But this is not so. Raleigh

[1] On Raleigh, Sir Charles Firth, "Sir Walter Raleigh's 'History of the World,' " in *Essays Historical & Literary*, ed. Godfrey Davies (Oxford, 1938), pp. 34–60; Ernest A. Strathmann, *Sir Walter Ralegh: A Study in Elizabethan Skepticism* (New York, 1951); and Christopher Hill, *Intellectual Origins of the English Revolution* (Oxford, 1965), pp. 131–224. Raleigh's whole career does not leave one with the feeling that he was essentially conservative: the interest in Machiavelli (discussed by Strathmann) and in science and exploration (discussed by Hill) preclude such an estimate. Nonetheless, I feel that Raleigh, in writing *The History of the World*, was preserving what he could of an older order while making use of the new where relevant.

tells us that he originally intended to write a history of England; his own predilections and the advice of friends enjoined him to begin with the history of the world and then shift his ground over to the history of England.[2] As it happens, this is precisely the way in which the *Brut* and the *Polychronicon* were written. What Raleigh would have produced had he finished his enormous self-imposed labor it is impossible to say: the large folio he finished was only the first of a projected three. That Raleigh was prepared to take so much space on what amounted to no more than part of the introduction to the complete work means that he was, in a sense, outplaying Higden and Caxton at their own game. Moreover, Raleigh's arrangement of the books within his *History* resembled the medieval: he began with the Seven Ages, then shifted to the third and fourth of the Four Monarchies. Admittedly, this line of argument must not be pushed too far. Unlike his predecessors, Raleigh did not write annals, nor did he object to including digressions of various lengths in order to discuss problems or give judgment or merely show the relation of what he was describing to the world he actually lived in.

Similarly, Raleigh's remarks on causation and on the utility of history at first glance resembled those of Higden and his followers. History shows the operations of God's judgment, is in fact the record of the workings of Providence. As such, it trains our consciences: "In a word, we may gather out of History a policy no less wise than eternal; by the comparison and application of other mens fore-passed miseries with our own errours and ill-deservings."[3] That Raleigh would choose to use the highly inflammatory word "policy" in such a connection is revealing, for the passage must be read as a rejection of the Machiavellian approach to political questions. Partly this is sheer pessimism. Machiavelli believed that some sort of "science of history" was possible; so did Bacon. But Raleigh, who had shared that view (and in some moods still did), had moved through optimism and back to a pessimism characterized once more by a strong be-

---

[2] Raleigh, *The History of the World* (London, 1676), Preface, fol. B1ʳ. Book and chapter numbers, as well as page numbers, are essential because of the idiosyncratic pagination of this edition.

[3] Ibid., Preface, fol. B1ᵛ.

lief in Providence. Thus he differed from the late medieval writers who began with Providence and never moved beyond it. Thus, too, he could write (as Higden, for example, never could have), "To say that GOD was pleased to have it so, were a true, but an idle answer (for his secret will is the cause of all things). . . ." [4] Second causes had to be probed. But how much could be made of them? Raleigh had read Sidney and agreed with him that in the matter of causes historians commonly borrowed their methods from the poets.[5] Provided that the historian did not derogate from the power of God, the search for second causes was both necessary and useful. But how successful could it be? "For the heart of Man is unsearchable: and Princes, howsoever their intents be seldom hidden from some those many eyes which pry both into them, and into such as live about them; yet sometimes either by their own close temper, by some subtil mists, they conceal the truth from all reports." [6] Only God could penetrate that darkness, and the historian who based his conclusions on such conjecture was building on sand. For him to commend policy on such evidence as this was madness, especially as history did demonstrate that kings too much interested in "reasons of State, and politick subtilty" eventually "pulled the vengeance of GOD upon themselves, upon theirs, and upon their prudent Ministers." [7]

Yet the conclusion of Raleigh's digression on conjecture was favorable, and if one examines his use of it, it is not difficult to see why. Like all the "politic" historians, even the somewhat disillusioned Raleigh held that men were at all times and places the same. Thus if two situations seem substantially similar, the causes of one might (with due caution) be applied to the other. Thus Guicciardini's account of the difficulties facing Charles VIII in ruling a reluctant Florence was a sure guide in determining the origins of Joash's tribulations in subduing Jerusalem.[8] With a case so clear-cut, Raleigh was willing to abandon his

[4] Ibid., II, xix, 6; p. 297.
[5] Ibid., II, xxi, 6 ("A digression wherein is maintained the liberty of using conjecture in Histories"); p. 311.
[6] Ibid., II, xxi, 6; p. 311.
[7] Ibid., Preface, fol. C1ᵛ.
[8] Ibid., II, xxii, 9; pp. 320–321.

usual caution and apply the method even to sacred history. If the problem came up in classical history, then Raleigh's reluctance faded and he used even his own military and naval experience in an attempt to elucidate what actually happened at a battle such as Cannae. Conjecture had to derive from something more than armchair psychology; if it did, its value was undoubted, though care was still required to prevent infringement on the power of God. What Raleigh accomplished was to tame "politic" history: he used the methods but saw their limitations, and he reiterated the importance of the first cause in a world where the understanding of second causes, however practically useful, could never come near perfection. It is no wonder that the Puritans, with their combination of the pious and the practical, found Raleigh's *History* praiseworthy.

To the techniques of the politic historians Raleigh added other parts of his inheritance from his Tudor predecessors. In criticism of sources he went further than most. By 1614 the application of the concept of anachronism had become well-nigh second nature. One result was that the historians of the early seventeenth century, for all that they still thought of history writing as didactic, were more concerned with the authenticity of the story than their medieval predecessors had been. Moreover, the idea of anachronism gave them a means to judge such authenticity. This in turn led to source criticism, as witness the theologians. Raleigh was aware of all this. He worried about which source was closest to the event, which author most trustworthy. He brought to bear his own experience, including his travels. Ancient accounts of Amazons became more credible when one had heard a modern "which was delivered me for truth by an ancient *Cacique* of *Guiana.*"[9] In the case of scriptural history it was necessary to tread warily, though that did not prevent Raleigh from indulging in very learned speculation on the location of the Garden of Eden or, still more interestingly, on whether the amount of water on the earth was sufficient to produce Noah's flood. Raleigh was unlikely to question a biblical story, however much he might amplify it; he was, however, quite

[9] Ibid., IV, ii, 15; p. 593.

capable of rejecting the Roman historians out of hand. These
men were so partial to their own cause, so eager to show their
own compatriots in a heroic stance, that their accounts of battles
not uncommonly degenerated into utter confusion. The soldier
in Raleigh found such chaos unbearable, and he kept only those
parts of the story which appeared coherent to a military mind.
Thus, far more than the professional scholars, many of whom
were crippled by an undue reverence for anything classical,
Raleigh was willing to sit in judgment on his sources. His history
of England would have been worth seeing: there, not even a ves-
tigial trace of inbred classical piety would have remained. But
it may not be entirely an accident of timing that prevented Raleigh from finishing: the historian who asserted "That whosoever
in writing a modern History, shall follow Truth too near the
heels, it may haply strike out his Teeth," [10] and who had already
suffered from the displeasure of King James for being too critical
of kings, may have suspended his work deliberately before his
distance from the flailing heels became dangerously short.

Raleigh as historian was far from being a complete radical,
and his value as a figure summing up the developments of the
sixteenth century is the result of the fact that he was inclined to
compromise and thus made some use of practically everything.
Beginning with the essential structure of the medieval world
chronicle (in its English version), he learned from the poets and
playwrights something of the art of compression and organization. But from the humanists and theologians he learned, too,
something of source analysis, and the *History* had now to carry
this new freight in place of the old comprehensiveness of detail
which the Tudor chroniclers eventually jettisoned. The idea of
politic history helped to weld the new material into place where
the problem was itself political; the antiquaries showed how this
could be done with geographic and "chorographic" problems.
Nonetheless, where Holinshed and his editors had carried inclusiveness too far in one direction, Raleigh carried it too far in another.
And here is another part of the explanation for Raleigh's failure
to finish his book. It required a folio to get to around 200 B.C., in

---

[10] Ibid., Preface, fol. D2ʳ.

other words, to a date before the documentation became really substantial. Raleigh's own estimate of three volumes strikes one as optimistic. A world history on that scale had become impossible. The age of specialization begins in the seventeenth century with the antiquaries, and Raleigh's experience indicates why. But he had summed up the sixteenth-century experience, and his political and religious biases, as well as the tragic end of his life, helped to insure that his work would be read and the legacy of his predecessors preserved.

It may be said that the two principal lessons learned by the historians of the sixteenth century concerned sources and selection. Beginning with Polydore Vergil, men began to look at where their information about the past came from. Polydore proved that much could be done merely by using common sense; Leland showed that seeking out any and all sources of information was an even better way of getting at the truth of the past, though not until the theologians were forced to defend their interpretations of church history did the use of criticism in the style of Valla become widespread. Gradually the new techniques were adopted by the chroniclers and antiquaries; the latter used them to answer a whole series of new questions. But antiquarianism rapidly became a specialty, and the more learned the antiquary, the smaller his audience. The chroniclers, however, required some principle of selection as much as, if not more than, new sources of information. Polydore and Hall proposed kingship as an organizing principle, coupled with the workings of the providence of God; Sir Thomas More demonstrated the advantages—and difficulties—of using psychology. Not until the poets and dramatists tamed More's ferocious picture of tyranny could psychology be harnessed to politics. Bacon and Hayward, already influenced by Machiavelli and Guicciardini, wrote to prove the primacy of politics and used the methods of their literary predecessors. But in the process the new use of sources tended to be lost, and some of the politic historians were almost as careless of historical background as the medieval chroniclers, and for much the same reason: the purpose of history overrode all other considerations. Camden in his *Annales* combined the two lessons of the sixteenth century best, by bringing to bear on politics the methods he had mastered in writing his *Britannia*. But Camden, in an age when passion was still fashionable in writing history, was too little impassioned for great popularity. He influenced the professionals, and it was left to Raleigh, who recapitulated the entire sixteenth-century development and did so with great verve, to educate the next generation of common readers in the achievements of the historians of the Tudor century.

Index

RENAISSANCE SOCIETY OF AMERICA
REPRINT TEXTS